THOMAS GRAY
AND
WILLIAM COLLINS

Poetical Works

THOMAS GRAY

Born in Cornhill, 26 December 1716
Died 30 July 1771

WILLIAM COLLINS

Born at Chichester, 25 December 1721
Died 12 June 1759

THOMAS GRAY
AND
WILLIAM COLLINS
Poetical Works

EDITED BY

Roger Lonsdale

OXFORD   LONDON   NEW YORK

OXFORD UNIVERSITY PRESS

1977

Oxford University Press, Walton Street, Oxford OX2 6DP

OXFORD LONDON GLASGOW NEW YORK
TORONTO MELBOURNE WELLINGTON CAPE TOWN
IBADAN NAIROBI DAR ES SALAAM LUSAKA ADDIS ABABA
KUALA LUMPUR SINGAPORE JAKARTA HONG KONG TOKYO
DELHI BOMBAY CALCUTTA MADRAS KARACHI

*First published in the Oxford Standard Authors series and simultaneously in the
Oxford Paperbacks series, 1977*

British Library Cataloguing in Publication Data

Thomas Gray and William Collins: poetical works.—
　(Oxford standard authors).
　I. Gray, Thomas, b.1716 II. Collins, William
　III. Lonsdale, Roger
　821'.6　　PR3501

　ISBN 0-19-254170-6
　ISBN 0-19-281169-X Pbk.

*Filmset in 'Monophoto' Ehrhardt 10 on 11 pt. by
Richard Clay (The Chaucer Press), Ltd., Bungay, Suffolk
and printed in Great Britain by
Fletcher & Son Ltd., Norwich*

CONTENTS

LIST OF ILLUSTRATIONS

PREFACE

THIS VOLUME IS INTENDED to replace Austin Lane Poole's edition of *The Poetical Works of Gray and Collins* (1917), frequent reprintings of which have served students of these two poets for more than fifty years. Poole's edition was revised in 1927 and, more significantly, in 1937, when Frederick Page corrected the poems of Collins, and Leonard Whibley, the editor with Paget Toynbee of Gray's *Correspondence* (3 vols., 1935), brought a considerable knowledge of recent Gray scholarship to bear on the text and annotation of that poet.

In re-editing these two poets for the Oxford Standard Authors, the most radical change I have made is the rearrangement of Gray's poems in chronological order of composition, in so far as that can be established. Poole printed the ten items of Gray's *Poems* (1768) in the poet's own arrangement, followed by the three other poems printed in his lifetime, and then placed all the posthumously published poems in a roughly chronological sequence, which nevertheless ended with Gray's earliest original English poem. The edition of Gray by H. W. Starr and J. R. Hendrickson (Oxford, 1966) retains a similar arrangement, although the posthumous poems are subdivided into various categories. Since Gray's own directions for the sequence of his poems in 1768 have an obvious interest, I have noted them in the list of 'Chief Editions' of his works. My experience has been, however, that students reading Gray for the first time have often been baffled by an arrangement of his poems which moves unpredictably backwards and forwards over a period of three decades, with the result, for example, that the poems which he wrote in the inspired summer of 1742 are widely separated and his group of translations from Norse and Welsh similarly scattered. With the aid of the chronological tables and the lists of chief editions, the present arrangement should enable the reader to obtain a clearer sense of the poetic career and development of both poets. The disposition of the poems of Collins has needed less alteration. As there is sparse evidence for dating the individual poems in his *Odes* (1746), I have followed Poole in retaining the published sequence.

The text and the textual apparatus, which records all substantive variants of significance, have been thoroughly revised for this edition and the biographical chronologies and lists of editions have been corrected and expanded in the light of recent scholarship. The head-note to each poem summarizes biographical and bibliographical information relevant to its composition and publication and indicates the text used. The headnotes have in general been expanded, partly to include explanatory information in particular cases, although all the footnotes to the poems remain those of the two poets (with the exception that references have occasionally been added or expanded in square brackets).*

I have retained a transcript of the Eton MS. of the *Elegy* as an appendix to Gray's poems, but have omitted the appendix on 'Gray's Removal from Peterhouse to Pembroke Hall', as this purely biographical matter has been adequately discussed elsewhere since the first appearance of Poole's edition by the editors of Gray's *Correspondence* and by R. W. Ketton-Cremer in his life of Gray (1955). I have omitted both of Poole's appendices to Collins's poems. Having printed Collins's revised second edition of his *Epistle to Hanmer*, I have placed variants from the first edition in the textual apparatus, rather than include the entire poem in an appendix. The discussion by Iolo A. Williams of 'A Song. Imitated from the Midsummer-Night's Dream of Shakespear' has been omitted, since recent evidence suggests that it is by Thomas Warton rather than by Collins. I have added an appendix on another poem dubiously attributed to Collins in the early nineteenth century only because the case for the attribution has recently been restated.

I have added a section to each poet which falls outside the general chronological arrangement. In the case of Gray, I have added to the edition his early translations from Latin and Italian, which represent almost all of his poetic output in English before 1742 to have survived. As an opening section in the main chronological arrangement, these early translations might have disheartened the reader, but I believe that the interested student should have the opportunity to consult them. To Collins's poems I have added the 'Drafts and Fragments' of poems discovered among the Warton MSS. in Trinity College, Oxford, and first edited by J. S. Cunningham (Oxford, 1956). The difficulty of dating these poems and their fragmentary nature have led me to place them in a separate section at the end of the main sequence. As will be clear from my transcription of these

* A full exposition of the facts summarized in the headnotes may be found in my edition of *The Poems of Gray, Collins and Goldsmith* (Longmans Annotated Poets, 1969), where I have also given an extensive selection of possible borrowings from and allusions to other poets, a text and translation of Gray's Latin poems, and a discussion of the lost or dubious poems attributed at various times to both poets.

poems, Collins's punctuation could be perfunctory or non-existent. This is equally true of the manuscript of what has long been known as Collins's *Ode on the Popular Superstitions of the Highlands*, which was rediscovered by Miss C. Lamont in 1967. This poem, unlike the 'Drafts and Fragments', must be considered one of Collins's finest achievements, unfinished as it is, and since a readable if not entirely accurate text has been available for almost two hundred years, it seems pointless now to include in this edition a transcript of the manuscript in which Collins's lack of punctuation will inevitably perplex the non-specialist reader. I have therefore added light punctuation to the text of the manuscript, most frequently at the ends of lines. Otherwise the text follows the manuscript, an exact transcription of which was given by Miss Lamont in *Review of English Studies*, XIX (1968). 137–47.

ROGER LONSDALE

September 1976

INTRODUCTION

I

THOMAS GRAY AND WILLIAM COLLINS were the most admired and influential lyric poets in the later eighteenth century. Although most of their poetry was written during the 1740s, that decade in which both poetry and the novel were seeking new directions, neither poet was at first particularly prominent among the young writers who emerged after the death of Pope in 1744. Collins was friendly with James Thomson, whose *The Seasons* (1726–30) provided an increasingly influential alternative to Popean ideals of 'correctness' in diction and metre, and to a witty, urbane tone and satiric content. Collins also knew the younger poets such as Mark Akenside and Joseph and Thomas Warton, all of whom enjoyed some success during the 1740s. Yet he himself, for all his intense poetic ambition, was to be largely ignored during his lifetime and his posthumous reputation did not begin until the 1760s.

Even Thomas Gray had greatness, in a manner, thrust upon him. He was certainly by temperament far from being a leader of new literary movements. A shy, defensive boy of relatively humble origins, he clung during his schooldays at Eton to a small group of friends, especially to Horace Walpole and Richard West. When he eventually left Cambridge, gloomily resigned to a legal career, he eagerly accepted an invitation from Walpole to accompany him on the Grand Tour to France and Italy. A means of postponing certain problems, the journey only brought Gray face to face with others, notably the social difference between himself and Walpole, who was after all the Prime Minister's son and who accordingly received very different treatment during their travels. In May 1741 the friends quarrelled in Italy and Gray returned alone to England.

Little detail about the quarrel was allowed to survive. Yet it can safely be assumed that its effect on Gray was shattering and, while it would be misleading to reduce his later poetry to this single biographical meaning, the impact of the quarrel undoubtedly affected much of his verse in one way or another. Walpole was not merely an unusually amusing and cultivated friend: he was also Gray's only means of access to the great world of power and influence. Without Walpole, he was virtually isolated and he returned to England at the age of twenty-four, financially insecure and totally uncertain about his future. For consolation Gray turned to literary correspondence with his other Eton friend, Richard West, and during the winter of 1741–2 began writing English poetry for virtually the first time. Apart from the early (but in their own way revealing) *Lines* addressed to Walpole from the underworld, Gray had hitherto written only in Latin or in English translation from Latin and Italian. He now embarked on an elaborate verse drama, *Agrippina*, modelled on Racine but stylistically heavily influenced by Shakespeare. It should be remembered that Gray's notorious assertion that 'the language of the age is never the language of poetry' was made in the context of West's criticism of the diction of this experimental verse drama, which he quickly abandoned, just as later in the decade, he would abandon another elaborate project, the didactic poem *Education and Government*.

Gray was in fact moving instinctively towards a concise, intense, lyric style. Many years later, in 1759, he would explain to William Mason that 'the true Lyric style with all its flights of fancy, ornaments & heightening of expression, & harmony of sound, is in its nature superior to every other style. wch is just the cause, why it could not be born in a work of great length'. He wrote his first exercise in such a style in the spring of 1742 when, in response to an *Ode on May* by Richard West, he sent in return his *Ode on the Spring*. For a first lyric effort in English, the poem is unusually accomplished, dense with felicities culled from classical and English poetry, which are blended into Gray's own allusive, evocative style with its choice diction and assured metrical control. It is the last stanza, however, which prevents the poem from being merely an elegant rehearsal of Augustan moral commonplaces. Gray finally reveals, behind the poet's complacent façade of superiority to the busy vernal world, his own insecurity and frustration. It is a significant moment in mid-century poetry, even if in origin it was no more than a rueful private admission to a close friend.

Yet the *Ode on the Spring* could not claim even Richard West as its audience, for Gray's friend had died of consumption at the age of twenty-five before receiving the poem. Deprived of his two closest friends within a year, Gray wrote more poetry during the summer of 1742 than at any other period of his life. The *Sonnet* in memory of West, for all Wordsworth's clumsy strictures on its diction, is a restrained but moving lament by the poet, isolated and sterile in a thriving natural world, for the loss of the one friend who would have read such a poem sympathetically. The *Eton Ode* provides a temporal as well as visual 'prospect' of the lost happy days of childhood.

Noticeably, Gray is unable or unwilling to explore the private predicament evoked in the opening stanzas, which is later generalized into the somewhat melodramatic account of the miseries of adult life. Once more the moralist's superior wisdom and experience are finally seen to be futile by comparison with the thoughtless if doomed innocence of the schoolchildren. According to the *Eton Ode*, all men are 'Condemn'd alike to groan'; the *Ode to Adversity* reads like a deliberate effort to emerge from such pessimism into the conviction that suffering has meaning, that it can lead to wisdom and sympathy for others. The closing lines might be taken to refer specifically to the quarrel with Walpole ('Teach me to love and to forgive . . .'). The verse and diction have a controlled austerity which appealed more to Samuel Johnson than those of any of Gray's other early poems.

The fragmentary *Hymn to Ignorance* is a derisive salute to Cambridge, where Gray returned in the autumn of 1742 and where he would remain in a state of mild dissatisfaction for the rest of his life. By late 1745 some kind of reconciliation with Horace Walpole had been brought about and Gray soon began diffidently showing him the intensely personal poems he had written during 1742. Walpole now became the 'audience' of Gray's poetry and, by one means or another, he was eventually to be responsible for ushering all Gray's important work into the world. In spite of his own diffidence about publication, Gray apparently resigned himself to this inevitable result of showing his poetry to his friend. By 1748 three of the poems had been published, including the *Ode* on the death of Walpole's cat. The elegant and amusing surface of the poem, a mock-heroic parody of instructive fables for the female sex, reflects the reconciliation with Walpole, even if there are also hints of themes associated in Gray's poetry with his complicated feelings about Walpole: ingratitude (the abandoned 'favourite') and the dangers of the glamorous great world.

This last theme is a central preoccupation of the *Elegy*, which Gray seems to have begun in 1746 and sent to Walpole as soon as he had completed it in June 1750. There are two versions of the poem, the earlier surviving in the Eton MS., which concludes with four stanzas which would later be omitted or reworked. At this stage the *Elegy* was clearly a personal meditation in which, as the poem's carefully balanced structure emphasized, the poet weighed the attractions and opportunities of worldly success and power against a life of humble, rural innocence and made his own unambiguous decision in favour of the latter. The much more familiar expanded conclusion to the poem in effect acknowledges the inadequacy of this solution and attempts a more complex and self-conscious projection of the poet's predicament into the figure of the melancholy, doomed young man, who is just as out of place in the simple, purposeful life of the village as he would be in the great world. This figure nevertheless deserves (and in the 'Epitaph' provides himself with) sympathetic respect, not merely for his mysterious sorrows but for his own sympathetic and benevolent sensibility, which is the more positive aspect of his melancholy.

After the superbly controlled opening of the *Elegy*, with its effective evocation of the fading sights and sounds of the village, and the powerfully eloquent generalizations about unchanging human experience at its centre, the poem's conclusion inevitably seems uneasy, the expansive balance of the quatrain less appropriate to the play of fancy and sensibility. Yet the doomed poet, decked as he is in the phrasing of Spenser, Shakespeare, and Milton, is Gray's best solution to the problem of expressing his private anxieties in an age dubious about the value of direct personal utterance: a means of escaping the frustrated, sterile self of the earlier poetry and of bestowing value on the poet's distinctive sensibility.

With the *Elegy* Gray ceased to use his poetry as a means, to whatever degree, of resolving personal anxieties. The immediate celebrity of the poem, once Walpole had arranged its publication, in itself solved some of Gray's problems, while simultaneously making continued poetic self-revelation impossible for so sensitive and fastidious a man. *A Long Story*, which Gray later tried to suppress, is a humorously self-derisive expression of the self-consciousness resulting from the fame of the *Elegy*. Gray's creative impulse, indeed, hardly survived his new fame. He failed to complete the *Ode on Vicissitude* which he began in about 1754 and there is an air of strain and will-power about his last serious poems, the two Pindaric *Odes* of 1757 (the first book to be printed at Walpole's press at Strawberry Hill).

In one aspect both the *Odes* clearly reflect the lively discussion of the nature of poetry, and the growing interest in primitive and exotic literature, which are characteristic of the period. The result, as with Collins, can be a sense of simultaneous poetic liberation and yet also of hampering self-consciousness. Gray knew perfectly well that he was cutting himself off in these poems from the common reader who had responded so directly to the *Elegy*. He himself could refer to *The Progress of Poesy* as 'a high Pindarick upon stilts'. Classical influence, it may be noted, has moved from the Roman and Virgilian or Horatian to the Greek and Pindaric (as it had already for Collins a decade earlier). Both Gray's poems are remarkable for their technical

virtuosity, their ambitious effort to imitate the obscurity, allu-
siveness, and lyric intensity of the elaborate Pindaric form. In lofty
and harmonious verse, which itself aspires to embody the poetic
qualities it describes, *The Progress of Poesy* traces the art from its
primitive origins and celebrates its powers and its importance to man
and society. In its imitation of Greek poetry, its emphasis on the
primitive origins of poetry, its praise of Spenser, Shakespeare, and
Milton as *the* English tradition, *The Progress of Poesy* offers, with
considerable technical brilliance, a view of poetry in which the
triumphs of earlier Augustan verse are suddenly diminished. Dryden,
it is noticeable, appears primarily as a lyric poet and Pope is unmen-
tioned.

 The Bard attempts even more directly to embody, rather than
merely to describe, the true sources of poetry identified by the age in
the prophetic, the medieval, the Celtic, the visionary, and the natural
sublime, and to dramatize the connection of poetry and political
liberty. It is as if Gray were trying to include in his depiction of the
medieval Welsh bard every possible prescription for the 'poetic', not
omitting even 'the Supreme Being', whose depiction by Raphael (as
he admitted in a footnote) influenced the opening of the poem. The
Bard is Gray's final version of the poet as an isolated and doomed
figure in an unsympathetic society and his defiant suicide also marks
the virtual end of Gray's own poetic career at the age of forty. For
many readers up to the end of the century, the sublime splendour of
the two Pindaric *Odes* would seem a greater achievement than the
Elegy, as is clear from the outrage which greeted Johnson's contemptuous comments in the *Lives of the Poets* in 1781 and from the
fascination which the Bard exerted over so many artists, from
William Blake to John Martin.

 Gray spent his remaining years in Cambridge as an aloof and
fastidious bachelor, increasingly devoted to antiquarian and botanical
studies. In some ways he always remained responsive to new
influences and interests, as is clear from his excited reaction in the
1760s to the 'discovery' of Ossian and from his travel letters a few
years later in the Lake District. The fragmentary (and highly influential) translations from Norse and Welsh poetry, which he added as a
makeweight to his collected *Poems* of 1768, are a remarkable
testimony to his interest in the primitive and violent. He supplied
epitaphs and occasional verses on request, some humorous verse, and
(reluctantly) an accomplished *Ode* for a university ceremony at
Cambridge. The outstanding poem of these last years, however, is
the still neglected *On Lord Holland's Seat near Margate*, a poem

whose satiric intensity comes as a final reminder of a side of Gray which is too easily forgotten. Walpole believed that Gray expressed himself most easily and naturally in comic verse and his brilliant letters display a wit and playfulness which will surprise those familiar only with his more melancholy lyric poems. His satiric and comic gifts are evident in a series of poems written throughout his career, from the undergraduate *Lines* to Walpole to the fierce epigram on *Tophet* and the contemptuous attack on Lord Sandwich in *The Candidate*.

Surveying his slender poetic output at the end of his career, Gray admitted that he would inevitably appear 'a shrimp of an author'. The explanation is partly his temperamental fastidiousness, which was in itself a kind of poetic integrity: when the genuine creative impulse failed, Gray refused to fall back on fluent repetition of his earlier successes. Yet there was another kind of inhibition. Gray's distinctive achievement is the tact with which he could at his best blend more traditional 'classical' qualities of clarity, balance, and restraint with the play of his own sensibility and the new inspiration he found in the earlier English poetic tradition. Yet for Gray, as for Collins, the rediscovery of sources of poetic vitality in Spenser, Shakespeare, and Milton led eventually only to a new sense of frustration, a pessimistic conviction that English poetry itself was in decline, that post-Enlightenment England had lost touch with the true, instinctive sources of poetic power. So Gray declared in the early 1750s in his *Stanzas to Mr Bentley*:

> But not to one in this benighted age
>   Is that diviner inspiration giv'n,
> That burns in Shakespear's or in Milton's page,
>   The pomp and prodigality of heav'n.

In *The Progress of Poesy*, that 'progress' can be traced to Spenser, Shakespeare, and Milton, and even as far as Dryden; but 'Thoughts, that breath, and words, that burn' are no longer available to the lyric poet. 'Oh! Lyre divine, what daring Spirit/Wakes thee now?' For all his youthful aspirations, the poet himself admits his inability to sustain the great tradition. In *The Bard* Gray can assume the robes of poetic power only by an act of historical imagination, and all he can finally imagine is poetic suicide.

II

The poetry of William Collins manifests an even less inhibited search for new sources of inspiration, a more impassioned aspiration to join

the great tradition of English poetry and even more explicit acknow-
ledgement of the difficulty of doing so. By comparison with Gray,
Collins is an obscure figure biographically, although his origins and
education are roughly similar. The son of a prosperous Chichester
tradesman, Collins was educated at Winchester and Oxford. At
school, where his friendship with Joseph Warton began, he wrote his
Persian Eclogues, which he published in 1742 while an undergraduate
at Oxford. In some respects the *Eclogues* are predictably conven-
tional, written as they are in couplets which often echo Pope's even
more youthful *Pastorals*. Yet Collins's pretence that he was translating from the Persian shows him already seeking to escape what his
Preface calls 'the naturally Strong and Nervous' style of Augustan
poetry in pursuit of the 'rich and figurative' manner he ascribes to
the Middle East. If there is little that is authentically 'Persian' about
the poems (Collins himself later admitted that they might as well
have been called *Irish Eclogues*) and if 'Informing Morals' and the
'useful Lesson' are still obtrusive, the youthful poet had given himself
an opportunity to indulge in at least two of the poems in extremes of
'desp'rate Sorrow wild' and 'wild'ring Fear', which stretched the
pastoral convention to its limits, and the verse itself foreshadows, in
its sensuous and emotional tendencies, Collins's later poetry.

Shortly before leaving Oxford in late 1743 or early 1744, Collins
addressed an *Epistle* (originally *Verses*) to Sir Thomas Hanmer, the
editor of a handsome new edition of Shakespeare. Still writing in
couplets strongly influenced by Pope, Collins's panegyric turns into a
critical verse essay on the progress and history of drama. Theor-
etically, the Augustan 'progress poem' led up steadily to a climactic
celebration of modern Britain itself. Yet, just as Gray's *Progress of
Poesy* had come to a halt in the later seventeenth century, so Collins
has to admit that English drama had made no obvious progress since
Shakespeare:

> *No second Growth the Western Isle could bear,*
> *At once exhausted with too rich a Year. . . .*

Yet Shakespeare's drama could still provide inspiration for the
modern painter and Collins's 'instructions' to the painter in effect
allow his own poetry to draw inspiration both from strikingly
emotional Shakespearean scenes and from pictorial effects. (The
'Drafts and Fragments' of poems which were probably written at this
period make quite explicit Collins's interest in painting and in the
connections between the 'Sister Arts', an interest manifested more
subtly in his best poetry.)

The *Epistle to Hanmer* contains one moment of personal appeal by the poet to Shakespeare himself:

> *O more than all in pow'rful Genius blest,*
> *Come, take thine Empire o'er the willing Breast!*
> *Whate'er the Wounds this youthful Heart shall feel,*
> *Thy Songs support me, and thy Morals heal!*

The *Song from Cymbelyne*, which Collins added to the second, extensively revised, edition of the *Epistle*, is a skilful pastiche, a pastoral elegy for Fidele. It is also revealing about Collins's willingness to surrender his 'youthful Heart' to Shakespeare's influence and not primarily, we may suspect, to his healing 'Morals'. Ostensibly an exorcism from the pastoral world of the magical, mysterious, demonic, and violent—ghosts, witches, goblins, and tempests—the *Song* makes clear Collins's fascination with these elements which, he already suspected, constituted the true sources of poetry and which had been all too successfully excluded from the world of modern poetry.

Collins spent the 1740s in or near London, friendly with such literary men as James Thomson, Johnson, and the Warton brothers, busy with numerous literary enterprises—translations, treatises, tragedies, periodicals—none of which came to anything. His one important publication resulted from Joseph Warton's suggestion in 1746 that they should publish a joint collection of *Odes*. In the event they published separate volumes towards the end of the year, but it has never been doubted that Warton's 'Advertisement' to his *Odes on Several Subjects* expressed views with which Collins essentially agreed. Warton believed that 'the fashion of moralising in verse has been carried too far' and claimed that the 'right channel' for poetry lay in the 'imagination'.

Collins's *Odes*, more original and more obscure than Warton's, were less popular and, indeed, were virtually forgotten until the 1760s. According to tradition, Collins himself bought and destroyed the unsold copies of the book in disgust. Yet these twelve poems were eventually to have considerable influence, one which survives into the second generation of Romantic poets. Following the example of the Wartons and Akenside (he would not then have seen Gray's early *Odes*), Collins was now exploring the relatively short, intense lyric, sensuous and emotional, although ranging from simpler stanzaic forms to elaborate Pindaric structures which aspired to the impassioned and sublime. Collins's *Odes* required no explanatory 'Advertisement' because so many of them are about poetry itself, about the poet's own aspirations and allegiances. What prevents this tendency to aesthetic self-absorption from remaining abstract and generalized is the intensity of Collins's concern about the direction English poetry should take and the distinctive structure of many of the poems.

In earlier eighteenth-century poetry, 'intensity' usually manifested itself as satiric contempt or the less familiar 'religious sublime'. Collins's instinct was to transfer religious emotion to aesthetic issues. The personified qualities of his *Odes*—Pity, Fear, or Simplicity—are addressed in a quasi-religious situation. The poem itself becomes a prayer by a supplicant offering his rite to the divinity, whose qualities are described, whose visitation on the poet himself may be implored, and to whose service the poet dedicates himself. The personified quality becomes a goddess, given reality not merely by pictorial and emblematic description or by an account of her literary manifestations, but by the earnestness of the poet's own aspirations and, finally, by the character of the particular poem itself, in so far as it succeeds in embodying the quality described.

The *Ode to Pity* illustrates many of these features in a simple form. The *Ode to Fear* is appropriately a more hectic evocation of the personification, which verges (as do all the *Odes* to a greater or lesser extent) on the mythical, symbolic, and visionary. Fear is an alarmed and alarming but essentially creative power, associated with popular superstition, with the emotions aroused by Greek tragedy and Shakespeare: it is the power both to feel the emotion and to arouse it in others. Collins's sense of demonic energies behind the surface of civilized life is nowhere clearer, yet there is an acute sense of frustration in his ability to identify and yet failure to possess this power. 'Be mine, to read the Visions old,/Which thy awak'ning Bards have told' is his plea, but the crux is the problem of belief. Collins yearns to 'Hold each strange Tale devoutly true', but senses the impossibility in an 'enlightened' age. While Shakespeare is once more celebrated as the supreme poet of emotional power, there is some desperation in Collins's earnest invocation to Fear: 'Hither again thy Fury deal,/ Teach me but once like Him to feel.'

The most original of the *Odes* is that on the *Poetical Character* itself. For Collins true poetry is inspired, visionary, and prophetic, a sacred gift granted to very few. The rarity of the true visionary, poetic power is established by means of an episode from (significantly) Spenser; the 'divine' character of the poetic imagination is elaborated by the analogy of the poet with God, the Creator of the universe by an imaginative act; the inaccessibility of true poetic imagination, such as Milton's, is finally conveyed in terms of Milton's own description of Eden, haunt of strange shades and holy genii, where the native strains of Heaven were still audible. Collins rejects the Augustan tradition initiated by Waller (line 69) only to discover that the inspired Spenser–Milton tradition is no longer available. He had earlier doubted the modern poet's claim to the magic 'cest' of poetic inspiration and must finally acknowledge that Milton's 'inspiring Bow'rs' are now 'curtain'd close . . . from ev'ry future View'. Countering such a pessimistic conclusion is, of course, the poem's own imaginative and visionary boldness, which constitutes its own claim to the true 'poetical character'. Less popular than several of the simpler *Odes*, the poem has had some notable admirers. Coleridge admitted in 1796 that it had 'inspired and whirled' him 'along with greater agitations of enthusiasm than any the most *impassioned* Scene in Schiller or Shakspere'.

Not all the *Odes* are concerned merely with poetry or literature, although their 'literariness' has often obscured the fact that several of those in the central group are concerned with specific public or national events, such as the war with France or the Jacobite rising of 1745. In 'How Sleep the Brave', patriotism, religious suggestion, and supernatural fiction are economically but delicately blended in Collins's pastoral consolation for the British dead. In the *Ode to Liberty*, another of Collins's ambitious 'progress poems', he makes his claim to be the 'new Alcæus', the poet of freedom, ranging with youthful virtuosity in an uninhibited if not always entirely lucid manner through huge geographical and historical perspectives. In contrast, the *Ode to Evening* is a skilful evocation of twilight and stillness. The invoked personification here merges inextricably with the darkening landscape, as do the mood and procedure of the poem itself, with its fluid and minimally assertive syntax and the music of its subtly controlled unrhymed metre. The natural description itself is composed of vivid details, hints of pictorial evocation, appropriate literary reminiscence (largely Miltonic), and mythical overtones. Only at the end, when Collins claims for evening a moral as well as a creative influence, is the mood (in the experience of most readers, at least) partly broken. The last of the *Odes*, *The Passions*, once one of Collins's most popular poems, shows him aspiring to bring his art, with considerable technical resourcefulness, to the condition of music and painting.

After the failure of the *Odes*, Collins was to publish only one further poem, his *Ode* (1749) on the death of James Thomson, of whose circle Collins had been a member for some years. Thereafter we can date with confidence only the so-called *Ode on the Popular Superstitions of the Highlands*, an unfinished draft of which Collins presented early in 1750 to the Scottish dramatist John Home. The poem was in fact to remain unpublished until 1788, almost thirty years after Collins's death. In its original context it is a poem of surprising boldness, in which Collins turns (as would Gray, quite independently, a few years later) for poetic inspiration to pre-Shakespearean literature and belief. Collins himself entitled the poem only an *Epistle* to John Home, but in both its imaginative range and elaborate stanzaic structure the poem bursts out of the traditional restraints of the Augustan verse-epistle. Home was returning from London to his native Scotland and Collins urges him to use as literary material traditional Scottish superstitions and legends and descriptions of Highland and Hebridean life.

In his own poem, of course, Collins himself is vicariously taking the opportunity to do just that. Scotland offers the poet 'copious Subjects' which 'ne'er shall fail'; the poet need only record 'what all believe who own thy Genial Land'. In fact, Collins's predicament, and that of his age, was precisely the loss of such unselfconscious belief. Thus the poem displays at times a disabling rift between the poet whose imagination longs to shed its inhibitions and the sophisticated metropolitan literary man. There is inevitable condescension in Collins's reassurance to Home that the beliefs and 'homelier thoughts' of 'th'untutor'd Swain' are 'Themes of simple sure Effect', which will 'add New conquests' to the 'boundless reign' of poetry. However attractive the new imaginative possibilities of such material – 'Unbounded is thy range' (of style and theme) – Collins still feels it necessary to persuade Home's 'gentle Mind' that such 'false Themes' deserve the attention of the modern literary world. The examples of Spenser and Shakespeare help to sanction such material, as does that of Tasso, Fairfax's Elizabethan translation of whom Collins greatly admired. The problem yet again is that Tasso, so Collins (probably mistakenly) thought, 'Believ'd the Magic Wonders which He sung!' In his heart Collins knew that the modern poet had been decisively cut off from the magical and supernatural basis of his art.

All of Collins's poetry, it should be remembered, was written before he was thirty. It is inevitably a poetry of excited aspiration rather than of final achievement. He left London in the early 1750s in ill-health and a state of depression which his contemporaries later decided to call insanity. He died in Chichester, his birthplace, in 1759, forgotten by all but a handful of friends and admirers. One such former friend was Samuel Johnson, who provided a short account of the poet (later reprinted in *The Lives of the Poets*) when Collins's poems were collected together for the first time in *The Poetical Calendar* in 1763. Johnson's assessment was in many ways shrewd, if not entirely sympathetic:

> He had employed his mind chiefly upon works of fiction, and subjects of fancy; and, by indulging some peculiar habits of thought, was eminently delighted with those flights of imagination which pass the bounds of nature, and to which the mind is reconciled only by a passive acquiescence in popular traditions . . .
>
> This was however the character rather of his inclination than his genius; the grandeur of wildness, and the novelty of extravagance, were always desired by him, but were not always attained. . . . This idea, which he had formed of excellence, led him to oriental fictions, and allegorical imagery; and, perhaps, while he was intent upon description, he did not sufficiently cultivate sentiment: his poems are the productions of a mind not deficient in fire, nor unfurnished with knowledge either of books or life, but somewhat obstructed in its progress by deviation in quest of mistaken beauties.

In fact the age was by now more eager to welcome Collins's 'mistaken beauties' than Johnson's 'sentiment'. In the previous year Richard Hurd, in his dissertation 'On the Idea of Universal Beauty', had expounded the attitude to poetry in which Collins would posthumously begin to flourish:

> there is something in the mind of man, sublime and elevated, which prompts it to overlook all obvious and familiar appearances, and to feign to itself other and more extraordinary; such as correspond to the extent of its own powers, and fill out all the faculties and capacities of our souls. This restless and aspiring disposition, poetry, first and principally, would indulge and flatter; and thence takes its name of *divine*, as if some power, above *human*, conspired to lift the mind to these exalted conceptions.

The collection of Collins's poems in *The Poetical Calendar* was enthusiastically reviewed by the poet John Langhorne, whose subsequent edition of Collins (1765), with an elaborate commentary, had a decisive influence on the poet's reputation. In answer to Johnson's rational reservations, Langhorne claimed for Collins, in words which significantly echo Hurd's paragraph, 'a luxuriance of imagination, a wild sublimity of fancy, and a felicity of expression so extraordinary, that it might be supposed to be suggested by some superior power, rather than to be the effect of human judgement, or capacity'. Extravagant as such a response must seem to a post-Romantic generation, Langhorne's enthusiasm emphasizes Collins's originality in his own day and explains why he had soon joined Gray as the dominant influence on lyric poetry at least until the end of the century.

POEMS
OF
THOMAS GRAY

LIST OF GRAY'S POEMS

TRANSLATIONS

1716   26 December. Born at the house of his father, Philip Gray, a scrivener, in Cornhill, where his mother, Dorothy, and her sister Mary Antrobus, also keep a milliner's shop. The only child of twelve to survive.

c. 1725–34   Educated at Eton, where his uncles, Robert and William Antrobus, are Assistants; becomes one of a group of friends (with Horace Walpole, Richard West, and Thomas Ashton) known as the 'Quadruple Alliance'. A few Latin exercises date from this period.

1734   4 July. Entered as pensioner at Peterhouse, Cambridge.

     9 October. Admitted at Peterhouse. (Ashton has already been admitted a Scholar of King's, 11 August; Walpole is to come up to King's on 11 March 1735; West matriculates at Christ Church, Oxford, 22 May 1735.)

     8 December. Sends his first extant poem in English, *Lines Spoken by the Ghost of John Dennis*, to Walpole.

1735   22 November. Admitted at the Inner Temple.

1736   12 February. His aunt Sarah Gray dies leaving him her small property.

     April–May. His *Hymeneal* on the marriage of the Prince of Wales published in the Cambridge *Gratulatio*.

1737   March. Writes the Tripos Verses, *Luna habitabilis*.

1738   14 September. Leaves Cambridge without taking his degree and lives at his father's house, at first intending to read for the Bar at the Inner Temple.

1739   29 March. Begins his tour to France and Italy with Horace Walpole, staying principally at Paris, Rheims, Lyons, Florence, and Rome. During this period sends several Latin poems to West and in the second half of 1740 begins *De Principiis Cogitandi*.

1741   c. 3 May   Quarrels with Walpole at Reggio.

     July–1 September. Travels back alone to England via Milan, Lyons, and Paris, visiting the Grande Chartreuse, where he writes an *Ode* in the album on 21 August.

     6 November. Death of his father, leaving the family in an insecure financial position.

1742   During the winter and early spring intends to study law, corresponds regularly with West, sending him Latin verses and translations, and begins his tragedy *Agrippina*.

     28 May. Visits his uncle Jonathan Rogers at Stoke Poges, Bucks., staying there until the autumn, except for a month (mid-June to mid-July) in London.

     1 June. Death of Richard West; Gray had just sent him his *Ode on the Spring*.

     August. Writes *Eton Ode*, *Sonnet on West*, *Ode to Adversity*.

     15 October. Returns to Peterhouse as a Fellow-commoner, remaining

in Cambridge, with a few protracted absences, for the rest of his life; at some point in the months preceding his return writes the unfinished *Hymn to Ignorance*.

21 October. Death of Jonathan Rogers.

? December. Gray's mother and Mary Antrobus retire from Cornhill to Stoke Poges to live with a third sister, Anna, widow of Jonathan Rogers. He accordingly divides his summers between Stoke and London in the following decade.

1743   October. Graduated as Bachelor of Laws.

1745   8 November. Reconciliation with Walpole.

1746   Autumn. Shows Walpole some of his earlier poetry and probably the beginning of the *Elegy* which he has recently started.

1747   1 March. Sends Walpole his *Ode on the Death of a Favourite Cat*.
        30 May. The *Eton Ode* published by Dodsley.

1748   15 January. Three of Gray's poems appear through Walpole in Dodsley's *Collection of Poems*.
        January or February. Speaks of William Mason as a new acquaintance.
        25 March. His house in Cornhill burned down in a fire.
        c. August. Begins writing *The Alliance of Education and Government*.

1749   March. Mason elected Fellow of Pembroke.
        5 November. Death of Mary Antrobus.

1750   12 June. Sends *Elegy*, completed at Stoke Poges, to Walpole, through whom it passes into manuscript circulation.
        ? August–September. Writes *A Long Story* for Lady Cobham.

1751   15 February. The *Elegy* published by Dodsley.

1752   Begins *Progress of Poesy*; projects a 'History of English Poetry' to be written in conjunction with William Mason.

1753   11 March. Death of Gray's mother.
        29 March. *Designs by Mr Bentley for Six Poems by Mr T. Gray* published by Dodsley.
        16 July–3 October. Travels to the north and visits Wharton at Old Park, Durham.

1754   December. Has completed *Progress of Poesy* and is starting *The Bard* (and probably *Ode on Vicissitude*).

1755   Declines an offer of the position of Secretary to the Earl of Bristol in Lisbon.

1756   5 March. Removes from Peterhouse to Pembroke Hall.

1757   8 August. *Odes* published, printed at the Strawberry Hill Press. This event marks the virtual end of his creative career: his interests hereafter are primarily historical and botanical.
        5 December. Declines the Poet Laureateship.

1758   *c.* January. Writes *Epitaph on Mrs Clerke*.
        c. June. Writes *Epitaph on a Child* for Thomas Wharton.
        September. Death of Mrs Rogers; Gray's connection with Stoke Poges ends in the following year. Hereafter his summers usually

include 'rambles' to visit friends in different parts of the country, only the more protracted of which are mentioned here.

1759   9 July. Takes up residence in London, in Southampton Row, to read at the British Museum, opened the previous January.

1760   28 June–21 July. Stays at Shiplake with Mrs Jennings and Miss Speed.

Summer. Is excited by Macpherson's *Fragments of Ancient Poetry* and Evan Evans's discoveries of Welsh poetry.

1761   5 May. By this date has written *The Fatal Sisters* and *The Descent of Odin* and probably his other imitations of Welsh and Norse poetry as well, with the intention of including them in his 'History of English Poetry'.

August. Writes *Epitaph on Sir William Williams*.

October. Writes *Song II* for Miss Speed, who is married on 12 November.

19 November. Leaves London and returns to Cambridge.

1762   11 June. Meets Norton Nicholls.

1 July–11 November. Visits Mason at York and Wharton at Old Park, Durham.

November. Fails to obtain the Regius Professorship of Modern History at Cambridge.

1764   January–March. During this period writes *The Candidate*.

1765   27 May–28 October. Visits York, Old Park, and the Highlands.

1766   16 May–4 July. Visits Kent.

1767   15 June–2 November. Visits York, Old Park, and the Lake District.

1768   12 March. Collected edition of his *Poems* published by Dodsley, including Norse and Welsh imitations.

4 May. *Poems* published at Glasgow by Foulis.

7 April–15 July. Visits Kent.

June. Writes *On Lord Holland's Seat near Margate*.

28 July. Appointed Regius Professor of Modern History at Cambridge.

1769   April. Completes his *Ode for Music*.

1 July. Performance of the *Ode for Music* at the Installation of the Duke of Grafton as Chancellor of the University.

18 July–15 October. Visits York, Old Park, and the Lake District.

December. Meets Charles-Victor Bonstetten, a young Swiss, and takes him to Cambridge.

1770   March. Bonstetten leaves England.

2 July. Makes his will.

2 July–3 August. Tour in West Country with Norton Nicholls.

1771   30 July. Dies at Cambridge; is buried at Stoke Poges.

POEMS

1. [*Lines Spoken by the Ghost of John Dennis at the Devil Tavern*]

[Gray sent this humorous communication from the underworld to Horace Walpole on 8 December 1734 (*Corresp.*, i. 9–11), two months after going up to Peterhouse, Cambridge. In his 'Memoir of Gray' (*Corresp.*, iii. 1287) Walpole stated that 'One of his first pieces of poetry was an answer in English verse to an epistle from H.W.' Gray introduced the poem in his letter as follows: 'I (tho' I say it) had too much modesty to venture answering your dear, diverting Letter, in the Poetical Strain myself: but, when I was last at the DEVIL, meeting by chance with the deceased M͏ʳ Dennis there, he offer'd his Service, &, being tip'd with a Tester, wrought, what follows—' John Dennis (1657–1734), poet, dramatist, and critic, and often satirized by Pope, had died on 6 January 1734. In lines 4, 8, and 41, Gray refers to the names used by the 'Quadruple Alliance' at Eton, 'Celadon' (Walpole) and 'Orozmades' (Gray): the others were 'Favonius' or 'Zephyrus' (Richard West) and 'Almanzor' (Thomas Ashton).

Atropos (line 3) was one of the Fates in Greek mythology, who cut the thread of life. Nicolino Grimaldi (line 35) had been a popular Italian opera-singer, a castrato. Anne Oldfield (line 43), who had died in 1730, was a famous actress and mistress of some prominent public figures. Artemisia (line 50) erected the Mausoleum in memory of her husband, Mausolus, King of Caria. She was said to have mixed ashes in her daily drink as a sign of her grief but, according to Gray, drinks bohea (a kind of tea) in the underworld. A 'ramilie' (line 51) was a kind of elaborate wig.

The poem was first printed by Paget Toynbee, *The Correspondence of Gray, Walpole, West and Ashton*, i.12–15, in 1915. The text followed here is that of the holograph letter in Pembroke College, Cambridge.]

From purling Streams & the Elysian Scene,
From Groves, that smile with never-fading Green
I reascend; in Atropos' despight
Restored to Celadon, & upper light:
Ye gods, that sway the Regions under ground,   5
Reveal to mortal View your realms profound;
At his command admit the eye of Day;
When Celadon commands, what God can disobey?
Nor seeks he your Tartarean fires to know,
The house of Torture, & th' Abyss of Woe;   10
But happy fields & Mansions free from Pain,
Gay Meads, & springing flowers best please yᵉ gentle Swain:

That little, naked, melancholy thing
My Soul, when first she tryed her flight to wing;
Began with speed new Regions to explore,   15
And blunder'd thro' a narrow Postern door:
First most devoutly having said its Prayers,
It tumbled down a thousand pair of [Stairs],
Thro' Entries long, thro' Cellars vast & deep,
Where ghostly Rats their habitations keep,   20
Where Spiders spread their Webs, & owlish Goblins sleep.
After so many Chances had befell,
It came into a mead of Asphodel:
Betwixt the Confines of ye light & dark
It lies, of 'Lyzium ye St James's park: 25
Here Spirit-Beaux flutter along the Mall,
And Shadows in disguise scate o'er ye Iced Canal:
Here groves embower'd, & more sequester'd Shades,
Frequented by ye Ghosts of Ancient Maids,
Are seen to rise: the melancholy Scene   30
With gloomy haunts, & twilight walks between
Conceals the wayward band: here spend their time
Greensickness Girls, that died in youthful prime,
Virgins forlorn, all drest in Willow-green-i
With Queen Elizabeth and Nicolini.   35
    More to reveal, or many words to use
Would tire alike your patience & my muse.
Believe, that never was so faithful found
Queen Proserpine to Pluto under ground,
Or Cleopatra to her Marc-Antony   40
As Orozmades to his Celadony.
    P:S: Lucrece for half a crown will shew you fun,
But Mrs Oldfield is become a Nun.
Nobles & Cits, Prince Pluto & his Spouse
Flock to the Ghost of Covent-Garden house: 45
Plays, which were hiss'd above, below revive;
When dead applauded, that were damn'd alive:
The People, as in life, still keep their Passions,
But differ something from the world in Fashions.
Queen Artemisia breakfasts on Bohea,   50
And Alexander wears a Ramilie.

2. *Agrippina, a Tragedy*

[Gray began this drama in the winter of 1741–42, partly under the influence of Racine, whose *Britannicus* he had seen in Paris in May 1739. By late March or early April 1742 he had sent Richard West the first scene, but West's criticism of the style caused Gray to abandon the play, as his letter of 23 April 1742, with its well-known discussion of the language of poetry, indicates. In December 1746 and January 1747 Gray sent the fragment to Walpole and may have written the twelve lines of Scene II at this time, but he soon dropped any plans of continuing it. No MS. has survived. The fragment was first printed posthumously in 1775 by Mason, who explained that he had put part of Agrippina's long speech 'into the mouth of Aceronia' and had broken it 'in a few other places'. Bradshaw and Tovey cut out Mason's obvious interpolations and conjecturally restored Gray's text: their suggestions are followed here, although the text is basically that of Mason, who also compiled the Argument for the whole play 'from two detached papers' of Gray. Most of Gray's historical material derives from Tacitus, *Annals*, Bks xiii–xiv, although he is also indebted to Racine for specific details and the general conception of the drama.]

DRAMATIS PERSONÆ

AGRIPPINA, the Empress mother
NERO, the Emperor
POPPÆA, believed to be in love with OTHO
OTHO, a young man of quality, in love with POPPÆA
SENECA, the Emperor's preceptor
ANICETUS, Captain of the guards
DEMETRIUS, the Cynic, friend to SENECA
ACERONIA, Confidant to AGRIPPINA

SCENE, the Emperor's villa at BAIÆ

THE ARGUMENT

The drama opens with the indignation of Agrippina, at receiving her son's orders from Anicetus to remove from Baiæ, and to have her guard taken from her. At this time Otho having conveyed Poppæa from the house of her husband Rufus Crispinus, brings her to Baiæ, where he means to conceal her among the croud; or, if his fraud is discovered, to have recourse to the Emperor's authority; but, knowing the lawless temper of Nero, he determines not to have recourse to that expedient but on the utmost necessity. In the meantime he commits her to the care of Anicetus, whom he takes to be his friend, and in whose age he thinks he may safely confide. Nero is not yet come to Baiæ; but Seneca, whom he sends before him, informs Agrippina of the accusation concerning Rubellius Plancus, and desires her to clear herself, which she does briefly; but demands to see her son, who, on his arrival,

acquits her of all suspicion, and restores her to her honours. In the mean-
while Anicetus, to whose care Poppæa had been entrusted by Otho, contrives
the following plot to ruin Agrippina: He betrays his trust to Otho, and brings
Nero, as it were by chance, to the sight of the beautiful Poppæa; the
Emperor is immediately struck with her charms, and she, by a feigned
resistance, increases his passion; tho', in reality, she is from the first dazzled
with the prospect of empire, and forgets Otho: She therefore joins with
Anicetus in his design of ruining Agrippina, soon perceiving that it will be
for her interest. Otho hearing that the Emperor had seen Poppæa, is much
enraged; but not knowing that this interview was obtained thro' the treachery
of Anicetus, is readily persuaded by him to see Agrippina in secret, and
acquaint her with his fears that her son Nero would marry Poppæa. Agrippina, to support her own power, and to wean the Emperor from the love of
Poppæa, gives Otho encouragement, and promises to support him. Anicetus
secretly introduces Nero to hear their discourse; who resolves immediately
on his mother's death, and, by Anicetus's means, to destroy her by drowning. A solemn feast, in honour of their reconciliation, is to be made; after
which she being to go by sea to Bauli, the ship is so contrived as to sink or
crush her; she escapes by accident, and returns to Baiæ.

In this interval Otho has an interview with Poppæa; and being duped a
second time by Anicetus and her, determines to fly with her into Greece, by
means of a vessel which is to be furnished by Anicetus; but he, pretending to
remove Poppæa on board in the night, conveys her to Nero's apartment: She
there encourages and determines Nero to banish Otho, and finish the horrid
deed he had attempted on his mother. Anicetus undertakes to execute his
resolves; and, under pretence of a plot upon the Emperor's life, is sent with a
guard to murder Agrippina, who is still at Baiæ in imminent fear, and
irresolute how to conduct herself. The account of her death, and the
Emperor's horrour and fruitless remorse, finishes the drama.

ACT I. SCENE I

AGRIPPINA, ACERONIA

AGRIPPINA

'Tis well, begone! your errand is perform'd:
           [Speaks as to Anicetus entering
The message needs no comment. Tell your master,
His mother shall obey him. Say you saw her
Yielding due reverence to his high command:
Alone, unguarded, and without a Lictor,   5

As fits the daughter of Germanicus.
Say, she retired to Antium; there to tend
Her houshold cares, a woman's best employment.
What if you add, how she turn'd pale, and trembled;
You think, you spied a tear stand in her eye,   10
And would have drop'd, but that her pride restrain'd it?
(Go! you can paint it well) 'twill profit you,
And please the stripling. Yet 'twould dash his joy
To hear the spirit of Britannicus
Yet walks on earth; at least there are who know   15
Without a spell to raise, and bid it fire
A thousand haughty hearts, unus'd to shake
When a boy frowns, nor to be lur'd with smiles
To taste of hollow kindness, or partake
His hospitable board: They are aware   20
Of th' unpledg'd bowl, they love not Aconite.

ACERONIA

He's gone; and much I hope these walls alone,
And the mute air are privy to your passion.
Forgive your servant's fears, who sees the danger
Which fierce resentment cannot fail to raise   25
In haughty youth, and irritated power.

AGRIPPINA

And dost thou talk to me, to me, of danger,
Of haughty youth, and irritated power,
To her that gave it being, her that arm'd
This painted Jove, and taught his novice hand   30
To aim the forked bolt; while he stood trembling
Scar'd at the sound, and dazzled with its brightness?
    'Tis like, thou hast forgot, when yet a stranger
To adoration, to the grateful steam
Of flattery's incense, and obsequious vows   35
From voluntary realms, a puny boy,
Deck'd with no other lustre, than the blood
Of Agrippina's race, he liv'd unknown
To fame, or fortune; haply eyed at distance
Some edileship, ambitious of the power   40
To judge of weights, and measures; scarcely dar'd

On expectation's strongest wing to soar
High as the consulate, that empty shade
Of long-forgotten liberty: When I
Oped his young eye to bear the blaze of greatness;   45
Shew'd him, where empire tower'd, and bad him strike
The noble quarry. Gods! then was the time
To shrink from danger; fear might then have worn
The mask of prudence; but a heart like mine,
A heart that glows with the pure Julian fire,   50
If bright Ambition from her craggy seat
Display the radiant prize, will mount undaunted,
Gain the rough heights, and grasp the dangerous honour.

ACERONIA

Thro' various life I have pursued your steps,
Have seen your soul, and wonder'd at its daring: 55
Hence rise my fears. Nor am I yet to learn
How vast the debt of gratitude, which Nero
To such a mother owes; the world, you gave him,
Suffices not to pay the obligation.
      I well remember too (for I was present)   60
When in a secret and dead hour of night,
Due sacrifice perform'd with barb'rous rites
Of mutter'd charms, and solemn invocation,
You bad the Magi call the dreadful powers,
That read futurity, to know the fate   65
Impending o'er your son: Their answer was,
If the son reign, the mother perishes.
Perish (you cry'd) the mother! reign the son!
He reigns, the rest is heav'n's; who oft has bad,
Ev'n when its will seem'd wrote in lines of blood,   70
Th' unthought event disclose a whiter meaning.
Think too how oft in weak and sickly minds
The sweets of kindness lavishly indulg'd
Rankle to gall; and benefits too great
To be repaid, sit heavy on the soul,   75
As unrequited wrongs. The willing homage
Of prostrate Rome, the senate's joint applause,
The riches of the earth, the train of pleasures,
That wait on youth, and arbitrary sway;
These were your gift, and with them you bestow'd   80
The very power he has to be ungrateful.

AGRIPPINA

Thus ever grave, and undisturb'd reflection
Pours its cool dictates in the madding ear
Of rage, and thinks to quench the fire it feels not.
Say'st thou I must be cautious, must be silent,   85
And tremble at the phantom I have rais'd?
Carry to him thy timid counsels. He
Perchance may heed 'em: Tell him too, that one,
Who had such liberal power to give, may still
With equal power resume that gift, and raise   90
A tempest, that shall shake her own creation
To its original atoms—tell me! say
This mighty Emperor, this dreaded Hero,
Has he beheld the glittering front of war?
Knows his soft ear the Trumpet's thrilling voice,   95
And outcry of the battle? Have his limbs
Sweat under iron harness? Is he not
The silken son of dalliance, nurs'd in Ease
And Pleasure's flowery lap?—Rubellius lives,
And Sylla has his friends, tho' school'd by fear   100
To bow the supple knee, and court the times
With shows of fair obeisance; and a call,
Like mine, might serve belike to wake pretensions
Drowsier than theirs, who boast the genuine blood
Of our imperial house. [Cannot my nod]   105
Rouse [up] eight hardy legions, wont to stem
With stubborn nerves the tide, and face the rigour
Of bleak Germania's snows[?] Four, not less brave,
That in Armenia quell the Parthian force
Under the warlike Corbulo, by [me]   110
Mark'd for their leader: These, by ties conform'd,
Of old respect and gratitude, are [mine].
Surely the Masians too, and those of Egypt,
Have not forgot [my] sire: The eye of Rome,
And the Prætorian camp have long rever'd   115
With custom'd awe, the daughter, sister, wife,
And mother of their Cæsars.
                           Ha! by Juno,
It bears a noble semblance. On this base
My great revenge shall rise; or say we sound
The trump of liberty; there will not want,   120
Even in the servile senate, ears to own

Her spirit-stirring voice; Soranus there,
And Cassius; Vetus too, and Thrasea,
Minds of the antique cast, rough, stubborn souls,
That struggle with the yoke. How shall the spark   125
Unquenchable, that glows within their breasts,
Blaze into freedom, when the idle herd
(Slaves from the womb, created but to stare,
And bellow in the Circus) yet will start,
And shake 'em at the name of liberty,   130
Stung by a senseless word, a vain tradition,
As there were magic in it? wrinkled beldams
Teach it their grandchildren, as somewhat rare
That anciently appear'd, but when, extends
Beyond their chronicle—oh! 'tis a cause   135
To arm the hand of childhood, and rebrace
The slacken'd sinews of time-wearied age.
  Yes, we may meet, ingrateful boy, we may!
Again the buried genius of old Rome
Shall from the dust uprear his reverend head,   140
Rous'd by the shout of millions: There before
His high tribunal thou and I appear.
Let majesty sit on thy awful brow,
And lighten from thy eye: Around thee call
The gilded swarm that wantons in the sunshine   145
Of thy full favour; Seneca be there
In gorgeous phrase of labour'd eloquence
To dress thy plea, and Burrhus strengthen it
With his plain soldier's oath, and honest seeming.
Against thee, liberty and Agrippina: 150
The world, the prize; and fair befall the victors.
  But soft! why do I waste the fruitless hours
In threats unexecuted? Haste thee, fly
These hated walls that seem to mock my shame,
And cast me forth in duty to their lord.   155
  My thought aches at him; not the basilisk
More deadly to the sight, than is to me
The cool injurious eye of frozen kindness.
I will not meet its poison. Let him feel
Before he sees me. Yes, I will be gone,   160
But not to Antium—all shall be confess'd,
Whate'er the frivolous tongue of giddy fame
Has spread among the crowd; things, that but whisper'd

Have arch'd the hearer's brow, and riveted
His eyes in fearful extasy: No matter   165
What; so't be strange, and dreadful.—Sorceries,
Assassinations, poisonings—the deeper
My guilt, the blacker his ingratitude.
  And you, ye manes of ambition's victims,
Enshrined Claudius, with the pitied ghosts   170
Of the Syllani, doom'd to early death,
(Ye unavailing horrours, fruitless crimes!)
If from the realms of night my voice ye hear,
In lieu of penitence, and vain remorse,
Accept my vengeance. Tho' by me ye bled,   175
He was the cause. My love, my fears for him
Dried the soft springs of pity in my heart,
And froze them up with deadly cruelty.
Yet if your injur'd shades demand my fate,
If murder cries for murder, blood for blood,   180
Let me not fall alone; but crush his pride,
And sink the traitor in his mother's ruin.   *Exeunt.*

SCENE II

OTHO, POPPÆA

OTHO

Thus far we're safe. Thanks to the rosy queen
Of amorous thefts: And had her wanton son
Lent us his wings, we could not have beguil'd   185
With more elusive speed the dazzled sight
Of wakeful jealousy. Be gay securely;
Dispell, my fair, with smiles, the tim'rous cloud
That hangs on thy clear brow. So Helen look'd,
So her white neck reclin'd, so was she borne   190
By the young Trojan to his gilded bark
With fond reluctance, yielding modesty,
And oft reverted eye, as if she knew not
Whether she fear'd, or wish'd to be pursued.

*   *   *   *   *   *   *

3. *Ode on the Spring*

[Gray's transcript in his Commonplace Book is entitled 'Noontide, an Ode'
and is dated 'at Stoke, the beginning of June, 1742. Sent to Fav: not knowing
he was then Dead'. 'Favonius' was Gray's Eton friend, Richard West (1716–
42), who had died on 1 June. Early in May he had sent Gray an 'Ode on
May' which asked him to 'invocate the tardy May' and the present poem was
Gray's response. On 20 October 1746 Gray sent the *Ode* to Walpole, through
whom it was first printed anonymously in Dodsley's *Collection of Poems by
Several Hands*, ii. 265–7, in January 1748. The text is that of 1768, with
variants from the Commonplace Book, the letter to Walpole, Dodsley, and a
fragmentary draft at Yale.]

Lo! where the rosy-bosom'd Hours,
Fair VENUS' train appear,
Disclose the long-expecting flowers,
And wake the purple year!
The Attic warbler pours her throat,   5
Responsive to the cuckow's note,
The untaught harmony of spring:
While whisp'ring pleasure as they fly,
Cool Zephyrs thro' the clear blue sky
Their gather'd fragrance fling.   10

Where'er the oak's thick branches stretch
A broader browner shade;
Where'er the rude and moss-grown beech
O'er-canopies the glade*
Beside some water's rushy brink   15
With me the Muse shall sit, and think
(At ease reclin'd in rustic state)
How vain the ardour of the Crowd,
How low, how little are the Proud,
How indigent the Great!   20

* —————————a bank
O'ercanopied with luscious woodbine.
        Shakesp. Mids. Night's Dream [II. i. 249–51].

Still is the toiling hand of Care:
The panting herds repose:
Yet hark, how thro' the peopled air
The busy murmur glows!
The insect youth are on the wing,   25
Eager to taste the honied spring,
And float amid the liquid noon:*
Some lightly o'er the current skim,
Some shew their gayly-gilded trim
Quick-glancing to the sun.†   30

To Contemplation's sober eye ‡
Such is the race of Man:
And they that creep, and they that fly,
Shall end where they began.
Alike the Busy and the Gay   35
But flutter thro' life's little day,
In fortune's varying colours drest:
Brush'd by the hand of rough Mischance,
Or chill'd by age, their airy dance
They leave, in dust to rest.   40

Methinks I hear in accents low
The sportive kind reply:
Poor moralist! and what art thou?
A solitary fly!
Thy Joys no glittering female meets,   45
No hive hast thou of hoarded sweets,
No painted plumage to display:
On hasty wings thy youth is flown;
Thy sun is set, thy spring is gone——
We frolick, while 'tis May.   50

* "Nare per æstatem liquidam————"
                         Virgil. Georg. lib. 4. [59].
† ————sporting with quick glance
  Shew to the sun their waved coats drop'd with gold.
                         Milton's Paradise Lost, book 7. [405–06].
‡ While insects from the threshold preach, &c.
                         M. GREEN, *in the Grotto* [57 ff].
                         Dodsley's Miscellanies, Vol. V. *p.* 161.

4. *Ode on a Distant Prospect of Eton College*

[Gray's transcript in his Commonplace Book is entitled 'Ode, on a distant
Prospect of Windsor, & the adjacent Country' and is dated 'at Stoke,
Aug.1742.' Another MS., once in the possession of Wordsworth and now at
Eton, has the same title with the omission of 'distant'. The *Ode* was the first
of Gray's English poems to appear in print. Walpole, who seems to have had
it in his possession by October 1746, was probably responsible for its anonymous publication in a folio pamphlet by Dodsley on 30 May 1747. Dodsley
also included it in his *Collection of Poems*, ii. 261–4, in January 1748. The
text is that of 1768, when the notes and the motto from Menander ('I am a
man; a sufficient excuse for being unhappy') were first printed with the
poem. Variants are recorded from the Commonplace Book, the Eton MS.,
and the Foulis edition (Glasgow, 1768) supervised by James Beattie.]

Ἄνθρωπος· ἱκανὴ πρόφασις εἰς τὸ δυστλχεῖν.

MENANDER.

Ye distant spires, ye antique towers,
That crown the watry glade,
Where grateful Science still adores
Her HENRY's* holy Shade;
And ye, that from the stately brow   5
Of WINDSOR's heights th' expanse below
Of grove, of lawn, of mead survey,
Whose turf, whose shade, whose flowers among
Wanders the hoary Thames along
His silver-winding way.   10

   Ah happy hills, ah pleasing shade,
Ah fields belov'd in vain,
Where once my careless childhood stray'd,
A stranger yet to pain!
I feel the gales, that from ye blow,   15
A momentary bliss bestow,
As waving fresh their gladsome wing,
My weary soul they seem to sooth,
And,† redolent of joy and youth,
To breathe a second spring.   20

---

* King HENRY the Sixth, Founder of the College.
† And bees their honey redolent of spring.
        Dryden's Fable on the Pythag. System. [110].

Say, Father THAMES, for thou hast seen
Full many a sprightly race
Disporting on thy margent green
The paths of pleasure trace,
Who foremost now delight to cleave   25
With pliant arm thy glassy wave?
The captive linnet which enthrall?
What idle progeny succeed
To chase the rolling circle's speed,
Or urge the flying ball?   30

While some on earnest business bent
Their murm'ring labours ply
'Gainst graver hours, that bring constraint
To sweeten liberty:
Some bold adventurers disdain   35
The limits of their little reign,
And unknown regions dare descry:
Still as they run they look behind,
They hear a voice in every wind,
And snatch a fearful joy.   40

Gay hope is theirs by fancy fed,
Less pleasing when possest;
The tear forgot as soon as shed,
The sunshine of the breast:
Theirs buxom health of rosy hue,   45
Wild wit, invention ever-new,
And lively chear of vigour born;
The thoughtless day, the easy night,
The spirits pure, the slumbers light,
That fly th' approach of morn.   50

Alas, regardless of their doom,
The little victims play!
No sense have they of ills to come,
Nor care beyond to-day:
Yet see how all around 'em wait   55
The Ministers of human fate,

And black Misfortune's baleful train!
Ah, shew them where in ambush stand
To seize their prey the murth'rous band!
Ah, tell them, they are men!   60

misery of human Condition

　These shall the fury Passions tear,
The vulturs of the mind,
Disdainful Anger, pallid Fear,
And Shame that sculks behind;
Or pineing Love shall waste their youth,   65
Or Jealousy with rankling tooth,
That inly gnaws the secret heart,
And Envy wan, and faded Care,
Grim-visag'd comfortless Despair,
And Sorrow's piercing dart.   70

　Ambition this shall tempt to rise,
Then whirl the wretch from high,
To bitter Scorn a sacrifice,
And grinning Infamy.
The stings of Falshood those shall try,   75
And hard Unkindness' alter'd eye,
That mocks the tear it forc'd to flow;
And keen Remorse with blood defil'd,
And moody Madness* laughing wild
Amid severest woe.   80

　Lo, in the vale of years beneath
A griesly troop are seen,
The painful family of Death,
More hideous than their Queen:
This racks the joints, this fires the veins,   85
That every labouring sinew strains,
Those in the deeper vitals rage:
Lo, Poverty, to fill the band,
That numbs the soul with icy hand,
And slow-consuming Age.   90

* ——Madness laughing in his ireful mood.
　　Dryden's Fable of Palamon and Arcite. [II. 582].

    To each his suff'rings: all are men,
Condemn'd alike to groan,
The tender for another's pain;
Th' unfeeling for his own.
Yet ah! why should they know their fate?   95
Since sorrow never comes too late,
And happiness too swiftly flies.
Thought would destroy their paradise.
No more; where ignorance is bliss,
'Tis folly to be wise.   100

5. *Sonnet* [*on the Death of Richard West*]

[Gray's transcript in his Commonplace Book, where it follows the *Eton Ode*, is dated 'at Stoke, Aug. 1742'. West had died on 1 June 1742. Gray also paid tribute to West during 1742 in his Latin poem, *De Principiis Cogitandi*, ii. 1–29. The *Sonnet* was first printed posthumously in 1775 by Mason, who provided the expanded title. The text followed is that of the Commonplace Book.]

        In vain to me the smileing Mornings shine,
        And redning Phœbus lifts his golden Fire:
        The Birds in vain their amorous Descant joyn;
        Or chearful Fields resume their green Attire:
        These Ears, alas! for other Notes repine,   5
        A different Object do these Eyes require.
        My lonely Anguish melts no Heart, but mine;
        And in my Breast the imperfect Joys expire.
        Yet Morning smiles the busy Race to chear,
        And new-born Pleasure brings to happier Men: 10
        The Fields to all their wonted Tribute bear:
        To warm their little Loves the Birds complain:
        I fruitless mourn to him, that cannot hear,
        And weep the more, because I weep in vain.

teach me that others in
adversity so that others in misery
I can relate to others in misery

6. *Ode to Adversity*

[Gray's transcript in his Commonplace Book is dated 'at Stoke, Aug. 1742'.
He did not send a copy of it to Walpole until 8 October 1751 and it was first
printed in *Designs by Mr R. Bentley for Six Poems by Mr T. Gray* in 1753.
The epigraph from Aeschylus, *Agamemnon* (176–7), may be translated,
'Zeus, who leads mortals in the way of understanding, Zeus, who has estab-
lished as a fixed ordinance that wisdom comes by suffering'. In the
Commonplace Book Gray gave a second epigraph from Aeschylus, *Eumenides*
(523) ('It profiteth through sorrow to get discretion'), which James Beattie
chose for the Glasgow edition of 1768. The poem has the present title in the
Commonplace Book and in Gray's instructions to Dodsley for the 1768
Poems (*Corresp.*, iii. 1004), but was entitled 'Hymn to Adversity' in the letter
to Walpole, the *Designs*, and in 1768. Otherwise the text followed is that of
1768, with variants from the Commonplace Book.]

———Ζῆνα
Τὸν φρονεῖν βροτοὺς ὁδώ-
σαντα, τῷ πάθει μάθαν
Θέντα κυρίως ἔχειν.

ÆSCHYLUS, in Agamemnone.

Daughter of Jove, relentless Power,
Thou Tamer of the human breast,
Whose iron scourge and tort'ring hour,
The Bad affright, afflict the Best!
Bound in thy adamantine chain   5
Ex. Newton — The Proud are taught to taste of pain,
etc. And purple Tyrants vainly groan
With pangs unfelt before, unpitied and alone.

When first thy Sire to send on earth
Virtue, his darling Child, design'd,   10
To thee he gave the heav'nly Birth,
And bad to form her infant mind.
Stern rugged Nurse! thy rigid lore
With patience many a year she bore:
What sorrow was, thou bad'st her know,   15
And from her own she learn'd to melt at others' woe.

Scared at thy frown terrific, fly
Self-pleasing Folly's idle brood,
Wild Laughter, Noise, and thoughtless Joy,
And leave us leisure to be good.   20
Light they disperse, and with them go
The summer Friend, the flatt'ring Foe;
By vain Prosperity received,
To her they vow their truth, and are again believed.

Wisdom in sable garb array'd   25
Immers'd in rapt'rous thought profound,
And Melancholy, silent maid
With leaden eye, that loves the ground,
Still on thy solemn steps attend:
Warm Charity, the gen'ral Friend,   30
With Justice to herself severe,
And Pity, dropping soft the sadly-pleasing tear.

Oh, gently on thy Suppliant's head,
Dread Goddess, lay thy chast'ning hand!
Not in thy Gorgon terrors clad,   35
Nor circled with the vengeful Band
(As by the Impious thou art seen)
With thund'ring voice, and threat'ning mien,
With screaming Horror's funeral cry,
Despair, and fell Disease, and ghastly Poverty.   40

Thy form benign, oh Goddess, wear,
Thy milder influence impart,
Thy philosophic Train be there
To soften, not to wound my heart,
The gen'rous spark extinct revive,   45
Teach me to love and to forgive,
Exact my own defects to scan,
What others are, to feel, and know myself a Man.

// Dunciad

7. [*Hymn to Ignorance. A Fragment*]

[In spite of line 11, which might suggest a date of 1741 (Gray had left Cambridge in 1738), this fragment was probably written during 1742 and not later than Gray's return to Cambridge in October 1742. Mason transcribed it into the Commonplace Book and first printed it posthumously in 1775, the text followed here, with variants recorded from his transcript.

Sesostris (line 37) was an Egyptian conqueror whose exploits were first described by Herodotus.]

Hail, Horrors, hail! ye ever gloomy bowers,
Ye gothic fanes, and antiquated towers,
Where rushy Camus' slowly-winding flood
Perpetual draws his humid train of mud:
Glad I revisit thy neglected reign,   5
Oh take me to thy peaceful shade again.
    But chiefly thee, whose influence breath'd from high
Augments the native darkness of the sky;
Ah, Ignorance! soft salutary Power!
Prostrate with filial reverence I adore.   10
Thrice hath Hyperion roll'd his annual race,
Since weeping I forsook thy fond embrace.
Oh say, successful do'st thou still oppose
Thy leaden Ægis 'gainst our antient foes?
Still stretch, tenacious of thy right divine,   15
The massy sceptre o'er thy slumb'ring line?
And dews Lethean thro' the land dispense
To steep in slumbers each benighted sense?
If any spark of Wit's delusive ray
Break out, and flash a momentary day,   20
With damp, cold touch forbid it to aspire,
And huddle up in fogs the dangerous fire.
    Oh say—she hears me not, but, careless grown,
Lethargic nods upon her ebon throne.
Goddess! awake, arise, alas, my fears!   25
Can powers immortal feel the force of years?
Not thus of old, with ensigns wide unfurl'd,
She rode triumphant o'er the vanquished world;
Fierce nations own'd her unresisted might,
And all was Ignorance, and all was Night.   30
    Oh! sacred Age! Oh Times for ever lost!
(The School-man's glory, and the Church-man's boast.)

Middle
Ages
(medieval
Revival)

aristotle

For ever gone—yet still to Fancy new,
Her rapid wings the transient scene pursue, }
And bring the buried ages back to view. ⎦   35
  High on her car, behold the Grandam ride
Like old Sesostris with barbaric pride;
* * * * a team of harness'd monarchs bend

                *   *   *   *   *

8. *Ode on the Death of a Favourite Cat, Drowned in a Tub of Gold Fishes*

[The poem was written between 22 February 1747, when Gray acknowledged Walpole's request for an epitaph on his drowned cat, and 1 March
1747, when he sent it to Walpole, a text which has not survived. Gray also
sent a copy to Thomas Wharton on 17 March and transcribed it into his
Commonplace Book (dated '1747. Cambr:'). The poem was first printed in
January 1748 in Dodsley's *Collection of Poems*, ii. 267–9, and small final
changes were made for its appearance in the *Designs* in 1753. The text
followed here is of 1768, with variants from the letter to Wharton, the
Commonplace Book, Dodsley, the Foulis edition (Glasgow, 1768), and the
Pery MS. (sold at Sotheby's on 18 July 1967).]

      'Twas on a lofty vase's side,
    Where China's gayest art had dy'd
      The azure flowers, that blow;
    Demurest of the tabby kind,
    The pensive Selima reclin'd,   5
      Gazed on the lake below.

    Her conscious tail her joy declar'd;
    The fair round face, the snowy beard,
      The velvet of her paws,
    Her coat, that with the tortoise vies,   10
    Her ears of jet, and emerald eyes,
      She saw; and purr'd applause.

    Still had she gaz'd; but 'midst the tide
    Two angel forms were seen to glide,
      The Genii of the stream: 15
    Their scaly armour's Tyrian hue
    Thro' richest purple to the view
      Betray'd a golden gleam.

The hapless Nymph with wonder saw:
A whisker first and then a claw,   20
  With many an ardent wish,
She stretch'd in vain to reach the prize.
What female heart can gold despise?
  What Cat's averse to fish?

Presumptuous Maid! with looks intent   25
Again she stretch'd, again she bent,
  Nor knew the gulf between.
(Malignant Fate sat by, and smil'd)
The slipp'ry verge her feet beguil'd,
  She tumbled headlong in.   30

Eight times emerging from the flood
She mew'd to ev'ry watry God,
  Some speedy aid to send.
No Dolphin came, no Nereid stirr'd:
Nor cruel *Tom*, nor *Susan* heard.   35
  ✗ A Fav'rite has no friend!

From hence, ye Beauties, undeceiv'd,
Know, one false step is ne'er retriev'd,
  And be with caution bold.
Not all that tempts your wand'ring eyes   40
And heedless hearts, is lawful prize;
  Nor all, that glisters, gold.
    ✗

9. [*The Alliance of Education and Government. A Fragment*]

[Gray had begun this poem by August 1748 and had probably abandoned it
by March 1749. He sent lines 1–57 to Wharton on 19 August 1748, introduc-
ing them as 'the Beginning of a Sort of Essay. what Name to give it I know
not, but the Subject is, the Alliance of Education & Government; I mean to
shew that they must necessarily concur to produce great & useful Men'
(*Corresp.*, i. 310). Wharton's transcript of the remaining lines accompanies
the letter in the British Museum. Gray also transcribed the fragment into his
Commonplace Book. It was first printed posthumously in 1775 by Mason,
who believed that Gray abandoned the poem when he discovered that
Montesquieu's *L'Esprit des Loix* (1748) had 'forestalled some of his best

thoughts'. Mason also printed (i. 193–200) 'a kind of commentary' which he
had put together from Gray's 'scattered papers in prose, which he writ, as
hints for his own use in the prosecution of this work'. This 'Commentary'
appears below. The epigraph from Theocritus, *Idylls* i. 62–3, can be translated, 'Begin, my friend, for to be sure thou canst in no wise carry thy song
with thee to Hades, that puts all things out of mind'. The text is that of the
Commonplace Book, with variants from the letter to Wharton and Wharton's
transcript.]

COMMENTARY

The Author's subject being (as we have seen) THE NECESSARY ALLIANCE BE-
TWEEN A GOOD FORM OF GOVERNMENT AND A GOOD MODE OF EDUCATION, IN
ORDER TO PRODUCE THE HAPPINESS OF MANKIND, the Poem opens with two
similes; an uncommon kind of exordium: but which I suppose the Poet
intentionally chose, to intimate the analogical method he meant to pursue in
his subsequent reasonings. 1st, He asserts that men without education are
like sickly plants in a cold or barren soil (line 1 to 5, and 8 to 12;) and, 2dly,
he compares them, when unblest with a just and well regulated government,
to plants that will not blossom or bear fruit in an unkindly and inclement air
(l. 5 to 9, and l. 13 to 22). Having thus laid down the two propositions he
means to prove, he begins by examining into the characteristics which (taking a general view of mankind) all men have in common one with another
(l. 22 to 39); they covet pleasure and avoid pain (l. 31); they feel gratitude for
benefits (l. 34); they desire to avenge wrongs, which they effect either by
force or cunning (l. 35); they are linked to each other by their common
feelings, and participate in sorrow and in joy (l. 36, 37). If then all the human
species agree in so many moral particulars, whence arises the diversity of
national characters? This question the Poet puts at line 38, and dilates upon
to l. 64. Why, says he, have some nations shown a propensity to commerce
and industry; others to war and rapine; others to ease and pleasure? (l. 42 to
46) Why have the Northern people overspread, in all ages, and prevailed over
the Southern? (l. 46 to 58) Why has Asia been, time out of mind, the seat of
despotism, and Europe that of freedom? (l. 59 to 64) Are we from these
instances to imagine men necessarily enslaved to the inconveniences of the
climate where they were born? (l. 64 to 72) Or are we not rather to suppose
there is a natural strength in the human mind, that is able to vanquish and
break through them? (l. 72 to 84) It is confest, however, that men receive an
early tincture from the situation they are placed in, and the climate which
produces them (l. 84 to 88). Thus the inhabitants of the mountains, inured to
labour and patience, are naturally trained to war (l. 88 to 96); while those of
the plain are more open to any attack, and softened by ease and plenty (l. 96
to 99). Again, the Ægyptians, from the nature of their situation, might be the
inventors of home-navigation, from a necessity of keeping up an intercourse
between their towns during the inundation of the Nile (l. 99, to * * * *).
Those persons would naturally have the first turn to commerce, who
inhabited a barren coast like the Tyrians, and were persecuted by some

neighbouring tyrant; or were drove to take refuge on some shoals, like the
Venetian and Hollander; their discovery of some rich island, in the infancy of
the world, described. The Tartar hardened to war by his rigorous climate
and pastoral life, and by his disputes for water and herbage in a country
without land-marks, as also by skirmishes between his rival clans, was con-
sequently fitted to conquer his rich Southern neighbours, whom ease and
luxury had enervated: Yet this is no proof that liberty and valour may not
exist in Southern climes, since the Syrians and Carthaginians gave noble
instances of both; and the Arabians carried their conquests as far as the
Tartars. Rome also (for many centuries) repulsed those very nations which,
when she grew weak, at length demolished her extensive Empire. * * * *

ESSAY I

. . . Πόταγ', ὦ 'γαθέ· τὰν γὰρ ἀοιδὰν
Οὔτι πω εἰς Ἀΐδαν γε τὸν ἐκλελάθοντα φυλαξεῖς.

THEOCRIT.

As sickly Plants betray a niggard Earth,
Whose barren Bosom starves her gen'rous Birth
Nor genial Warmth, nor genial Juice retains
Their Roots to feed, & fill their verdant Veins:
And as in Climes, where Winter holds his Reign, 5
The Soil, tho' fertile, will not teem in vain,
Forbids her Gems to swell, her Shades to rise,
Nor trusts her Blossoms to the churlish Skies.
So draw Mankind in vain the vital Airs,
Unform'd, unfriended, by those kindly Cares, 10
That Health & Vigour to the Soul impart,
Spread the young Thought, & warm the opening Heart.
So fond Instruction on the growing Powers
Of Nature idly lavishes her Stores,
If equal Justice with unclouded Face 15
Smile not indulgent on the rising Race,
And scatter with a free, tho' frugal, Hand
Light golden Showers of Plenty o'er the Land:
But Tyranny has fix'd her Empire there ⎫
To check their tender Hopes with chilling Fear, ⎬ 20
And blast the blooming Promise of the Year. ⎭
  This spacious animated Scene survey,
From where the rolling Orb, that gives the Day,

His sable Sons with nearer Course surrounds
To either Pole, & Life's remotest Bounds.   25
How rude soe'er th' exterior Form we find,
Howe'er Opinion tinge the varied Mind,
Alike to all the Kind impartial Heav'n
The Sparks of Truth & Happiness has given:
With Sense to feel, with Mem'ry to retain,   30
They follow Pleasure, & they fly from Pain;
Their Judgement mends the Plan their Fancy draws,
Th' Event presages, & explores the Cause;
The soft Returns of Gratitude they know,
By Fraud elude, by Force repell the Foe;   35
While mutual Wishes, mutual Woes, endear
The social Smile & sympathetic Tear.
   Say then, thro' Ages by what Fate confined
To diff'rent Climes seem different Souls assign'd?
Here measured Laws & philosophic Ease   40
Fix, & improve the polish'd Arts of Peace.
There Industry & Gain their Vigils keep,
Command the Winds, & tame th' unwilling Deep.
Here Force & hardy Deeds of Blood prevail;
There languid Pleasure sighs in every Gale.   45
Oft o'er the trembling Nations from afar
Has Scythia breath'd the living Cloud of War;
And, where the Deluge burst, with sweepy Sway
Their Arms, their Kings, their Gods were roll'd away.
As oft have issued, Host impelling Host,   50
The blue-eyed Myriads from the Baltick Coast.
The prostrate South to the Destroyer yields
Her boasted Titles, & her golden Fields:
With grim Delight the Brood of Winter view
A brighter Day, & Heavens of azure Hue,   55
Scent the new Fragrance of the breathing Rose,
And quaff the pendent Vintage, as it grows.
Proud of the Yoke, & pliant to the Rod,
Why yet does Asia dread a Monarch's nod,
While European Freedom still withstands   60
Th' encroaching Tide, that drowns her less'ning Lands,
And sees far off with an indignant Groan
Her native Plains, & Empires once her own.
Can opener Skies & Suns of fiercer Flame
O'erpower the Fire, that animates our Frame;   65

As Lamps, that shed at Ev'n a chearful Ray,
Fade & expire beneath the Eye of Day?
Need we the Influence of the Northern Star
To string our Nerves & steel our Hearts to War?
And, where the Face of Nature laughs around,   70
Must sick'ning Virtue fly the tainted Ground?
Unmanly Thought! what Seasons can controul,
What fancied Zone can circumscribe the Soul,
Who, conscious of the Source from whence she springs,
By Reason's Light on Resolution's Wings,   75
Spite of her frail Companion, dauntless goes
O'er Libya's Deserts & thro' Zembla's snows?
She bids each slumb'ring Energy awake,
Another Touch, another Temper take,
Suspends th' inferiour Laws, that rule our Clay: 80
The stubborn Elements confess her Sway;
Their little Wants, their low Desires, refine,
And raise the Mortal to a Height divine.

   Not but the human Fabrick from the Birth
Imbibes a flavour of its parent Earth   85
As various Tracts enforce a various Toil,
The Manners speak the Idiom of their Soil.
An Iron-Race the Mountain-Cliffs maintain,
Foes to the gentler Genius of the Plain:
For where unwearied Sinews must be found   90
With sidelong Plough to quell the flinty Ground,
To turn the Torrent's swift-descending Flood,
To brave the Savage rushing from the Wood,
What wonder, if to patient Valour train'd
They guard with Spirit, what by Strength they gain'd?   95
And while their rocky Ramparts round they see,
The rough Abode of Want & Liberty,
(As lawless Force from Confidence will grow)
Insult the Plenty of the Vales below?
What wonder, in the sultry Climes, that spread,   100
Where Nile redundant o'er his summer-bed
From his broad bosom life & verdure flings,
And broods o'er Egypt with his wat'ry wings,
If with advent'rous oar & ready sail
The dusky people drive before the gale,   105
Or on frail floats to distant cities ride,
That rise & glitter o'er the ambient tide.

10. [*Tophet*]. *Inscription on a Portrait*

[Gray probably wrote this epigram in about 1749. 'Tophet' is a phonetic anagram of Etough. The Rev. Henry Etough, Rector of Therfield, Herts., was widely disliked in Cambridge for his interference in university affairs and for his supposed religious hypocrisy, since he had originally been a Dissenting Minister who came over to the Church of England. Gray's letters of this period make several references to him. The epigram seems to have been written to accompany a drawing of Etough made in about 1749 by William Mason, of which an etching was made in 1769 by Michael Tyson of St Benet's College. It was first printed posthumously in the *London Magazine*, lii. 296, in June 1783 and, with some variants, in the *Gentleman's Magazine*, lv. 759, in October 1785. The text followed here is that transcribed by Mason into Gray's Commonplace Book, in which lines 3-4 are written below the six lines found in all other texts and described as 'additions in the first copy' to be inserted after line 2. A pen and ink copy of the etching in the Cole MSS. in the British Museum has several variants and a copy of the same text, also with the drawing of Etough, is in Pembroke College, Cambridge.]

> Such *Tophet* was; so looked the grinning Fiend
> Whom many a frighted Prelate calld his friend;
> I saw them bow & while they wishd him dead
> With servile simper nod the mitred head.
> Our Mother-Church with half-averted sight   5
> Blushd as she blesst her griesly proselyte:
> Hosannahs rung thro Hells tremendous borders
> And Satans self had thoughts of taking orders.

11. *Elegy Written in a Country Church-Yard*

[Mason believed that the *Elegy* was at least begun in August 1742, in spite of Walpole's initial conviction that Gray began writing it 'three or four years' after the death of Richard West in 1742 (an event with which later critics have often connected the closing stanzas). Careful examination of all the evidence, external and internal, suggests that most of the poem at least was written between the summer or autumn of 1746 and 12 June 1750, when Gray sent the complete poem to Walpole. By 18 December 1750, when Gray sent a copy to Wharton, the *Elegy* was circulating widely in manuscript, as a result of Walpole's enthusiasm for it. On 11 February 1751 Gray told Walpole that the editors of the *Magazine of Magazines* had informed him of their intention of printing it. Gray's response was to commission Walpole to have it published immediately by Dodsley and the poem duly appeared as a quarto pamphlet on 15 February 1751, with the following 'Advertisement' by Walpole:

> *The following POEM came into my hands by Accident, if the general Approbation with which this little Piece has been spread, may be call'd by so slight a term as Accident. It is this Approbation which makes it unnecessary for me to make any Apology but to the Author: As he cannot but feel some Satisfaction in having pleas'd so many Readers already, I flatter myself he will forgive my communicating that Pleasure to many more.*
>
> The *EDITOR*

Gray himself later made the following note in the margin of his transcript of the *Elegy* in his Commonplace Book, evidently adding to it from time to time:

> 1750. publish'd in Feb:^{ry} 1751. by Dodsley; and went through four [five *deleted*] editions; in two months; and afterwards a fifth, 6th, 7th, & 8th 9th & 10th & 11th. printed also in 1753 with Mr Bentley's Designs, of wch there is a 2^d Edition & again by Dodsley in his Miscellany Vol. 4th & in a Scotch Collection call'd the *Union*. translated into Latin by Ch^r Anstey Esq. & the Rev. Mr Roberts, & publish'd in 1762, & again in the same year by Rob: Lloyd M:A:

Most of the numerous appearances of the poem in Gray's lifetime are described in detail by F. G. Stokes in his edition (Oxford, 1929).

The text followed is that of 1768. Of the three holograph MSS., the Eton College MS. is clearly the earliest and its variants from the printed version, especially the original ending planned by Gray, are significant enough to deserve a full transcription and separate textual apparatus (see Appendix, p. 101). Variants are recorded from the Commonplace Book, the letter to Wharton, the quarto editions printed by Dodsley (the 3rd and 8th editions were significantly corrected by Gray), Dodsley's *Collection*, vol. iv (1755), and the Foulis edition (Glasgow, 1768).]

> The Curfew tolls* the knell of parting day,
> The lowing herd wind slowly o'er the lea,
> The plowman homeward plods his weary way,
> And leaves the world to darkness and to me.
>
> Now fades the glimmering landscape on the sight,   5
> And all the air a solemn stillness holds,
> Save where the beetle wheels his droning flight,
> And drowsy tinklings lull the distant folds;

---

*   ———squilla di lontano,
Che paia 'l giorno pianger, che si muore.
           Dante. Purgat. [*Canto*] 8. [ll. 5–6].

Save that from yonder ivy-mantled tow'r
The mopeing owl does to the moon complain   10
Of such, as wand'ring near her secret bow'r,
Molest her ancient solitary reign.

Beneath those rugged elms, that yew-tree's shade,
Where heaves the turf in many a mould'ring heap,
Each in his narrow cell for ever laid,   15
The rude Forefathers of the hamlet sleep.

The breezy call of incense-breathing Morn,
The swallow twitt'ring from the straw-built shed,
The cock's shrill clarion, or the ecchoing horn,
No more shall rouse them from their lowly bed.   20

For them no more the blazing hearth shall burn,
Or busy houswife ply her evening care:
No children run to lisp their sire's return,
Or climb his knees the envied kiss to share.

Oft did the harvest to their sickle yield,   25
Their furrow oft the stubborn glebe has broke;
How jocund did they drive their team afield!
How bow'd the woods beneath their sturdy stroke!

Let not Ambition mock their useful toil,
Their homely joys, and destiny obscure;   30
Nor Grandeur hear with a disdainful smile,
The short and simple annals of the poor.

The boast of heraldry, the pomp of pow'r,
And all that beauty, all that wealth e'er gave,
Awaits alike th' inevitable hour.   35
The paths of glory lead but to the grave.

Nor you, ye Proud, impute to These the fault,
If Mem'ry o'er their Tomb no Trophies raise,
Where thro' the long-drawn isle and fretted vault
The pealing anthem swells the note of praise.   40

Can storied urn or animated bust
Back to its mansion call the fleeting breath?
Can Honour's voice provoke the silent dust,
Or Flatt'ry sooth the dull cold ear of Death?

Perhaps in this neglected spot is laid   45
Some heart once pregnant with celestial fire,
Hands, that the rod of empire might have sway'd,
Or wak'd to extasy the living lyre.

But Knowledge to their eyes her ample page
Rich with the spoils of time did ne'er unroll;   50
Chill Penury repress'd their noble rage,
And froze the genial current of the soul.

Full many a gem of purest ray serene,
The dark unfathom'd caves of ocean bear:
Full many a flower is born to blush unseen,   55
And waste its sweetness on the desert air.

Some village-Hampden, that with dauntless breast
The little Tyrant of his fields withstood;
Some mute inglorious Milton here may rest,
Some Cromwell guiltless of his country's blood.   60

Th' applause of list'ning senates to command,
The threats of pain and ruin to despise,
To scatter plenty o'er a smiling land,
And read their hist'ry in a nation's eyes,

Their lot forbad: nor circumscrib'd alone   65
Their growing virtues, but their crimes confin'd;
Forbad to wade through slaughter to a throne,
And shut the gates of mercy on mankind,

The struggling pangs of conscious truth to hide,
To quench the blushes of ingenuous shame,   70
Or heap the shrine of Luxury and Pride
With incense kindled at the Muse's flame.

Far from the madding crowd's ignoble strife,
Their sober wishes never learn'd to stray;
Along the cool sequester'd vale of life   75
They kept the noiseless tenor of their way.

Yet ev'n these bones from insult to protect
Some frail memorial still erected nigh,
With uncouth rhimes and shapeless sculpture deck'd,
Implores the passing tribute of a sigh.   80

Their name, their years, spelt by th' unletter'd muse,
The place of fame and elegy supply:
And many a holy text around she strews,
That teach the rustic moralist to die.

For who to dumb Forgetfulness a prey,   85
This pleasing anxious being e'er resign'd,
Left the warm precincts of the chearful day,
Nor cast one longing ling'ring look behind?

On some fond breast the parting soul relies,
Some pious drops the closing eye requires;   90
Ev'n from the tomb the voice of Nature cries,
*Ev'n in our Ashes live their wonted Fires.

For thee, who mindful of th' unhonour'd Dead
Dost in these lines their artless tale relate;
If chance, by lonely contemplation led,   95
Some kindred Spirit shall inquire thy fate,

old person

Haply some hoary-headed Swain may say,
'Oft have we seen him at the peep of dawn
'Brushing with hasty steps the dews away
'To meet the sun upon the upland lawn.   100

* Ch'i veggio nel pensier, dolce mio fuoco,
  Fredda una lingua, & due begli occhi chiusi
  Rimaner doppo noi pien di faville.
                              Petrarch. Son. 169. [170].

Part of Gray's *Elegy* from the MS. at Pembroke College, Cambridge.

'There at the foot of yonder nodding beech
'That wreathes its old fantastic roots so high,
'His listless length at noontide wou'd he stretch,
'And pore upon the brook that babbles by.

'Hard by yon wood, now smiling as in scorn,   105
'Mutt'ring his wayward fancies he wou'd rove,
'Now drooping, woeful wan, like one forlorn,
'Or craz'd with care, or cross'd in hopeless love.

'One morn I miss'd him on the custom'd hill,
'Along the heath and near his fav'rite tree;   110
'Another came; nor yet beside the rill,
'Nor up the lawn, nor at the wood was he;

'The next with dirges due in sad array
'Slow thro' the church-way path we saw him born.
'Approach and read (for thou can'st read) the lay,   115
'Grav'd on the stone beneath yon aged thorn.'

The EPITAPH. *to poet of this poem — — not Gray, but perhaps Gray romanticised*

Here rests his head upon the lap of Earth
A Youth to Fortune and to Fame unknown,
Fair Science frown'd not on his humble birth,
And Melancholy mark'd him for her own.   120

Large was his bounty, and his soul sincere,
Heav'n did a recompence as largely send:
He gave to Mis'ry all he had, a tear,
He gain'd from Heav'n ('twas all he wish'd) a friend.

No farther seek his merits to disclose,   125
Or draw his frailties from their dread abode,
(* There they alike in trembling hope repose)
The bosom of his Father and his God.

---

* ——paventosa speme.
        Petrarch. Son. 114. [115].

12. *A Long Story*

[Gray's transcript in his Commonplace Book is dated 'Aug: 1750', when the events described in the poem no doubt took place, although line 120 refers to the trial of a highwayman which did not occur until 13 September 1750. (A note referring to Macleane's execution on 3 October 1750 could no doubt have been added later.) The poem dates from the period when the *Elegy* was already circulating in manuscript. Lady Cobham, who lived in the Manor House at Stoke Poges with her niece Henrietta Speed, was an early admirer of the poem. *A Long Story* humorously describes a visit to the poet by Miss Speed and Lady Schaub (53 ff.), their leaving an invitation (77–84) since the poet was out (or, according to the poem, in 'a small closet in the garden'), and his return visit to the Manor House (85 ff.). Gray invokes the history of the Manor House throughout the poem. Henry Hastings, Earl of Huntingdon, rebuilt it in about 1555 and is supposed to have mortgaged it in about 1580 to Sir Christopher Hatton, Lord Chancellor 1587–91. At line 41 Gray refers to Robert Purt, a clergyman who had first mentioned him to Lady Cobham and in lines 103 and 115–16, as his own notes indicate, to various members of the household at the Manor.

The poem was printed only once with Gray's approval, in *Designs by Mr R. Bentley* in 1753, merely for the sake of the illustrations, according to the poet. Thereafter Gray was anxious to suppress it, although it continued to appear in Irish editions of his poems during his lifetime. The text followed is that in the *Designs*, with variants from the Commonplace Book and a MS. now in the J. W. Garrett Library of Johns Hopkins University, which contains some additional explanatory notes.]

    In Britain's Isle, no matter where,
    An ancient pile of building stands:
    The Huntingdons and Hattons there
    Employ'd the power of Fairy hands

    To raise the cieling's fretted height,   5
    Each pannel in achievements cloathing,
    Rich windows that exclude the light,
    And passages, that lead to nothing.

    Full oft within the spatious walls,
    When he had fifty winters o'er him,   10
    My grave *Lord-Keeper led the Brawls:
    The Seal, and Maces, danc'd before him.

* [Sir Christopher] Hatton, prefer'd by Queen Elizabeth for his graceful Person and fine Dancing.

His bushy beard, and shoe-strings green,
His high-crown'd hat, and sattin-doublet,
Mov'd the stout heart of England's Queen,   15
Tho' Pope and Spaniard could not trouble it.

What, in the very first beginning!
Shame of the versifying tribe!
Your Hist'ry whither are you spinning?
Can you do nothing but describe?   20

A House there is, (and that's enough)
From whence one fatal morning issues
A brace of Warriors, not in buff,
But rustling in their silks and tissues.

The first came cap-a-pee from France   25
Her conqu'ring destiny fulfilling,
Whom meaner Beauties eye askance,
And vainly ape her art of killing.

The other Amazon kind Heaven
Had arm'd with spirit, wit, and satire: 30
But COBHAM had the polish given,
And tip'd her arrows with good-nature.

To celebrate her eyes, her air - - - - -
Coarse panegyricks would but teaze her.
Melissa is her Nom de Guerre.   35
Alas, who would not wish to please her!

With bonnet blue and capucine,
And aprons long they hid their armour,
And veil'd their weapons bright and keen
In pity to the country-farmer.   40

Fame in the shape of Mr. P - - - t
(By this time all the Parish know it)
Had told, that thereabouts there lurk'd
A wicked Imp they call a Poet,

Who prowl'd the country far and near,   45
Bewitch'd the children of the peasants,
Dried up the cows, and lam'd the deer,
And suck'd the eggs, and kill'd the pheasants.

My Lady heard their joint petition,
Swore by her coronet and ermine,   50
She'd issue out her high commission
To rid the manour of such vermin.

The Heroines undertook the task,
Thro' lanes unknown, o'er stiles they ventur'd,
Rap'd at the door, nor stay'd to ask,   55
But bounce into the parlour enter'd.

The trembling family they daunt,
They flirt, they sing, they laugh, they tattle,
Rummage his Mother, pinch his Aunt,
And up stairs in a whirlwind rattle.   60

Each hole and cupboard they explore,
Each creek and cranny of his chamber,
Run hurry-skurry round the floor,
And o'er the bed and tester clamber,

Into the Drawers and China pry,   65
Papers and books, a huge Imbroglio!
Under a tea-cup he might lie,
Or creased, like dogs-ears, in a folio.

On the first marching of the troops
The Muses, hopeless of his pardon,   70
Convey'd him underneath their hoops
To a small closet in the garden.

So Rumor says. (Who will, believe.)
But that they left the door a-jarr,
Where, safe and laughing in his sleeve,   75
He heard the distant din of war.

Short was his joy. He little knew,
The power of Magick was no fable.
Out of the window, whisk, they flew,
But left a spell upon the table.   80

The words too eager to unriddle
The Poet felt a strange disorder:
Transparent birdlime form'd the middle,
And chains invisible the border.

So cunning was the Apparatus,   85
The powerful pothooks did so move him,
That, will he, nill he, to the Great-house
He went, as if the Devil drove him.

Yet on his way (no sign of grace,
For folks in fear are apt to pray)   90
To Phœbus he prefer'd his case,
And beg'd his aid that dreadful day.

The Godhead would have back'd his quarrel,
But with a blush on recollection
Own'd, that his quiver and his laurel   95
'Gainst four such eyes were no protection.

The Court was sate, the Culprit there,
Forth from their gloomy mansions creeping
The Lady *Janes* and *Joans* repair,
And from the gallery stand peeping: 100

Such as in silence of the night
Come (sweep) along some winding entry
(* *Styack* has often seen the sight)
Or at the chappel-door stand sentry;

In peaked hoods and mantles tarnish'd,   105
Sour visages, enough to scare ye,
High Dames of honour once, that garnish'd
The drawing-room of fierce Queen Mary!

---

* The HOUSE-KEEPER.

The Peeress comes. The Audience stare,
And doff their hats with due submission: 110
She curtsies, as she takes her chair,
To all the People of condition.

The Bard with many an artful fib,
Had in imagination fenc'd him,
Disproved the arguments of *Squib,   115
And all that †Groom could urge against him.

But soon his rhetorick forsook him,
When he the solemn hall had seen;
A sudden fit of ague shook him,
He stood as mute as poor ‡Macleane.   120

Yet something he was heard to mutter,
'How in the park beneath an old-tree
'(Without design to hurt the butter,
'Or any malice to the poultry,)

'He once or twice had pen'd a sonnet;   125
'Yet hoped, that he might save his bacon:
'Numbers would give their oaths upon it,
'He ne'er was for a conj'rer taken.'

The ghostly Prudes with hagged face
Already had condemn'd the sinner.   130
My Lady rose, and with a grace - - - -
She smiled, and bid him come to dinner.

'Jesu-Maria! Madam Bridget,
'Why, what can the Vicountess mean?
(Cried the square Hoods in woful fidget)   135
'The times are alter'd quite and clean!

'Decorum's turn'd to mere civility;
'Her air and all her manners shew it.
'Commend me to her affability!
'Speak to a Commoner and Poet!   140
          [Here 500 Stanzas are lost]

* Groom of the Chambers.   † The Steward.
‡ A famous Highwayman hang'd the week before.

And so God save our noble King,
And guard us from long-winded Lubbers,
That to eternity would sing,
And keep my Lady from her Rubbers.

13. *Stanzas to Mr Bentley*

[Probably written in 1752, when Richard Bentley (1708–81) was preparing
his drawings for *Designs . . . for Six Poems by Mr T. Gray*, published on 29
March 1753. Mason transcribed these lines into the Commonplace Book and
first printed them in 1775, the text followed here except that Mason's attempts to supply the final words of the last three lines, missing because of a
torn corner in Gray's MS., have been confined to the textual notes.]

In silent gaze the tuneful choir among,
  Half pleas'd, half blushing let the muse admire,
While Bentley leads her sister-art along,
  And bids the pencil answer to the lyre.
See, in their course, each transitory thought   5
  Fix'd by his touch a lasting essence take;
Each dream, in fancy's airy colouring wrought,
  To local symmetry and life awake!
The tardy rhymes that us'd to linger on,
  To censure cold, and negligent of fame,   10
In swifter measures animated run,
  And catch a lustre from his genuine flame.
Ah! could they catch his strength, his easy grace,
  His quick creation, his unerring line;
The energy of Pope they might efface,   15
  And Dryden's harmony submit to mine.
But not to one in this benighted age
  Is that diviner inspiration giv'n,
That burns in Shakespear's or in Milton's page,
  The pomp and prodigality of heav'n.   20
As when conspiring in the diamond's blaze,
  The meaner gems, that singly charm the sight,
Together dart their intermingled rays,
  And dazzle with a luxury of light.
Enough for me, if to some feeling breast   25
  My lines a secret sympathy [   ]
And as their pleasing influence [   ]
  A sigh of soft reflection [   ]

14. *The Progress of Poesy. A Pindaric Ode*

[In July 1752 Gray described this poem as lacking only the final 17 lines, but his transcript in his Commonplace Book, where it is entitled 'Ode in the Greek Manner', states that it was 'Finish'd in 1754'. Gray sent the poem, with the same title, to Wharton on 26 December 1754. A letter to Edward Bedingfield on 29 April 1756 refers to it as *'the Powers of Poetry'*. On 29 December 1756 Gray sent lines 1–24 to Bedingfield, who had apparently already seen the rest of the poem. Originally intended for Vol. IV of Dodsley's *Collection of Poems* (1755), Gray finally decided that the poem should be published, together with *The Bard*, in a separate quarto pamphlet by Dodsley. It was the first book to be printed at Horace Walpole's newly established press at Strawberry Hill and appeared on 8 August 1757.

Gray begins by describing the different kinds of poetry, its sources and powers, and its importance to mankind (1–53). After dwelling on its primitive origins and ubiquity and its connection with political liberty (54–65), he describes the progress of the art from Ancient Greece to Italy and finally to Britain (66–82). In particular, Shakespeare, the poet of the passions, Milton, the poet of the sublime, and Dryden, the poet of harmony and energy, are celebrated (83–111). Finally, Gray speaks of his own poetic powers and aspirations, and his daring in imitating Pindar in an age unfavourable to lyric poetry (112–23).

The text follows 1768, when the 'Advertisement' and notes first appeared. Variants are recorded from the Commonplace Book and the letters to Wharton and Bedingfield. Gray himself translated his motto to the two *Odes*, *'vocal to the Intelligent alone'*.]

Φωνᾶντα συνετοῖσιν· ἐς
Δὲ τὸ πᾶν ἑρμηνέων χατίζει.

PINDAR, Olymp. II. [85].

ADVERTISEMENT

When the Author first published this and the following Ode, he was advised, even by his Friends, to subjoin some few explanatory Notes: but had too much respect for the understanding of his Readers to take that liberty.

I. 1

*Awake, Æolian lyre, awake,
And give to rapture all thy trembling strings.
From Helicon's harmonious springs
A thousand rills their mazy progress take:
The laughing flowers, that round them blow,   5
Drink life and fragrance as they flow.
Now the rich stream of music winds along
Deep, majestic, smooth, and strong,
Thro' verdant vales, and Ceres' golden reign:
Now rowling down the steep amain,   10
Headlong, impetuous, see it pour:
The rocks, and nodding groves rebellow to the roar.

I. 2

† Oh! Sovereign of the willing soul,
Parent of sweet and solemn-breathing airs,
Enchanting shell! the sullen Cares,   15
And frantic Passions hear thy soft controul.
On Thracia's hills the Lord of War,
Has curb'd the fury of his car,
And drop'd his thirsty lance at thy command.
‡ Perching on the scept'red hand   20
Of Jove, thy magic lulls the feather'd king
With ruffled plumes, and flagging wing:
Quench'd in dark clouds of slumber lie
The terror of his beak, and light'nings of his eye.

* Awake, my glory: awake, lute and harp.
                              David's Psalms. [LVII. 9].

Pindar styles his own poetry with its musical accompanyments, Αἰολῇς μολπή,
Αἰολίδες χορδαί, Αἰολίδων πνοαὶ αὐλῶν, Æolian song, Æolian strings, the breath of
the Æolian flute.

  The subject and simile, as usual with Pindar, are united. The various sources of
poetry, which gives life and lustre to all it touches, are here described; its quiet
majestic progress enriching every subject (otherwise dry and barren) with a pomp of
diction and luxuriant harmony of numbers; and its more rapid and irresistible course,
when swoln and hurried away by the conflict of tumultuous passions.

  † Power of harmony to calm the turbulent sallies of the soul. The thoughts are
borrowed from the first Pythian of Pindar [5–12].

  ‡ This is a weak imitation of some incomparable lines in the same Ode.

I. 3

*Thee the voice, the dance, obey,   25
Temper'd to thy warbled lay.
O'er Idalia's velvet-green
The rosy-crowned Loves are seen
On Cytherea's day
With antic Sports, and blue-eyed Pleasures,   30
Frisking light in frolic measures;
Now pursuing, now retreating,
Now in circling troops they meet:
To brisk notes in cadence beating
†Glance their many-twinkling feet.   35
Slow melting strains their Queen's approach declare:
Where'er she turns the Graces homage pay.
With arms sublime, that float upon the air,
In gliding state she wins her easy way:
O'er her warm cheek, and rising bosom, move   40
‡The bloom of young Desire, and purple light of Love.

II. 1

§Man's feeble race what Ills await,
Labour, and Penury, the racks of Pain,
Disease, and Sorrow's weeping train,
And Death, sad refuge from the storms of Fate!   45
The fond complaint, my Song, disprove,
And justify the laws of Jove.
Say, has he giv'n in vain the heav'nly Muse?
Night, and all her sickly dews,
Her Spectres wan, and Birds of boding cry,   50
He gives to range the dreary sky:
‖Till down the eastern cliffs afar
Hyperion's march they spy, and glitt'ring shafts of war.

---

* Power of harmony to produce all the graces of motion in the body.

† Μαρμαρυγὰς θηεῖτο ποδῶν, θαύμαζε δὲ θυμῷ.   HOMER. Od. Θ. [VIII, 265].

‡ Λάμπει δ' ἐπὶ πορφυρέῃσι
Παρείῃσι φῶς ἔρωτος.
                PHRYNICHUS, apud Athenæum. [*Deipnosophistae*, XIII. 604a].

§ To compensate the real and imaginary ills of life, the Muse was given to Mankind by the same Providence that sends the Day by its chearful presence to dispel the gloom and terrors of the Night.

‖ Or seen the Morning's well-appointed Star
Come marching up the eastern hills afar.
                    Cowley [*Brutus, an ode*. st. IV].

II. 2

* In climes beyond the solar † road,
Where shaggy forms o'er ice-built mountains roam,   55
The Muse has broke the twilight-gloom
To chear the shiv'ring Native's dull abode.
And oft, beneath the od'rous shade
Of Chili's boundless forests laid,
She deigns to hear the savage Youth repeat   60
In loose numbers wildly sweet
Their feather-cinctured Chiefs, and dusky Loves.
Her track, where'er the Goddess roves,
Glory pursue, and generous Shame,
Th' unconquerable Mind, and Freedom's holy flame.   65

II. 3

‡ Woods, that wave o'er Delphi's steep,
Isles, that crown th' Egæan deep,
Fields, that cool Ilissus laves,
Or where Mæander's amber waves
In lingering Lab'rinths creep,   70
How do your tuneful Echoes languish,
Mute, but to the voice of Anguish?
Where each old poetic Mountain
Inspiration breath'd around:
Ev'ry shade and hallow'd Fountain   75
Murmur'd deep a solemn sound:
Till the sad Nine in Greece's evil hour
Left their Parnassus for the Latian plains.
Alike they scorn the pomp of tyrant-Power,
And coward Vice, that revels in her chains.   80
When Latium had her lofty spirit lost,
They sought, oh Albion! next thy sea-encircled coast.

---

* Extensive influence of poetic Genius over the remotest and most uncivilized nations: its connection with liberty, and the virtues that naturally attend on it. [See the Erse, Norwegian, and Welch Fragments, the Lapland and American songs.]

   † "Extra anni solisque vias——"   *Virgil* [*Aeneid*, VI. 796].
   "Tutta lontana dal camin del sole."   *Petrarch, Canzon* 2. [48].

  ‡ Progress of Poetry from Greece to Italy, and from Italy to England. Chaucer was not unacquainted with the writings of Dante or of Petrarch. The Earl of Surrey and Sir Tho. Wyatt had travelled in Italy, and formed their taste there; Spenser imitated the Italian writers; Milton improved on them: but this School expired soon after the Restoration, and a new one arose on the French model, which has subsisted ever since.

III. 1

Far from the sun and summer-gale,
In thy green lap was Nature's *Darling laid,
What time, where lucid Avon stray'd,   85
To Him the mighty Mother did unveil
Her aweful face: The dauntless Child
Stretch'd forth his little arms, and smiled.
This pencil take (she said) whose colours clear
Richly paint the vernal year: 90
Thine too these golden keys, immortal Boy!
This can unlock the gates of Joy;
Of Horrour that, and thrilling Fears,
Or ope the sacred source of sympathetic Tears.

III. 2

Nor second He,† that rode sublime   95
Upon the seraph-wings of Extasy,
The secrets of th' Abyss to spy.
‡ He pass'd the flaming bounds of Place and Time:
§ The living Throne, the saphire-blaze,
Where Angels tremble, while they gaze,   100
He saw; but blasted with excess of light,
‖ Closed his eyes in endless night.
Behold, where Dryden's less presumptuous car,
Wide o'er the fields of Glory bear
¶ Two Coursers of ethereal race,   105
** With necks in thunder cloath'd, and long-resounding pace.

---

* Shakespear.
† Milton.
‡ "——flammantia mœnia mundi."   *Lucretius* [I. 73].
§ For the spirit of the living creature was in the wheels—And above the firmament,
that was over their heads, was the likeness of a throne, as the appearance of a saphire-
stone.—This was the appearance of the glory of the Lord.   *Ezekiel* i. 20, 26, 28.
‖ Ὀφθαλμῶν μὲν ἄμερσε· δίδου δ' ἡδεῖαν ἀοιδήν.   HOMER. Od. [VIII. 64].
¶ Meant to express the stately march and sounding energy of Dryden's rhimes.
** Hast thou cloathed his neck with thunder?   *Job* [XXXIX. 19].

III. 3

Hark, his hands the lyre explore!
Bright-eyed Fancy hovering o'er
Scatters from her pictur'd urn
*Thoughts, that breath, and words, that burn.   110
†But ah! 'tis heard no more——
Oh! Lyre divine, what daring Spirit
Wakes thee now? tho' he inherit
Nor the pride, nor ample pinion,
‡That the Theban Eagle bear   115
Sailing with supreme dominion
Thro' the azure deep of air:
Yet oft before his infant eyes would run
Such forms, as glitter in the Muse's ray
With orient hues, unborrow'd of the Sun: 120
Yet shall he mount, and keep his distant way
Beyond the limits of a vulgar fate,
Beneath the Good how far—but far above the Great.

---

* Words, that weep, and tears that speak.   *Cowley* [*The Prophet*, 20].

† We have had in our language no other odes of the sublime kind, than that of Dryden on St. Cecilia's day: for Cowley (who had his merit) yet wanted judgment, style, and harmony, for such a task. That of Pope is not worthy of so great a man. Mr. Mason indeed of late days has touched the true chords, and with a masterly hand, in some of his Choruses,—above all in the last of Caractacus,

> Hark! heard ye not yon footstep dread? &c.

‡ Διὸς πρὸς ὄρνιχα θεῖον. Olymp. 2. [88]. Pindar compares himself to that bird, and his enemies to ravens that croak and clamour in vain below, while it pursues its flight, regardless of their noise.

15. *The Bard. A Pindaric Ode*

[Written between 1755 and mid-June 1757. During August 1755 Gray sent passages from the first hundred lines to Wharton and Stonhewer but could make no further progress with the poem. In May 1757 his interest in it was reawakened by hearing a performance in Cambridge by John Parry, a blind Welsh harper: he sent a draft of the conclusion of the poem to Mason before the end of the month and had extensively revised it by mid-June. *The Bard* was published, together with *The Progress of Poesy*, on 8 August 1757. Gray's source for the tradition that Edward I ordered the suppression of the Welsh bards was a short passage in Thomas Carte's *General History of England*, ii (1750) 196. A long essay on Anglo-Welsh relations, entitled 'Cambri', in Gray's Commonplace Book written before 1759, shows that he had come to have some doubts about the historical accuracy of the tradition.

The poem begins with the Bard denouncing Edward I and his army as they return across Snowdonia from the subjugation of Wales in 1283. He then laments his bardic companions supposedly slaughtered by Edward (1–48). The ghosts of the slaughtered bards prophetically describe the fate which awaits 'Edward's race', the Plantagenets, down to Richard III (49–100). After this vision, the Bard himself resumes to foretell the return of the House of Tudor, which will restore the political liberty essential to poetry, resulting in the poetic revival of the reign of Queen Elizabeth. After this defiance of the tyrant, the Bard commits triumphant suicide (100–44).

The text is that of 1768, where the historical notes appeared in full for the first time. Variants are recorded from passages included or discussed before publication in letters to Wharton, Bedingfield, and Mason.]

ADVERTISEMENT

The following Ode is founded on a Tradition current in Wales, that EDWARD THE FIRST, when he compleated the Conquest of that country, ordered all the Bards, that fell into his hands, to be put to death.

I. 1

'Ruin seize thee, ruthless King!
'Confusion on thy banners wait,
'Tho' fann'd by Conquest's crimson wing
'*They mock the air with idle state.
'Helm, nor †Hauberk's twisted mail,   5
'Nor even thy virtues, Tyrant, shall avail
'To save thy secret soul from nightly fears,
'From Cambria's curse, from Cambria's tears!'
Such were the sounds, that o'er the ‡crested pride
Of the first Edward scatter'd wild dismay,   10
As down the steep of §Snowdon's shaggy side
He wound with toilsome march his long array.
Stout ‖ Glo'ster stood aghast in speechless trance:
To arms! cried ¶ Mortimer, and couch'd his quiv'ring lance.

I. 2

On a rock, whose haughty brow   15
Frowns o'er old Conway's foaming flood,
Robed in the sable garb of woe,
With haggard eyes the Poet stood;
**Loose his beard, and hoary hair
††Stream'd, like a meteor, to the troubled air)   20

* Mocking the air with colours idly spread.   *Shakespear's King John* [V. i. 72].
   † The Hauberk was a texture of steel ringlets, or rings interwoven, forming a coat of mail, that sate close to the body, and adapted itself to every motion.
   ‡ ——The crested adder's pride.   *Dryden's Indian Queen* [III. i].
   § *Snowdon* was a name given by the Saxons to that mountainous tract, which the Welch themselves call *Craigian-eryri*: it included all the highlands of Caernarvonshire and Merionethshire, as far east as the river Conway. R. Hygden speaking of the castle of Conway built by King Edward the first, says, 'Ad ortum amnis Conway ad clivum montis Erery;' and Matthew of Westminster, (ad ann. 1283,) 'Apud Aberconway ad pedes montis Snowdoniæ fecit erigi castrum forte.'
   ‖ Gilbert de Clare, surnamed the Red, Earl of Gloucester and Hertford, son-in-law to King Edward.
   ¶ Edmond de Mortimer, Lord of Wigmore.
   They both were *Lords-Marchers*, whose lands lay on the borders of Wales, and probably accompanied the King in this expedition.
   ** The image was taken from a well-known picture of Raphaël, representing the Supreme Being in the vision of Ezekiel: there are two of these paintings (both believed original), one at Florence, the other at Paris.
   †† Shone, like a meteor, streaming to the wind.
                                           Milton's Paradise Lost [I. 537].

And with a Master's hand, and Prophet's fire,
Struck the deep sorrows of his lyre.
'Hark, how each giant-oak, and desert cave,
'Sighs to the torrent's aweful voice beneath!
'O'er thee, oh King! their hundred arms they wave,   25
'Revenge on thee in hoarser murmurs breath;
'Vocal no more, since Cambria's fatal day,
'To high-born Hoël's harp, or soft Llewellyn's lay.

I. 3

'Cold is Cadwallo's tongue,
'That hush'd the stormy main: 30
'Brave Urien sleeps upon his craggy bed:
'Mountains, ye mourn in vain
'Modred, whose magic song
'Made huge Plinlimmon bow his cloud-top'd head.
'*On dreary Arvon's shore they lie,   35
'Smear'd with gore, and ghastly pale:
'Far, far aloof th' affrighted ravens sail;
'The famish'd †Eagle screams, and passes by.
'Dear lost companions of my tuneful art,
'‡Dear, as the light that visits these sad eyes,   40
'‡Dear, as the ruddy drops that warm my heart,
'Ye died amidst your dying country's cries—
'No more I weep. They do not sleep.
'On yonder cliffs, a griesly band,
'I see them sit, they linger yet,   45
'Avengers of their native land:
'With me in dreadful harmony §they join,
'And §weave with bloody hands the tissue of thy line.'

---

* The shores of Caernarvonshire opposite to the isle of Anglesey.

† Cambden and others observe, that eagles used annually to build their aerie among
the rocks of Snowdon, which from thence (as some think) were named by the Welch
Craigian-eryri, or the crags of the eagles. At this day (I am told) the highest point of
Snowdon is called *the eagle's nest*. That bird is certainly no stranger to this island, as
the Scots, and the people of Cumberland, Westmoreland, *&c.* can testify: it even has
built its nest in the Peak of Derbyshire. [See Willoughby's Ornithol. published by
Ray.]

‡ As dear to me as are the ruddy drops,
    That visit my sad heart——
                              Shakesp. Jul. Cæsar [II. i. 289–90].
§ See the Norwegian Ode, that follows [*The Fatal Sisters*].

II. 1

"Weave the warp, and weave the woof,
"The winding-sheet of Edward's race.   50
"Give ample room, and verge enough
"The characters of hell to trace.
"Mark the year, and mark the night,
"*When Severn shall re-eccho with affright
"The shrieks of death, thro' Berkley's roofs that ring,   55
"Shrieks of an agonizing King!
"† She-Wolf of France, with unrelenting fangs,
"That tear'st the bowels of thy mangled Mate,
"‡ From thee be born, who o'er thy country hangs
"The scourge of Heav'n. What Terrors round him wait!   60
"Amazement in his van, with Flight combined,
"And Sorrow's faded form, and Solitude behind.

II. 2

"Mighty Victor, mighty Lord,
"§ Low on his funeral couch he lies!
"No pitying heart, no eye, afford   65
"A tear to grace his obsequies.
"Is the sable ‖ Warriour fled?
"Thy son is gone. He rests among the Dead.
"The Swarm, that in thy noon-tide beam were born?
"Gone to salute the rising Morn.   70
"Fair ¶ laughs the Morn, and soft the Zephyr blows,
"While proudly riding o'er the azure realm
"In gallant trim the gilded Vessel goes;
"Youth on the prow, and Pleasure at the helm;
"Regardless of the sweeping Whirlwind's sway,   75
"That, hush'd in grim repose, expects his evening-prey.

* Edward the Second, cruelly butchered in Berkley-Castle [1327].
† Isabel of France, Edward the Second's adulterous Queen.
‡ Triumphs of Edward the Third in France.
§ Death of that King, abandoned by his Children, and even robbed in his last moments by his Courtiers and his Mistress [1377].
‖ Edward, the Black Prince, dead some time before his Father [1376].
¶ Magnificence of Richard the Second's reign. See Froissard, and other contemporary Writers.

II. 3

"*Fill high the sparkling bowl,
"The rich repast prepare,
"Reft of a crown, he yet may share the feast:
"Close by the regal chair   80
"Fell Thirst and Famine scowl
"A baleful smile upon their baffled Guest.
"Heard ye the din of †battle bray,
"Lance to lance, and horse to horse?
"Long Years of havock urge their destined course,   85
"And thro' the kindred squadrons mow their way.
"Ye Towers of Julius,‡ London's lasting shame,
"With many a foul and midnight murther fed,
"Revere his §Consort's faith, his Father's ‖fame,
"And spare the meek ¶ Usurper's holy head.   90
"Above, below, the **rose of snow,
"Twined with her blushing foe, we spread:
"The bristled ††Boar in infant-gore
"Wallows beneath the thorny shade.
"Now, Brothers, bending o'er th' accursed loom   95
"Stamp we our vengeance deep, and ratify his doom.

* Richard the Second, (as we are told by Archbishop Scroop and the confederate
Lords in their manifesto, by Thomas of Walsingham, and all the older Writers,) was
starved to death [1400]. The story of his assassination by Sir Piers of Exon, is of much
later date.

  † Ruinous civil wars of York and Lancaster.

  ‡ Henry the Sixth, George Duke of Clarence, Edward the Fifth, Richard Duke of
York, &c. believed to be murthered secretly in the Tower of London. The oldest part
of that structure is vulgarly attributed to Julius Cæsar.

  § Margaret of Anjou, a woman of heroic spirit, who struggled hard to save her
Husband and her Crown.

  ‖ Henry the Fifth.

  ¶ Henry the Sixth very near being canonized. The line of Lancaster had no right of
inheritance to the Crown.

  ** The white and red roses, devices of York and Lancaster.

  †† The silver Boar was the badge of Richard the Third; whence he was usually
known in his own time by the name of *the Boar*.

III. 1

"Edward, lo! to sudden fate
"(Weave we the woof. The thread is spun)
"*Half of thy heart we consecrate.
"(The web is wove. The work is done.)"   100
'Stay, oh stay! nor thus forlorn
'Leave me unbless'd, unpitied, here to mourn:
'In yon bright track, that fires the western skies,
'They melt, they vanish from my eyes.
'But oh! what solemn scenes on Snowdon's height   105
'Descending slow their glitt'ring skirts unroll?
'Visions of glory, spare my aching sight,
'Ye unborn Ages, crowd not on my soul!
'No more our long-lost † Arthur we bewail.
'All-hail, ‡ ye genuine Kings, Britannia's Issue, hail!   110

III. 2

'Girt with many a Baron bold
'Sublime their starry fronts they rear;
'And gorgeous Dames, and Statesmen old
'In bearded majesty, appear.
'In the midst a Form divine!   115
'Her eye proclaims her of the Briton-Line;
'Her lyon-port§, her awe-commanding face,
'Attemper'd sweet to virgin-grace.

* Eleanor of Castile died [1290] a few years after the conquest of Wales. The heroic proof she gave of her affection for her Lord is well known. The monuments of his regret, and sorrow for the loss of her, are still to be seen at Northampton, Geddington, Waltham, and other places.

† It was the common belief of the Welch nation, that King Arthur was still alive in Fairy-Land, and should return again to reign over Britain.

‡ Both Merlin and Taliessin had prophesied, that the Welch should regain their sovereignty over this island; which seemed to be accomplished in the House of Tudor.

§ Speed relating an audience given by Queen Elizabeth to Paul Dzialinski, Ambassadour of Poland, says, 'And thus she, lion-like rising, daunted the malapert Orator no less with her stately port and majestical deporture, than with the tartnesse of her princelie checkes.'

'What strings symphonious tremble in the air,
'What strains of vocal transport round her play!   120
'Hear from the grave, great Taliessin*, hear;
'They breathe a soul to animate thy clay.
'Bright Rapture calls, and soaring, as she sings,
'Waves in the eye of Heav'n her many-colour'd wings.

III. 3

   'The verse adorn again   125
'† Fierce War, and faithful Love,
'And Truth severe, by fairy Fiction drest.
'In ‡ buskin'd measures move
'Pale Grief, and pleasing Pain,
'With Horrour, Tyrant of the throbbing breast.   130
'A § Voice, as of the Cherub-Choir,
'Gales from blooming Eden bear;
'‖ And distant warblings lessen on my ear,
'That lost in long futurity expire.
'Fond impious Man, think'st thou, yon sanguine cloud,   135
'Rais'd by thy breath, has quench'd the Orb of day?
'To-morrow he repairs the golden flood,
'And warms the nations with redoubled ray.
'Enough for me: With joy I see
'The different doom our Fates assign.   140
'Be thine Despair, and scept'red Care,
'To triumph, and to die, are mine.'
He spoke, and headlong from the mountain's height
Deep in the roaring tide he plung'd to endless night.

---

  * Taliessin, Chief of the Bards, flourished in the VIth Century. His works are still preserved, and his memory held in high veneration among his Countrymen.
  † Fierce wars and faithful loves shall moralize my song.
                         Spenser's Proëme to the Fairy Queen [I. 9].
  ‡ Shakespear.
  § Milton.
  ‖ The succession of Poets after Milton's time.

16. [*Ode on the Pleasure Arising from Vicissitude*]

[Mason transcribed these lines into Gray's Commonplace Book, where he entitled them 'Fragment of an Ode found amongst Mr. Grays papers after his decease and here transcribed from the corrected Copy'. Mason also copied out a note from Gray's pocketbook for 1754: 'Contrast between the Winter past & coming spring Joy owing to that vicissitude. many that never feel that delight. Sloth envy Ambition. how much happier the rustic that feels it tho he knows not how.' The incomplete poem appears to date therefore from 1754 or 1755. Mason added, after transcribing Gray's note, 'Then follow a few lines of the Ode now the golden Morn &c so that the note above appears to be a kind of argument to the fragment. Four lines also, as follow, are among the others.' These four lines, sometimes printed after stanza 2, have been confined here to the textual note to line 17. Mason also recorded a number of variants and the fragments of lines 49–59. Mason printed the poem for the first time in 1775 (i. 236–7), but he also offered in the 'Poems' (ii. 76–81) his own reconstructed version of the poem expanded to 96 lines, and with the present title. The text followed here is that of his transcript in the Commonplace Book.]

Now the golden Morn aloft
   Waves her dew-bespangled wing;
With vermeil cheek and whisper soft
   She woo's the tardy spring:
Till April starts, and calls around   5
The sleeping fragrance from the ground,
And lightly o'er the living scene
Scatters his freshest, tenderest green.

New-born flocks in rustic dance
   Frisking ply their feeble feet.   10
Forgetful of their wintry trance
   The birds his presence greet.
But chief the Sky-lark warbles high
His trembling thrilling ecstasy;
And, less'ning from the dazzled sight,   15
Melts into air and liquid light.

Yesterday the sullen year
  Saw the snowy whirlwind fly;
Mute was the musick of the air,
  The Herd stood drooping by: 20
Their raptures now that wildly flow,
No yesterday, nor morrow know;
'Tis Man alone that Joy descries
With forward and reverted eyes.

Smiles on past Misfortune's brow   25
  Soft Reflection's hand can trace;
And o'er the cheek of Sorrow throw
  A melancholy grace;
While Hope prolongs our happier hour,
Or deepest shades, that dimly lour   30
And blacken round our weary way,
Gilds with a gleam of distant day.

Still, where rosy Pleasure leads,
  See a kindred Grief pursue;
Behind the steps that Misery treads,   35
  Approaching Comfort view:
The hues of Bliss more brightly glow,
Chastised by sabler tints of woe;
And blended form, with artful strife,
The strength and harmony of Life.   40

See the Wretch, that long has tost
  On the thorny bed of Pain,
At length repair his vigour lost,
  And breathe and walk again:
The meanest flowret of the vale,   45
The simplest note that swells the gale,
The common Sun, the air, and skies,
To him are opening Paradise.

Humble Quiet builds her cell,
  Near the source whence Pleasure flows;   50
She eyes the clear chrystalline well,
  And tastes it as it goes.
Far below   the crowd.

Broad & turbulent it grows

  with resistless sweep   55
They perish in the boundless deep

Mark where Indolence and Pride,
Softly rolling, side by side,
Their dull, but daily round.

17. [*Epitaph on Mrs Clerke*]

[The epitaph is on a mural tablet in St George's Church, Beckenham, in Kent. John Clerke (1717–90), who became a Fellow of Peterhouse, Cambridge, in 1740, practised as a physician in Epsom. His wife, Jane Clerke, had died on 27 April 1757 at the age of thirty-one. Gray sent a text of the poem to Bedingfield on 31 January 1758. It was first printed in the *Gentleman's Magazine*, xxix. 485, in October 1759. Its only other publication in Gray's lifetime was in the *Poetical Calendar*, 1763, viii. 121. The text is that of the tablet in Beckenham Church, with variants from the letter to Bedingfield.]

  Lo! where this silent marble weeps,
  A friend, a wife, a mother sleeps:
  A heart, within whose sacred cell
  The peaceful virtues lov'd to dwell,
  Affection warm, and faith sincere,   5
  And soft humanity were there.
  In agony, in death resign'd,
  She felt the wound she left behind.
  Her infant image, here below,
  Sits smiling on a father's woe: 10
  Whom what awaits, while yet he strays
  Along the lonely vale of days?
  A pang, to secret sorrow dear;
  A sigh; an unavailing tear;
  Till time shall every grief remove,   15
  With life, with memory, and with love.

18. [*Epitaph on a Child*]

[This is presumably the epitaph which Gray wrote in 1758 for his friend Dr Thomas Wharton, whose eldest son Robert died in April 1758 at the age of four or five. It was first printed by Gosse in 1884 from a copy made by Alexander Dyce when the original MS. was sold in 1854. The text followed here is that of Gray's untitled holograph MS. now in the Pierpont Morgan Library, with variants from two transcripts in the Mitford MSS. and Gosse's text.]

> Here, free'd from pain, secure from misery, lies
> A Child the Darling of his Parent's eyes:
> A gentler Lamb ne'er sported on the plain,
> A fairer Flower will never bloom again!
> Few were the days allotted to his breath;   5
> Here let him sleep in peace his night of death.

19. *The Fatal Sisters. An Ode*

[Gray's transcript in his Commonplace Book is dated 1761 and the poem had been written by 5 May 1761 when Walpole referred to it and to *The Descent of Odin* in a letter to Montagu. Like all Gray's translations from Norse and Welsh, it was associated with a plan, dating back to 1752, to write with Mason a 'History of English Poetry'. Articles in Gray's Commonplace Book indicate that he did collect material for this work from time to time and his enthusiasm for the project revived temporarily in 1760–61; but the 'Advertisement' which preceded the translations in 1768 indicates that he had by then abandoned the plan to make way for Thomas Warton, whose *History of English Poetry* was to appear between 1774 and 1781.

In the Commonplace Book the poem is entitled 'The Song of the Valkyries'. A transcript by Wharton in the British Museum is entitled 'The Song of the weird Sisters, translated from the Norwegian about 1029'. The present title appeared in 1768, where another expanded version describes it as '(From the NORSE-TONGUE,) IN THE ORCADES of THOR-MODUS TORFÆUS; HAFNIÆ, 1697. Folio: and also in BAR-THOLINUS. VITT ER ORPIT FYRIR VALFALLI, &C.' Although both Thorfaeus and Bartholin (1689) gave the Norse text, Gray in fact translated their Latin versions of the poem. The original poem, *Daraðar Ljóð* or 'Lay of the Darts' was probably written soon after the Battle of Clontarf, fought on Good Friday 1014. It was later absorbed into the *Njáls Saga*. Gray's paraphrase, with the two following poems, was first published in 1768 to replace the omitted *A Long Story*. The text is that of 1768, which followed that sent by Gray to James Dodsley in early February 1768, except that the stanzas were not separated in the letter. Variants are given from the Commonplace Book and the transcript by Wharton.]

ADVERTISEMENT

The Author once had thoughts (in concert with a Friend) of giving *the History of English Poetry:* In the Introduction to it he meant to have produced some specimens of the Style that reigned in ancient times among the neighbouring nations, or those who had subdued the greater part of this Island, and were our Progenitors: the following three Imitations made a part of them. He has long since drop'd his design, especially after he had heard, that it was already in the hands of a Person well qualified to do it justice, both by his taste, and his researches into antiquity.

PREFACE

In the Eleventh Century *Sigurd*, Earl of the Orkney-Islands, went with a fleet of ships and a considerable body of troops into Ireland, to the assistance of *Sictryg with the silken beard*, who was then making war on his father-in-law *Brian*, King of Dublin: the Earl and all his forces were cut to pieces, and *Sictryg* was in danger of a total defeat; but the enemy had a greater loss by the death of *Brian*, their King, who fell in the action. On Christmas-day, (the day of the battle,) a Native of *Caithness* in Scotland saw at a distance a number of persons on horseback riding full speed towards a hill, and seeming to enter into it. Curiosity led him to follow them, till looking through an opening in the rocks he saw twelve gigantic figures resembling women: they were all employed about a loom; and as they wove, they sung the following dreadful Song; which when they had finished, they tore the web into twelve pieces, and (each taking her portion) galloped Six to the North and as many to the South.

> Now the storm begins to lower,
> (Haste, the loom of Hell prepare,)
> * Iron-sleet of arrowy shower
> † Hurtles in the darken'd air.

Note—The *Valkyriur* were female Divinities, Servants of *Odin* (or *Woden*) in the Gothic mythology. Their name signifies *Chusers of the slain.* They were mounted on swift horses, with drawn swords in their hands; and in the throng of battle selected such as were destined to slaughter, and conducted them to *Valhalla*, the hall of *Odin*, or paradise of the Brave; where they attended the banquet, and served the departed Heroes with horns of mead and ale.

* How quick they wheel'd; and flying, behind them shot
  Sharp sleet of arrowy shower——   *Milton's Par. Regained* [III. 323–4].
† The noise of battle hurtled in the air.   *Shakesp. Jul. Cæsar* [II. ii. 22].

Glitt'ring lances are the loom,   5
Where the dusky warp we strain,
Weaving many a Soldier's doom,
Orkney's woe, and *Randver*'s bane.

See the griesly texture grow,
('Tis of human entrails made,)   10
And the weights, that play below,
Each a gasping Warriour's head.

Shafts for shuttles, dipt in gore,
Shoot the trembling cords along.
Sword, that once a Monarch bore,   15
Keep the tissue close and strong.

Mista black, terrific Maid,
Sangrida, and *Hilda* see,
Join the wayward work to aid:
'Tis the woof of victory.   20

Ere the ruddy sun be set,
Pikes must shiver, javelins sing,
Blade with clattering buckler meet,
Hauberk crash, and helmet ring.

(Weave the crimson web of war)   25
Let us go, and let us fly,
Where our Friends the conflict share,
Where they triumph, where they die.

As the paths of fate we tread,
Wading thro' th' ensanguin'd field: 30
Gondula, and *Geira*, spread
O'er the youthful King your shield.

We the reins to slaughter give,
Ours to kill, and ours to spare:
Spite of danger he shall live.   35
(Weave the crimson web of war.)

They, whom once the desart-beach
Pent within its bleak domain,
Soon their ample sway shall stretch
O'er the plenty of the plain.   40

Low the dauntless Earl is laid,
Gor'd with many a gaping wound:
Fate demands a nobler head;
Soon a King shall bite the ground.

Long his loss shall Eirin weep,   45
Ne'er again his likeness see;
Long her strains in sorrow steep,
Strains of Immortality!

Horror covers all the heath,
Clouds of carnage blot the sun.   50
Sisters, weave the web of death;
Sisters, cease, the work is done.

Hail the task, and hail the hands!
Songs of joy and triumph sing!
Joy to the victorious bands;   55
Triumph to the younger King.

Mortal, thou that hear'st the tale,
Learn the tenour of our song.
Scotland, thro' each winding vale
Far and wide the notes prolong.   60

Sisters, hence with spurs of speed:
Each her thundering faulchion wield;
Each bestride her sable steed.
Hurry, hurry to the field.

20. *The Descent of Odin. An Ode*

[Written by 5 May 1761 and first published in 1768 (see headnote to *The Fatal Sisters*), with the source named in the expanded title: '(From the NORSE-TONGUE,) IN BARTHOLINUS, de causis contemnendæ mortis; HAFNIÆ, 1689, Quarto. UPREIS ODINN ALLDA GAUTR, &c.' Gray had transcribed the poem into his Commonplace Book and there is also a transcript by Wharton in the British Museum, entitled 'The Vegtams Kwitha from Bartholinus'. Known in its earliest sources as *Baldrs Draumar* ('Balder's Dream'), this Icelandic poem was later entitled *Vegtamskviða* ('Lay of the Wayfarer'). The text is that of 1768, which follows that in Gray's letter to James Dodsley in early February 1768, except that occasional intervals were introduced into the printed text. Variants are from the Commonplace Book and Wharton's transcript.]

Uprose the King of Men with speed,
And saddled strait his coal-black steed;
Down the yawning steep he rode,
That leads to * HELA's drear abode.
Him the Dog of Darkness spied,   5
His shaggy throat he open'd wide,
While from his jaws, with carnage fill'd,
Foam and human gore distill'd:
Hoarse he bays with hideous din,
Eyes that glow, and fangs, that grin;   10
And long pursues, with fruitless yell,
The Father of the powerful spell.
Onward still his way he takes,
(The groaning earth beneath him shakes,)
Till full before his fearless eyes   15
The portals nine of hell arise.

Right against the eastern gate,
By the moss-grown pile he sate;
Where long of yore to sleep was laid
The dust of the prophetic Maid.   20
Facing to the northern clime,
Thrice he traced the runic rhyme;

---

* *Niflheimr*, the hell of the Gothic nations, consisted of nine worlds, to which were devoted all such as died of sickness, old-age, or by any other means than in battle: Over it presided HELA, the Goddess of Death.

Thrice pronounc'd, in accents dread,
The thrilling verse that wakes the Dead;
Till from out the hollow ground   25
Slowly breath'd a sullen sound.

    PR. What call unknown, what charms presume
To break the quiet of the tomb?
Who thus afflicts my troubled sprite,
And drags me from the realms of night?   30
Long on these mould'ring bones have beat
The winter's snow, the summer's heat,
The drenching dews, and driving rain!
Let me, let me sleep again.
Who is he, with voice unblest,   35
That calls me from the bed of rest?

    O. A Traveller, to thee unknown,
Is he that calls, a Warriour's Son.
Thou the deeds of light shalt know;
Tell me what is done below,   40
For whom yon glitt'ring board is spread,
Drest for whom yon golden bed.

    PR. Mantling in the goblet see
The pure bev'rage of the bee,
O'er it hangs the shield of gold;   45
'Tis the drink of *Balder* bold:
Balder's head to death is giv'n.
Pain can reach the Sons of Heav'n!
Unwilling I my lips unclose:
Leave me, leave me to repose.   50

    O. Once again my call obey.
Prophetess, arise, and say,
What dangers *Odin*'s Child await,
Who the Author of his fate.

    PR. In *Hoder*'s hand the Heroe's doom: 55
His Brother sends him to the tomb.
Now my weary lips I close:
Leave me, leave me to repose.

    O. Prophetess, my spell obey,
Once again arise, and say,   60

Who th' Avenger of his guilt,
By whom shall *Hoder*'s blood be spilt.

Pr. In the caverns of the west,
By *Odin*'s fierce embrace comprest,
A wond'rous Boy shall *Rinda* bear,   65
Who ne'er shall comb his raven-hair,
Nor wash his visage in the stream,
Nor see the sun's departing beam;
Till he on *Hoder*'s corse shall smile
Flaming on the fun'ral pile.   70
Now my weary lips I close:
Leave me, leave me to repose.

O. Yet a while my call obey.
Prophetess, awake, and say,
What Virgins these, in speechless woe,   75
That bend to earth their solemn brow,
That their flaxen tresses tear,
And snowy veils, that float in air.
Tell me, whence their sorrows rose:
Then I leave thee to repose.   80

Pr. Ha! no Traveller art thou,
King of Men, I know thee now,
Mightiest of a mighty line——

O. No boding Maid of skill divine
Art thou, nor Prophetess of good;   85
But Mother of the giant-brood!

Pr. Hie thee hence, and boast at home,
That never shall Enquirer come
To break my iron-sleep again;
Till * *Lok* has burst his tenfold chain.   90
Never, till substantial Night
Has reassum'd her ancient right;
Till wrap'd in flames, in ruin hurl'd,
Sinks the fabric of the world.

---

* *Lok* is the evil Being, who continues in chains till the *Twilight of the Gods*
approaches, when he shall break his bonds; the human race, the stars, and sun, shall
disappear; the earth sink in the seas, and fire consume the skies: even Odin himself and
his kindred-deities shall perish. For a farther explanation of this mythology, see
Mallet's Introduction to the History of Denmark, 1755, Quarto.

21. *The Triumphs of Owen. A Fragment*

[Written in 1760 or 1761 and transcribed into the Commonplace Book with *The Fatal Sisters* and *The Descent of Odin*. When Gray first printed the translation in 1768, he misleadingly described it as 'FROM Mr. EVANS'S Specimens of the Welch Poetry; LONDON, 1764, Quarto'. Gray had in fact seen in MS. a Latin translation by Evan Evans (a pioneer of Welsh studies) of Gwalchmai ap Meilyr's 'Arwyain Owain Gwynnedd', the source of the present poem, as early as April 1760. By about 20 June 1760 he had been shown the MS. of Evans's 'De Bardis Dissertatio', the source of his translations from the *Gododdin*. Gray's translations were made therefore from Evans's Latin versions and not the English translations given by Evans in his *Specimens* in 1764.

The poem probably celebrates the victory of Owen, Prince of North Wales, over three fleets sent against him by Henry II in 1157. The text is that of 1768, which follows that in Gray's letter to James Dodsley in early February 1768, except that two intervals were introduced into the printed text. Four additional lines from the Commonplace Book are recorded in the textual notes.]

ADVERTISEMENT
Owen succeeded his Father GRIFFIN in the Principality of North-Wales, A.D. 1120. This battle was fought near forty Years afterwards.

> OWEN's praise demands my song,
> OWEN swift, and OWEN strong;
> Fairest flower of Roderic's stem,
> * Gwyneth's shield, and Britain's gem.
> He nor heaps his brooded stores,   5
> Nor on all profusely pours;
> Lord of every regal art,
> Liberal hand, and open heart.
>
> Big with hosts of mighty name,
> Squadrons three against him came;   10
> This the force of Eirin hiding,
> Side by side as proudly riding,
> On her shadow long and gay
> † Lochlin plows the the watry way;

* North-Wales.
† Denmark.

There the Norman sails afar   15
Catch the winds, and join the war:
Black and huge along they sweep,
Burthens of the angry deep.

    Dauntless on his native sands
* The Dragon-Son of Mona stands;   20
In glitt'ring arms and glory drest,
High he rears his ruby crest.
There the thund'ring strokes begin,
There the press, and there the din;
Talymalfra's rocky shore   25
Echoing to the battle's roar.
Where his glowing eye-balls turn,
Thousand Banners round him burn.
Where he points his purple spear,
Hasty, hasty Rout is there,   30
Marking with indignant eye
Fear to stop, and shame to fly.
There Confusion, Terror's child,
Conflict fierce, and Ruin wild,
Agony, that pants for breath,   35
Despair and honourable Death.

            *   *   *

* The red Dragon is the device of Cadwallader, which all his descendents bore on
their banners.

22. [*The Death of Hoël*]

[Written in 1760 or 1761 (see headnote to *The Triumphs of Owen*). Gray's transcript in the Commonplace Book is entitled 'From Aneurin, Monarch of the Bards, extracted from the Gododin'. Gray had seen a Latin translation of fragments of the *Gododdin*, the sixth-century Welsh poem, in Evan Evans's MS. 'De Bardis Dissertatio' by June 1760. This poem and the two following fragments were first printed, with their present titles, by Mason in 1775. The text is that of the Commonplace Book.]

Had I but the torrent's might,
With headlong rage & wild affright
Upon Deïra's squadrons hurl'd,
To rush, & sweep them from the world!
  Too, too secure in youthful pride 5
By them my Friend, my Hoël, died,
Great Cian's Son: of Madoc old
He ask'd no heaps of hoarded gold;
Alone in Nature's wealth array'd
He ask'd, & had the lovely Maid. 10
  To Cattraeth's vale in glitt'ring row
Thrice two hundred Warriors goe;
Every Warrior's manly neck
Chains of regal honour deck,
Wreath'd in many a golden link: 15
From the golden cup they drink
Nectar, that the bees produce,
Or the grape's extatic juice.
Flush'd with mirth & hope they burn:
But none from Cattraeth's vale return, 20
Save Aeron brave, & Conan strong,
(Bursting thro' the bloody throng)
And I, the meanest of them all,
That live to weep, & sing their fall.

23. [*Caradoc*]

[See the headnote to *The Death of Hoël*, in his notes to which Mason first printed these two translations of fragments of the *Gododdin* in 1775. There is no MS. source.]

> Have ye seen the tusky Boar,
> Or the Bull, with sullen roar,
> On surrounding Foes advance?
> So Carádoc bore his lance.

24. [*Conan*]

[See headnotes to 22 and 23.]

> Conan's name, my lay, rehearse,
> Build to him the lofty verse,
> Sacred tribute of the Bard,
> Verse, the Hero's sole reward.
> As the flame's devouring force;   5
> As the whirlwind in its course;
> As the thunder's fiery stroke,
> Glancing on the shiver'd oak;
> Did the sword of Conan mow
> The crimson harvest of the foe.   10

25. [*Sketch of His Own Character*]

[First printed in 1775 by Mason, who noted: 'In one of his pocket-books I find a slight sketch in verse of his own character. . . . It was written in 1761.' The date is confirmed by the references in line 6 to Charles Townshend (1725–67), who was appointed Secretary at War on 24 March 1761, and Dr Samuel Squire (1713–66), who became Bishop of St David's on 14 April 1761. The text is that of 1775, with variants from Mason's transcript of the lines in the Commonplace Book.]

> Too poor for a bribe, and too proud to importune;
> He had not the method of making a fortune:
> Could love, and could hate, so was thought somewhat odd;
> NO VERY GREAT WIT, HE BELIEV'D IN A GOD:
> A Post or a Pension he did not desire,   5
> But left Church and State to Charles Townshend and Squire.

26. [*Epitaph on Sir William Williams*]

[Written between May and August 1761. Sir William Williams (*c.* 1730–61), whom Gray had known in Cambridge, was killed in the expedition against Belle Isle off the coast of Brittany on 27 April 1761. Frederick Montagu, who planned to erect a monument to Williams at Belle Isle, asked Gray to write the epitaph in May 1761. It was first printed in 1775 by Mason, who stated that the monument had not been erected. The text is that sent by Gray to Mason in August 1761, with variants from Mason's transcript in the Commonplace Book, the text printed by Mason in 1775, and Mitford.]

Here foremost in the dang'rous paths of fame
Young Williams fought for England's fair renown:
His mind each Muse, each Grace adorn'd his frame,
Nor Envy dared to view him with a frown.
    At Aix uncall'd his maiden-sword he drew   5
(There first in blood his infant-glory seal'd)
From fortune, pleasure, science, love, he flew,
And scorn'd repose, when Britain took the field.
    With eyes of flame & cool intrepid breast
Victor he stood on Bellisle's rocky steeps: 10
Ah gallant Youth!—this marble tells the rest,
Where melancholy Friendship bends, & weeps.

27. *Song* [*I*]

[Since *Song* [*II*] can be dated October 1761, the present poem probably dates from the same period. According to John Penn, *An Historical and Descriptive Account of Stoke Park* (1813), these two songs were given by the Comtesse de Viry (Gray's former friend Henrietta Speed) to the Rev. Mr Leman in 1780. *Song* [*I*] was first printed in Joseph Warton's edition of *The Works of Pope*, ii. 285 n., in 1797, but had been in MS. circulation previously. Mrs Thrale-Piozzi had copied it into her journal (*Thraliana*, ii. 774) in 1790, having obtained it from Gray's friend Norton Nicholls. The text is that of Mason's transcript from 'an interlined & corrected Copy' in the Commonplace Book (with punctuation added at the end of lines 2, 5, 6, 7), with variants from Warton and Mrs Piozzi. (Variants attributed to Mitford by earlier editors stem from Warton.)]

Midst Beauty & Pleasures gay triumphs to languish
And droop without knowing the source of my anguish,
To start from short slumbers & look for the morning
Yet close my dull eyes when I see it returning.

Sighs sudden & frequent, Looks ever dejected,   5
Sounds that steal from my tongue by no meaning connected:
Ah say Fellow-swains how these symptoms befell me.
They smile, but reply not. sure Delia will tell me.

28. Song [II]

[Walpole sent this song to the Countess of Ailesbury on 28 November 1761
and dated it October 1761 in his 'Memoir of Gray' (*Corresp.*, iii. 1288).
According to Walpole, Gray wrote the poem for Miss Speed and 'the
thought is from the French'. It was first printed in the *European Magazine*,
xix. 152, in February 1791. The text is that of Gray's holograph MS. in the
Pierpont Morgan Library, which has no title. Variants are from Mason's
transcript (entitled 'Song') in the Commonplace Book, Walpole's letter,
Mrs Piozzi's transcript in *Thraliana* in July 1790, and Mitford.]

Thyrsis, when we parted, swore,
E'er the spring he would return.
Ah, what means yon violet-flower,
And the buds, that deck the thorn?
'Twas the lark, that upward sprung!   5
'Twas the nightingale, that sung!

Idle notes, untimely green,
    Why such unavailing haste?
Western gales, & skies serene
Prove not always Winter past.   10
Cease my doubts, my fears to move;
Spare the honour of my Love.

29. *The Candidate*

[Probably written between January and March 1764. John Montagu, 4th Earl of Sandwich (1718–92), First Lord of the Admiralty and a notorious rake, was the Government candidate in a remarkable contest for the High Stewardship of the University of Cambridge in the early months of 1764. The poem describes Sandwich's 'courtship' of the three Faculties of Medicine, Law, and Divinity. Gray's point is that, in spite of Sandwich's reputation, much of his support came from clergymen hoping for ecclesiastical preferment. The nickname of Jemmy Twitcher (from *The Beggar's Opera*) was applied to Sandwich after his hypocritical denunciation of John Wilkes for immorality in November 1763. Gray apparently sent Walpole a MS. of the poem which has not survived, but there are copies by Walpole in the Pierpont Morgan Library and the W. S. Lewis Collection. It was first printed in the *London Evening Post* in February 1777 and in two magazines and an anthology in the 1780s. The present text is from a flysheet, several copies of which survive, which is close to the texts recorded by Walpole and includes the final couplet elsewhere omitted. It may have been printed by Walpole as late as 1787. The final word is supplied from its unique appearance in the Pierpont Morgan MS. Variants are recorded from the Lewis MS., the *London Evening Post*, the *Gentleman's Magazine*, lii. 39–40, for January 1782, and the *London Magazine*, lii. 296, for June 1783 (obvious misprints from these last two texts are omitted).]

When sly Jemmy Twitcher had smugg'd up his face
With a lick of court white-wash, and pious grimace,
A wooing he went, where three Sisters of old
In harmless society guttle and scold.

    Lord! Sister, says Physic to Law, I declare   5
Such a sheep-biting look, such a pick-pocket air,
Not I, for the Indies! you know I'm no prude;
But his nose is a shame, and his eyes are so lewd!
Then he shambles and straddles so oddly, I fear—
No; at our time of life, 'twould be silly, my dear.   10

    I don't know, says Law, now methinks, for his look,
'Tis just like the picture in Rochester's book.
But his character, Phyzzy, his morals, his life;
When she died, I can't tell, but he once had a wife.

    They say he's no Christian, loves drinking and whoring,   15
And all the town rings of his swearing and roaring,
His lying, and filching, and Newgate-bird tricks:—
Not I,—for a coronet, chariot and six.

    Divinity heard, between waking and dozing,
Her sisters denying, and Jemmy proposing;   20

From dinner she rose with her bumper in hand,
She stroked up her belly, and stroked down her band.
     What a pother is here about wenching and roaring!
Why David loved catches, and Solomon whoring.
Did not Israel filch from th' Ægyptians of old   25
Their jewels of silver, and jewels of gold?
The prophet of Bethel, we read, told a lie:
He drinks; so did Noah: he swears; so do I.
To refuse him for such peccadillos, were odd;
Besides, he repents, and he talks about G[od].   30
     Never hang down your head, you poor penitent elf!
Come, buss me, I'll be Mrs. Twitcher myself.
D[am]n ye both for a couple of Puritan bitches!
He's Christian enough, that repents, and that [stitches].

30. *William Shakespeare to Mrs Anne, Regular Servant to the Revd Mr Precentor of York*

[Gray sent these lines to William Mason, Canon Residentiary and Precentor of York since 1762, in a letter of about 8 July 1765. Mason had apparently been annotating an interleaved edition of Shakespeare, although he did not publish his observations. Lines 5–8 allude to earlier eighteenth-century editors and critics of Shakespeare. 'Clouët' (21) was the Duke of Newcastle's famous French cook.

     The poem was first printed by Mitford in the *Gray–Mason Correspondence* in 1853. There is a transcript in the Mitford MSS. in the British Museum and an earlier draft by Gray in a notebook described by Paget Toynbee in *Modern Language Review*, xxv (1930) 83–5. The text is that of Gray's letter, with variants from Mitford, and the Murray MS. described by Toynbee.]

A moment's patience, gentle Mistris Anne!
(But stint your clack for sweet St Charitie)
'Tis Willy begs, once a right proper Man,
Tho' now a Book, and interleav'd, you see.
     Much have I born from canker'd Critick's spite,   5
From fumbling Baronets, and Poets small,
Pert Barristers, & Parsons nothing bright:
But, what awaits me now, is worst of all!
     'Tis true, our Master's temper natural
Was fashion'd fair in meek & dovelike guise: 10
But may not honey's self be turn'd to gall
By residence, by marriage, & sore eyes?

If then he wreak on me his wicked will:
Steal to his closet at the hour of prayer,
And (when thou hear'st the organ piping shrill)   15
Grease his best pen, & all he scribbles, tear.
    Better to bottom tarts & cheesecakes nice,
Better the roast-meat from the fire to save,
Better be twisted into caps for spice,
Than thus be patch'd, & cobbled in one's grave!   20
    So York shall taste, what Clouët never knew;
So from *our* works sublimer fumes shall rise:
While Nancy earns the praise to Shakespear due
For glorious puddings, & immortal pies.

31. [*Invitation to Mason*]

[Gray sent these lines to Mason from Cambridge in a letter of 8 January
1768 (first printed by Mitford in 1853). The references are to common
friends, all at various times Fellows of Cambridge colleges, and, in lines 6–7,
to women employed in the coffee-house Gray frequented.]

Prim *Hurd* attends your call, & *Palgrave* proud,
Stonhewer the lewd, & *Delaval* the loud.
For thee does *Powel* squeeze, & *Marriot* sputter,
And *Glyn* cut phizzes, & Tom *Nevile* stutter.
Brown sees thee sitting on his nose's tip,   5
The *Widow* feels thee in her aching hip
For thee fat *Nanny* sighs, & handy *Nelly*,
And *Balguy* with a Bishop in his belly!

32. *On L[or]d H[ollan]d's Seat near M[argat]e. K[en]t*

[Written in June 1768, when Gray was staying with the Rev. William Robinson of Denton Court in Kent. Sir Egerton Brydges told Mitford that they were 'found in the drawer of Gray's dressing table after he was gone'. Henry Fox, Lord Holland (1705–74), had amassed a huge fortune as Paymaster-General from 1757 to 1765 and had the reputation of being an unscrupulous and corrupt politician. After quarrelling with and being deserted by his former political colleagues (named in lines 17–18, as they had been in a privately published poem by Holland himself in 1767), he had retired to ornament his estate at Kingsgate, near Margate, with mock ruins. Gray's poem describes this decadent taste as a frustrated manifestation of Holland's ambition to ruin the nation.

The poem was first published without Gray's permission in the *New Foundling Hospital for Wit*, iii. 34–5, in 1769, a text closely related to a transcript by Wharton in the British Museum. Wharton's text is followed here, with variants from the *New Foundling Hospital*, a transcript in the Cole MSS. in the British Museum, the *Gentleman's Magazine*, xlvii. 624 and xlviii. 88 (December 1777–January 1778), Nichols's *Select Collection of Poems*, vii (1781) 350–1, and the 2nd edition of Stephen Jones's edition of Gray (1800).]

Old and abandon'd by each venal friend
    Here H[olland] took the pious resolution
To smuggle some few years and strive to mend
    A broken character and constitution.
On this congenial spot he fix'd his choice,   5
    Earl Godwin trembled for his neighbouring sand,
Here Seagulls scream and cormorants rejoice,
    And Mariners tho' shipwreckt dread to land,
Here reign the blustring north and blighting east,
    No tree is heard to whisper, bird to sing,   10
Yet nature cannot furnish out the feast,
    Art he invokes new horrors still to bring;
Now mouldring fanes and battlements arise,
    Arches and turrets nodding to their fall,
Unpeopled palaces delude his eyes,   15
    And mimick desolation covers all.
Ah, said the sighing Peer, had Bute been true
    Nor Shelburn's, Rigby's, Calcraft's friendship vain,
Far other scenes than these had bless'd our view
    And realis'd the ruins that we feign.   20

Purg'd by the sword and beautifyed by fire,
  Then had we seen proud London's hated walls,
Owls might have hooted in S! Peters Quire,
  And foxes stunk and litter'd in S! Pauls.

33. [*Ode for Music*]

[Written between February and April 1769. The Duke of Grafton, who as
Prime Minister had been directly responsible for Gray's appointment as
Regius Professor of Modern History at Cambridge in July 1768, was elected
Chancellor of the University on 29 November 1768. Gray therefore reluctantly felt obliged to write the Ode which was to be performed to a musical
setting at the Installation ceremony on 1 July 1769. The knowledge that the
Ode would be derided (as it was) by Grafton's political opponents did not
make the task easier, but he had completed it by 20 April 1769, as he told
Wharton. It was published anonymously at Cambridge in July 1769,
entitled, *Ode performed in the Senate-House at Cambridge, July 1, 1769, at the
installation of His Grace Augustus-Henry Fitzroy, Duke of Grafton, Chancellor
of the University. Set to music by Dr Randal, Professor of Music.*
  After celebrating Milton and Newton as famous sons of Cambridge, Gray
introduces a series of royal founders or benefactors of colleges: Edward III,
the Countess of Pembroke, the Countess of Clare, Margaret of Anjou,
Elizabeth Woodville (wife of Edward IV), Henry VI, Henry VIII, and
Margaret, mother of Henry VII. The compliment to Grafton in lines 68–70
depends on the fact that he was a descendant of an illegitimate son of Charles
II. The text is that of the original edition, which Gray did not alter.]

AIR
  "Hence, avaunt, ('tis holy ground)
  "Comus, and his midnight-crew,
  "And Ignorance with looks profound,
  "And dreaming Sloth of pallid hue,
  "Mad Sedition's cry profane,   5
  "Servitude that hugs her chain,
  "Nor in these consecrated bowers
  "Let painted Flatt'ry hide her serpent-train in flowers.

CHORUS
  "Nor Envy base, nor creeping Gain
  "Dare the Muse's walk to stain,   10
  "While bright-eyed Science watches round:
  "Hence, away, 'tis holy Ground!

RECITATIVE

From yonder realms of empyrean day
Bursts on my ear th' indignant lay:
There sit the sainted Sage, the Bard divine,   15
The Few, whom Genius gave to shine
Through every unborn age, and undiscovered clime.
Rapt in celestial transport they,   (*accomp*.)
Yet hither oft a glance from high
They send of tender sympathy   20
To bless the place, where on their opening soul
First the genuine ardor stole.
'Twas *Milton* struck the deep-toned shell,
And, as the choral warblings round him swell,
Meek *Newton's* self bends from his state sublime,   25
And nods his hoary head, and listens to the rhyme.

AIR

"Ye brown o'er-arching Groves,
"That Contemplation loves,
"Where willowy *Camus* lingers with delight!
"Oft at the blush of dawn   30
"I trod your level lawn,
"Oft woo'd the gleam of *Cynthia* silver-bright
"In cloisters dim, far from the haunts of Folly,
"With Freedom by my Side, and soft-ey'd Melancholy.

RECITATIVE

But hark! the portals sound, and pacing forth   35
With solemn steps and slow
High Potentates and Dames of royal birth
And mitred Fathers in long order go:
Great *Edward* with the lillies on his brow
From haughty *Gallia* torn,   40
And sad *Chatillon*, on her bridal morn
That wept her bleeding Love, and princely *Clare*,
And *Anjou's* Heroine, and the paler Rose,
The rival of her crown, and of her woes,
And either *Henry* there,   45
The murther'd Saint, and the majestic Lord,
That broke the bonds of *Rome*.
(Their tears, their little triumphs o'er,   (*accomp*.)
Their human passions now no more,

Save Charity, that glows beyond the tomb)   50
All that on *Granta's* fruitful plain
Rich streams of regal bounty pour'd,
And bad these aweful fanes and turrets rise,
To hail their *Fitzroy's* festal morning come;
And thus they speak in soft accord   55
The liquid language of the skies.

QUARTETTO
"What is Grandeur, what is Power?
"Heavier toil, superior pain.
"What the bright reward we gain?
"The grateful mem'ry of the Good.   60
"Sweet is the breath of vernal shower,
"The bee's collected treasures sweet,
"Sweet music's melting fall, but sweeter yet
"The still small voice of Gratitude.

RECITATIVE
Foremost and leaning from her golden cloud   65
The venerable *Marg'ret* see!
"Welcome, my noble Son, (she cries aloud)
"To this, thy kindred train, and me:
"Pleas'd in thy lineaments we trace
"A *Tudor's* fire, a *Beaufort's* grace.   70

AIR
"Thy liberal heart, thy judging eye,
"The flower unheeded shall descry,
"And bid it round heaven's altars shed
"The fragrance of it's blushing head:
"Shall raise from earth the latent gem   75
"To glitter on the diadem.

RECITATIVE
"Lo, *Granta* waits to lead her blooming band,
"Not obvious, not obtrusive, She
"No vulgar praise, no venal incense flings;
"Nor dares with courtly tongue refin'd   80
"Profane thy inborn royalty of mind:
"She reveres herself and thee.

"With modest pride to grace thy youthful brow
"The laureate wreath, that *Cecil* wore, she brings,
"And to thy just, thy gentle hand   85
"Submits the Fasces of her sway,
"While Spirits blest above and Men below
"Join with glad voice the loud symphonious lay.

GRAND CHORUS
"Thro' the wild waves as they roar
"With watchful eye and dauntless mien   90
"Thy steady course of honor keep,
"Nor fear the rocks, nor seek the shore:
"The Star of *Brunswick* smiles serene,
"And gilds the horrors of the deep."

FRAGMENTARY
AND UNDATED POEMS

34. [*Lines Written at Burnham*]

[Written by August 1736, if the letter to Walpole in which they appear is correctly dated by Toynbee and Whibley (*Corresp.*, i. 47). First printed by Mason in 1775, where the letter is dated September 1737. The same letter contains the lines '—the tim'rous Hare, & sportive Squirrel/Gambol around me—', perhaps only a reminiscence of *Paradise Lost*, iv. 340–5.]

> And, as they bow their hoary Tops, relate
> In murm'ring Sounds the dark Decrees of Fate;
> While Visions, as Poetic eyes avow,
> Cling to each Leaf, & swarm on ev'ry Bough:

35. [*Lines on Dr Robert Smith*]

[This epigram cannot be dated more precisely than between 1742 and 1768. Robert Smith (1689–1768) was Master of Trinity College, Cambridge, from 1740 and author of *A Compleat System of Optics* (1738), from which he gained the nickname 'Old Focus'. Smith seems to have intended to cut down the Chestnut Walk at Trinity. Gosse printed the epigram for what was thought to be the first time in 1902 from a MS. preserved by Prof. Adam Sedgewick; but it had in fact appeared in print in George Pryme's *Autobiographic Recollections*, Cambridge, 1870, p. 277. Pryme stated that he heard the epigram from William Selwyn (1775–1855), a lawyer, who had been at Cambridge in the 1790s. Pryme's text is followed here, with variants from Gosse's text.]

> Do you ask why old Focus Sylvanus defies,
> And won't suffer a Chestnut in being?
> 'Tis not for the prospect, because he's no eyes,
> But because he has writ about seeing.

36. *Satire on the Heads of Houses;*
or, Never a Barrel the Better Herring

[First printed by Gosse in 1884 from the holograph MS. then owned by
Lord Houghton. No particular date has ever been assigned to the poem,
though it may have some connection with *The Capitade*, a satiric attack on
the Heads of Houses at Cambridge by Thomas Nevile or James Devie,
published in the *London Evening Post* for 1 November 1750. (See the
Gentleman's Magazine, li (1781), 530–1, where the poem is annotated by
John Duncombe.) Variants are recorded here from a copy by Mitford.]

O Cambridge, attend
To the Satire I've pen'd
On the Heads of thy Houses,
Thou Seat of the Muses!

Know the Master of Jesus   5
Does hugely displease us;
The Master of Maudlin
In the same dirt is dawdling;
The Master of Sidney
Is of the same kidney;   10
The Master of Trinity
To him bears affinity;
As the Master of Keys
Is as like as two pease,
So the Master of Queen's   15
Is as like as two beans;
The Master of King's
Copies them in all things;
The Master of Catherine
Takes them all for his pattern;   20
The Master of Clare
Hits them all to a hair;
The Master of Christ
By the rest is enticed;
But the Master of Emmanuel   25
Follows them like a spaniel;
The Master of Benet
Is of the like tenet;
The Master of Pembroke
Has from them his system took;   30

The Master of Peter's
Has all the same features;
The Master of St John's
Like the rest of the Dons.

P.S.—As to Trinity Hall   35
We say nothing at all.

37. [*Impromptus*]

[These spontaneous epigrams were preserved by Wharton (British Museum, Egerton MS. 2400 ff. 233–4). The second was printed by Joseph Cradock, *Literary Memoirs*, iv. 224, in 1828; the remainder were first printed by Gosse in 1884. Three of them refer to Edmund Keene (1714–81), Master of Peterhouse 1749–54, when Gray would have known him best, and Bishop of Chester from 1752. Raby Castle, not far from Wharton's home at Old Park, Co. Durham, was the seat of the Vane family. Wharton may have recorded these epigrams during Gray's visit to Old Park in 1753, but he made later visits in the 1760s.]

Extempore by Mr Gr⟨ay⟩ on Dr K⟨eene⟩. B⟨ishop⟩ of C⟨hester⟩.

The Bishop of Chester
Tho' wiser than Nestor
And fairer than Esther,
If you scratch him will fester.

one day the Bishop having offered to give a Gentleman a Goose Mr Gr⟨ay⟩ composed his Epitaph, thus.

Here lies Edmund Keene Lord Bishop of Chester,
He eat a fat goose, and could not digest her—

And this upon his Lady—

Here lies Mrs Keene the Bishop of Chester,
She had a bad face which did sadly molest her.

Impromptu by Mr Gray going out of Raby Castle

Here lives Harry Vane,
Very good claret and fine Champaign

A Couplet by Mr Gray

When you rise from your dinner as light as before
'Tis a sign you have eat just enough and no more.

38. [*Verse Fragments*]

[These fragments were copied from Gray's pocketbook for 1754 by Mason into the Commonplace Book. They were first printed in 1890 by Tovey, *Gray and His Friends*, pp. 269–70.]

> Gratitude
> > The Joy that trembles in her eye
> > She bows her meek & humble head
> > > in silent praise
> > > beyond the power of Sound.

> (Mr Pope dead)
> > and smart beneath the visionary scourge

> > —'tis Ridicule & not reproach that wounds
> > Their vanity & not their conscience feels'.

> > a few shall
> > The cadence of my song repeat
> > & hail thee in my words.

39. [*Couplet about Birds*]

[Norton Nicholls, who met Gray on 11 June 1762, records in his 'Reminiscences of Gray' (*Corresp.*, iii. 1290), first published by Mitford in 1843, that this couplet was 'made by Mr Gray as we were walking in the spring in the neighbourhood of Cambridge'.]

> There pipes the wood-lark, & the song thrush there
> Scatters his loose notes in the waste of air.

40. [Epitaph on Mrs Mason]

[Norton Nicholls in his 'Reminiscences of Gray' (Corresp., iii. 1294) states that Gray wrote the last four lines of Mason's epitaph on his wife, who died on 27 March 1767, and that he had seen them in Gray's handwriting. This assertion is confirmed by references in Gray's letter to Mason of 23 May 1767. The text of Gray's quatrain is from the tablet in Bristol Cathedral.]

> Tell them, tho 'tis an awful thing to die
> ('Twas ev'n to thee) yet the dread path once trod,
> Heav'n lifts its everlasting portals high
> And bids "the pure in heart behold their God."

41. [Parody on an Epitaph]

[Presumably written about 3 September 1767, when Gray visited Brough and Appleton during a tour of the Lake District with Wharton. Gray's holograph MS. is in the British Museum, inscribed by Wharton, 'Extempore Epitaph on Ann Countess of Dorset, Pembroke, and Montgomery, made by Mr Gray on reading the Epitaph on her mothers tomb in the Church at Appleby composed by the Countess in the same manner'. The epitaph (1617) was on the Countess's mother, Margaret, widow of George Clifford, 3rd Earl of Cumberland. The parody was first published by Gosse in 1884.]

> Now clean, now hideous, mellow now, now gruff,
> She swept, she hiss'd, she ripen'd & grew rough,
> At Broom, Pendragon, Appleby & Brough.

TRANSLATIONS

[Apart from the first (an early school exercise), these translations are all dated between 1736 and 1742, a period when Gray's poetry was otherwise written almost entirely in Latin. Textual variants have been recorded only from Gray's own MSS.]

42. Translation from Statius, *Thebaid, IX. 319–27*

[Walpole wrote on Gray's MS., now at Pembroke College, 'This written when he was very young', and the handwriting suggests that it was an early exercise at Eton. The lines are preceded in the MS. by a rough draft with corrections (not recorded here) of the same passage. First printed by Paget Toynbee, *Corresp. of Gray, Walpole, West and Ashton*, ii. 299–300, in 1915. Full stops have been inserted after lines 4, 16.]

> Crenæus, whom the Nymph Ismenis bore
> To Faunus on the Theban Rivers shore
> With new-born heat amidst his native stream
> Exults in arms, which cast an iron gleam.
> In this clear wave he first beheld the day   5
> On the green bank first taught his steps to stray,
> To skim the parent flood & on the margin play:
> Fear he disdains & scorns the power of fate,
> Secure within his mothers watry state.
> The youth exulting stems the bloody tide,   10
> Visits each bank & stalks with martial pride,
> While old Ismenus' gently-rolling wave,
> Delights the favourite youth within its flood to lave.
> Whither the youth obliquely steers his course
> Or cuts the downward stream with equal force   15
> Th' indulgent river strives his steps to aid.

43. Translation from Statius, *Thebaid, VI. 646–88, 704–28*

[Gray sent lines 1–59 to Richard West in a letter of 8 May 1736 and the remaining 27 lines before 24 May 1736. The text of lines 1–59 is that of the MS. first printed by Mitford in 1853; Mason printed lines 60–86 in 1775, and his text is the only authority. In the margin of the MS. Gray wrote 'Adrastus' against line 1 and 'Hippomedon' against line 13.]

Then thus the King, 'whoe'er the Quoit can wield,
And furthest send its weight athwart the field;
Let him stand forth his brawny arm to boast.'
Swift at the word, from out the gazing host
Young Pterelas with strength unequal drew   5
Labouring the Disc, & to small distance threw:
The Band around admire the mighty Mass,
A slipp'ry weight, & form'd of polish'd Brass;
The love of honour bad two Youths advance,
Achaians born, to try the glorious chance;   10
A third arose, of Acarnania he,
Of Pisa one, & three from Ephyre;
Nor more for now Nesimachus's Son,
By Acclamations roused, came towring on;
Another Orb upheaved his strong right hand,   15
Then thus, "Ye Argive flower, ye warlike band,
Who trust your arms shall rase the Tyrian towers,
And batter Cadmus' Walls with stony Showers,
Receive a worthier load; yon puny Ball
Let Youngsters toss:"   20
He said, & scornful flung th' unheeded weight
Aloof; the champions trembling at the sight
Prevent disgrace, the palm despair'd resign;
All, but two youths, th' enormous Orb decline,
These conscious Shame withheld, & pride of noble line: 25
As bright & huge the spatious circle lay
With doubled light it beam'd against the Day;
So glittering shews the Thracian Godheads shield,
With such a gleam affrights Pangæa's field,
When blazing 'gainst the Sun it shines from far,   30
And clash'd rebellows with the Din of war:
   Phlegyas the long-expected play began,
Summon'd his strength, & call'd forth all the Man;

All eyes were bent on his experienced hand,
For oft in Pisa's sports his native land   35
Admired that arm, oft on Alpheus' Shore
The pond'rous brass in exercise he bore;
Where flow'd the widest Stream he took his stand;
Sure flew the Disc from his unerring hand;
Nor stop'd till it had cut the further strand: 40
And now in Dust the polish'd Ball he roll'd,
Then grasp'd its weight, elusive of his hold;
Now fitting to his gripe, & nervous Arm
Suspends the crowd with expectation warm;
Nor tempts he yet the plain, but hurl'd upright   45
Emits the mass, a prelude of his might;
Firmly he plants each knee, & o'er his head,
Collecting all his force, the circle sped;
It towers to cut the clouds; now thro' the Skies
Sings in its rapid way, & strengthens, as it flies;   50
Anon with slack'ned rage comes quivering down,
Heavy & huge, & cleaves the solid ground.

　　So from th' astonish'd Stars, her nightly train,
The Sun's pale sister, drawn by magic strain,
Deserts precipitant [her] darken'd Sphere;   55
In vain the Nations [wi]th officious fear
Their cymbals toss, & sounding brass explore;
Th' Æmonian Hag enjoys her dreadful hour,
And smiles malignant on the labouring Power.

Third in the labours of the Disc came on,   60
With sturdy step and slow, Hippomedon;
Artful and strong he pois'd the well-known weight,
By Phlegyas warn'd, and fir'd by Mnestheus' fate,
That to avoid, and this to emulate.
His vigorous arm he try'd before he flung,   65
Brac'd all his nerves, and every sinew strung;
Then with a tempest's whirl and wary eye,
Pursu'd his cast, and hurl'd the orb on high;
The orb on high tenacious of its course,
True to the mighty arm that gave it force,   70
Far overleaps all bound, and joys to see
Its antient lord secure of victory.

The theatre's green height and woody wall
Tremble ere it precipitates its fall,
The ponderous mass sinks in the cleaving ground,   75
While vales and woods and echoing hills rebound.
As when from Ætna's smoking summit broke,
The eyeless Cyclops heav'd the craggy rock;
Where Ocean frets beneath the dashing oar,
And parting surges round the vessel roar;   80
'Twas there he aim'd the meditated harm,
And scarce Ulysses scap'd his giant arm.
A tyger's pride the victor bore away,
With native spots and artful labour gay,
A shining border round the margin roll'd,   85
And calm'd the terrors of his claws in gold.

44. Translation from Tasso, *Gerusalemme Liberata, XIV. 32–9*

[Gray's transcript in his Commonplace Book is dated 1738. He had been reading Tasso and learning Italian in the previous year. First printed by Mathias, ii. 90–2, in 1814.]

Dismiss'd at length they break thro' all delay
To tempt the dangers of the doubtful way;
And first to Ascalon their steps they bend,
Whose walls along the neighbouring Sea extend:
Nor yet in prospect rose the distant shore,   5
Scarce the hoarse waves from far were heard to roar;
When thwart the road a River roll'd its flood
Tempestuous, and all further course withstood:
The torrent-stream his ancient bounds disdains,
Swoll'n with new force, & late-descending rains.   10
Irresolute they stand, when lo! appears
The wondrous Sage; vigorous he seem'd in years,
Awful his mien; low as his feet there flows
A vestment unadorn'd, tho' white as new-fal'n Snows:
Against the stream the waves secure he trod,   15
His head a chaplet bore, his hand a Rod.
    As on the Rhine when Boreas' fury reigns,
And Winter binds the floods in icy chains

Swift shoots the Village-maid in rustick play
Smooth, without step, adown the shining way: 20
Fearless in long excursion loves to glide,
And sports, & wantons o'er the frozen tide.
 So moved the Seer, but on no harden'd plain:
The river boil'd beneath & rush'd towards the Main.
Where fixed in wonder stood the warlike pair,   25
His course he turn'd, & thus relieved their care.
 "Vast, oh my friends, & difficult the toil
To seek your Hero in a distant Soil!
No common helps, no common guide ye need,
Art it requires, and more than winged speed.   30
What length of sea remains, what various lands,
Oceans unknown, inhospitable Sands!
For adverse fate the captive chief has hurl'd
Beyond the confines of our narrow world.
Great things and full of wonder in your ears   35
I shall unfold; but first dismiss your fears;
Nor doubt with me to tread the downward road,
That to the grotto leads, my dark abode."
 Scarce had he said, before the warriors' eyes,
When mountain-high the waves disparted rise: 40
The flood on either hand its billows rears,
And in the midst a spacious arch appears.
Their hands he seized and down the steep he led
Beneath the obedient river's inmost bed.
The watry glimmerings of a fainter day   45
Discover'd half, & half conceal'd their way.
As when athwart the dusky woods by night
The uncertain Crescent gleams a sickly light.
Thro' subterraneous passages they went
Earth's inmost cells, & caves of deep descent.   50
Of many a flood they view'd the secret source
The birth of rivers, riseing to their course;
Whate'er with copious train its channel fills,
Floats into Lakes, or bubbles into rills.
The Po was there to see, Danubius' bed,   55
Euphrates' fount, & Nile's mysterious head.
Further they pass; where ripening minerals flow,
And embryon metals undigested glow:
Sulphureous veins & liveing silver shine,
Which soon the parent Sun's warm powers refine;   60

In one rich mass unite the precious store,
The parts combine & harden into Ore.
Here gems break thro' the night with glitt'ring beam,
And paint the margin of the costly stream.
All stones of lustre shoot their vivid ray,   65
And mix attemper'd in a various day.
   Here the soft emerald smiles of verdant hue,
And rubies flame, with sapphires heavenly blue;
The diamond there attracts the wond'ring sight
Proud of its thousand dies, & luxury of light.   70

45. Translation from Dante, *Inferno, XXXIII. 1–78*

[Probably written in 1737 or 1738, when Gray was learning Italian and
reading and translating Tasso. It was first printed in full by Gosse in 1884,
from a MS. in the handwriting of Mitford in the possession of Lord
Houghton. The text followed here is in Mitford's Notebook, vol. iii, in the
British Museum.]

From his dire food the greisly Fellon raised
His gore-dyed lips, which on the clotter'd locks
Of th' half devoured Head he wiped, & thus
Began; "Wouldst thou revive the deep despair
The Anguish, that unutter'd nathless wrings   5
My inmost Heart? yet if the telling may
Beget the Traitour's infamy, whom thus
I ceaseless gnaw insatiate, thou shalt see me
At once give loose to Utterance & to Tears.
   I know not who thou art nor on what errand   10
Sent hither; but a Florentine my ear
Won by thy tongue, declares thee. Know, thou seest
In me Count Ugolino, & Ruggieri
Pisa's perfidious Prelate, this: now hear
My Wrongs & from them judge of my revenge.   15
   That I did trust him, that I was betrayd
By trusting, & by Treachery slain, it rekes not
That I advise Thee; that which yet remains
To thee & all unknown (a horrid Tale)
The bitterness of Death, I shall unfold.   20
Attend, & say if he have injurd me.

   Thro' a small Crevice opening, what scant light
That grim & antique Tower admitted (since
Of me the Tower of Famine hight & known
To many a Wretch) already 'gan the dawn   25
To send; the whilst I slumbring lay, A Sleep
Prophetic of my Woes with direful Hand
Oped the dark Veil of fate. I saw methought
Toward Pisa's Mount, that intercepts the view
Of Lucca chas'd by Hell-hounds gaunt & bloody   30
A Wolf full grown; with fleet & equal speed
His young ones ran beside him, Lanfranc there
And Sigismundo & Gualandi rode
Amain, my deadly foes! headed by this
The deadliest; he their Chief, the foremost he   35
Flashed to pursue & chear the eager Cry:
Nor long endured the Chase: the panting Sire
Of Strength bereft, his helpless offspring soon
Oerta'en beheld, & in their trembling flanks
The hungry Pack their sharp-set Fangs embrued.   40
   The Morn had scarce commencd, when I awoke:
My Children (they were with me) Sleep as yet
Gave not to know their Sum of Misery
But yet in low & uncompleated Sounds
I heard 'em wail for bread. oh! thou art cruel   45
Or thou dost mourn to think, what my poor Heart
Foresaw, foreknew: oh! if thou weep not now,
Where are thy Tears? too soon they had arousd them
Sad with the fears of Sleep, & now the Hour
Of timely food approached: when at the gate   50
Below I heard the dreadful Clank of bars,
And fastning bolts; then on my Children's eyes
Speechless my Sight I fix'd, nor wept, for all
Within was Stone: they wept, unhappy boys!
They wept, & first my little dear Anselmo   55
Cried, 'Father, why, why do you gaze so sternly?
What would you have?' yet wept I not, or answerd
All that whole day, or the succeeding Night
Till a new Sun arose with weakly gleam
And wan, such as mought entrance find within   60
That house of Woe: but oh! when I beheld
My sons & in four faces saw my own
Despair reflected, either hand I gnawed

For Angeuish, which they construed Hunger; straight
Ariseing all they cried, 'far less shall be   65
Our sufferings, Sir, if you resume your gift;
These miserable limbs with flesh you cloathed;
Take back what once was yours.' I swallowd down
My struggling Sorrow, nor to heighten theirs.
That day & yet another, mute we sate   70
And motionless: O! Earth! couldst thou not gape
Quick to devour me? yet a fourth day came
When Gaddo at my feet outstretchd, implor'ng
In vain my Help, expir'd: ee'r the sixth Morn
Had dawnd, my other three before my eyes   75
Died one by one; I saw 'em fall: I heard
Their doleful Cries; for three days more I grop'd
About among their cold remains (for then
Hunger had reft my eyesight) often calling
On their dear Names, that heard me now no more: 80
The fourth, what Sorrow could not, Famine did."
  He finished; then with unrelenting eye
Askaunce he turn'd him, hasty to renew
The hellish feast, & rent his trembling Prey.

46. Translation from Propertius, *Elegies, III. V. 1–2, 19–48*

[The translation is dated December 1738 in Gray's Commonplace Book, the text followed here. Mathias printed lines 5–56 in 1814; the remainder was first printed by Gosse in 1884.]

Love, gentle Power! to Peace was e'er a friend:
Before the Goddess' shrine we too, love's vot'ries, bend.
Still may his Bard in softer fights engage;
Wars hand to hand with Cynthia let me wage.

                    *   *   *   *

Long as of youth the joyous hours remain;   5
Me may Castalia's sweet recess detain,
Fast by th' umbrageous Vale lull'd to repose,
Where Aganippe warbles as it flows;
Or roused by sprightly sounds from out the trance
I'd in the ring knit hands, & joyn the Muses' Dance.   10

Give me to send the laughing bowl around,
My soul in Bacchus' pleasing fetters bound:
Let on this head unfadeing flowers reside
There bloom the vernal rose's earliest pride;
And when, our flames commission'd to destroy,   15
Age step 'twixt love & me, and intercept the joy;
When my changed head these locks no more shall know,
And all it's jetty honours turn to Snow:
Then let me rightly spell of nature's ways
To Providence, to Him my thoughts I'd raise   20
Who taught this vast machine its stedfast laws,
That first, eternal, universal Cause:
Search to what regions yonder Star retires,
Who monthly waneing hides her paly fires;
And whence anew revived, with silver light   25
Relumes her crescent Orb to chear the dreary Night.
How riseing winds the face of Ocean sweep:
Where lie th' eternal fountains of the deep:
And whence the cloudy Magazines maintain
Their wintry war, or pour the autumnal rain: 30
How flames perhaps with dire confusion hurl'd
Shall sink this beauteous fabric of the world:
What colours paint the vivid arch of Jove:
What wondrous force the solid earth can move;
When Pindus' self approaching ruin dreads,   35
Shakes all his Pines, & bows his hundred heads:
Why does yon Orb, so exquisitely bright
Obscure his radiance in a short-lived night:
Whence the seven Sisters' congregated fires;
And what Bootes' lazy waggon tires: 40
How the rude Surge its sandy Bounds controul;
Who measured out the year, & bad the seasons roll:
If realms beneath those fabled torments know;
Pangs without respite, fires that ever glow;
Earth's monster-brood stretch'd on their iron bed;   45
The hissing terrours round Alecto's head;
Scarce to nine acres Tityus' bulk confined;
The triple dog, that scares the shadowy kind;
All angry heaven inflicts, or hell can feel,
The pendent rock, Ixion's whirling wheel,   50
Famine at feasts, & thirst amid the stream:
Or are our fears th' enthusiast's empty dream,

And all the scenes, that hurt the grave's repose,
But pictured horrour, & poëtic woes.
    These soft, inglorious joys my hours engage;   55
Be love my youth's pursuit, & science crown my Age.
You whose young bosoms feel a nobler flame
Redeem, what Crassus lost, & vindicate his name.

47. Translation from Propertius, *Elegies, II.I*

[Gray sent this translation to West on 23 April 1742 and transcribed it into
his Commonplace Book (dated 'April 1742'), the text followed here.
Mathias printed lines 31–108 in 1814 and the translation was first printed in
full by Gosse in 1884. Variants from the letter to West are recorded.]

You ask, why thus my Loves I still rehearse,
Whence the soft Strain & ever-melting Verse?
From Cynthia all, that in my Numbers shines:
She is my Genius, she inspires the Lines;
No Phœbus else, no other Muse I know;   5
She tunes my easy Rhime, & gives the Lay to flow.
If the loose Curls around her Forehead play,
Or lawless o'er their Ivory Margin stray:
If the thin Coan Web her Shape reveal,
And half disclose those Limbs it should conceal: 10
Of those loose Curls, that Ivory front I write;
Of the dear Web whole Volumes I indite:
Or if to Musick she the Lyre awake,
That the soft Subject of my Song I make,
And sing with what a careless Grace she flings   15
Her artful hand across the sounding Strings.
If sinking into Sleep she seem to close
Her languid Lids, I favour her repose
With lulling Notes, & thousand beauties see,
That Slumber brings to aid my Poetry.   20
When less averse, & yielding to Desires
She half accepts, & half rejects my Fires;
While to retain the envious Lawn she tries,
And struggles to elude my longing Eyes:
The fruitful Muse from that auspicious Night   25
Dates the long Iliad of the amorous Fight.
In brief whate'er she do, or say, or look:
'Tis ample Matter for a Lover's Book:

And many a copious Narrative you'll see
Big with the important Nothing's History.   30
   Yet would the Tyrant Love permit me raise
My feeble Voice to sound the Victor's Praise,
To paint the Hero's Toil, the Ranks of War,
The laurel'd Triumph, & the sculptured Carr:
No Giant-Race, no Tumult of the Skies,   35
No Mountain-Structures in my Verse should rise,
Nor Tale of Thebes, or Ilium there should be,
Or how the Persian trod the indignant Sea;
Not Marius' Cimbrian Wreaths would I relate;
Nor lofty Carthage struggleing with her Fate.   40
Here should Augustus great in Arms appear,
And Thou, Mecænas, be my second Care:
Here Mutina from flames & famine free,
And there th' ensanguined Wave of Sicily:
And sceptred Alexandria's captive Shore;   45
And sad Philippi red with Roman Gore:
Then, while the vaulted Skies loud Io's rend,
In golden Chains should loaded Monarchs bend,
And hoary Nile with pensive Aspect seem
To mourn the Glories of his sevenfold Stream   50
While Prows, that late in fierce Encounter mett,
Move thro' the Sacred Way, and vainly threat.
Thee too the Muse should consecrate to Fame,
And with his Garlands weave thy ever-faithful Name.
But nor Callimachus' enervate Strain   55
May tell of Jove, & Phlegra's blasted Plain:
Nor I with unaccustom'd Vigour trace
Back to it's Source divine the Julian Race.
Sailors to tell of Winds & Seas delight,
The Shepherd of his flocks, the Soldier of the Fight,   60
A milder Warfare I in Verse display;
Each in his proper Art should waste the Day:
Nor thou my gentle Calling disapprove;
To die is glorious in the Bed of Love.
Happy the Youth, & not unknown to Fame,   65
Whose heart has never felt a second flame.
Oh, might that envied Happiness be mine!
To Cynthia all my Wishes I confine,
Or if, alas! it be my Fate to try
Another Love, the quicker let me die.   70

But she, the Mistress of my faithful breast,
Has oft the Charms of Constancy confest,
Condemns her fickle Sexe's fond Mistake,
And hates the Tale of Troy for Helen's Sake.
Me from myself the soft Enchantress stole;   75
Ah! let her ever my Desires controul,
Or if I fall the Victim of her Scorn,
From her loved Door may my pale Coarse be born.
The Power of Herbs can other Harms remove,
And find a Cure for every Ill, but Love.   80
The Melian's Hurt Machaon could repair,
Heal the slow Chief, & send again to War;
To Chiron Phœnix owed his long-lost Sight,
And Phœbus' Son recall'd Androgeon to the Light.
Here Arts are vain, even Magick here must fail,   85
The powerful Mixture, & the midnight Spell:
The Hand, that can my captive heart release,
And to this bosom give it's wonted Peace,
May the long Thirst of Tantalus allay,
Or drive the infernal Vulture from his Prey.   90
For Ills unseen what Remedy is found,
Or who can probe the undiscover'd Wound?
The Bed avails not, or the Leeche's Care,
Nor changeing Skies can hurt, nor sultry Air.
'Tis hard th' elusive Symptoms to explore.   95
To day the Lover walks, tomorrow is no more:
A Train of mourning Friends attend his Pall,
And wonder at the sudden Funeral.
    When then my Fates, that breath they gave, shall claim;
When the short Marble but preserves a Name,   100
A little Verse, my All, that shall remain:
Thy passing Courser's slacken'd Speed retain;
(Thou envied Honour of thy Poet's Days,
Of all our Youth the Ambition, & the Praise!)
Then to my quiet Urn awhile draw near,   105
And say, while o'er the Place You drop a Tear,
Love & the Fair were of his Life the Pride;
He lived, while she was kind; & when she frown'd, he died.

APPENDIX

Stanza's Wrote in a Country Church-Yard

[This MS., preserved at Eton College, clearly contains the earliest surviving version of the *Elegy*. The four bracketed stanzas represent the original ending of the poem, and the evidence suggests that there was an interval of indefinite length before Gray returned to the poem, either omitting these stanzas or reworking them in his continuation.]

> The Curfeu tolls the Knell of parting Day,
> The lowing Herd wind slowly o'er the Lea,
> The Plowman homeward plods his weary Way,
> And leaves the World to Darkness & to me.
>
> Now fades the glimm'ring Landscape on the Sight,   5
> And now the Air a solemn Stillness holds;
> Save, where the Beetle wheels his droning Flight,
> Or drowsy Tinklings lull the distant Folds.
>
> Save, that from yonder ivy-mantled Tower
> The mopeing Owl does to the Moon complain   10
> Of such as wandring near her secret Bower
> Molest her ancient solitary Reign.
>
> Beneath those rugged Elms, that Yewtree's Shade,
> Where heaves the Turf in many a mould'ring Heap,
> Each in his narrow Cell for ever laid   15
> The rude Forefathers of the Hamlet sleep.
>
> For ever sleep. the breezy Call of Morn,
> Or Swallow twitt'ring from the strawbuilt Shed,
> Or Chaunticleer so shrill or ecchoing Horn,
> No more shall rouse them from their lowly Bed.   20
>
> For them no more the blazeing Hearth shall burn,
> Or busy Huswife ply her Evening Care;
> No Children run to lisp their Sire's Return,
> Nor climb his Knees the coming Kiss to share.

11 *wandring*] with *stray* written above.
12 *Molest her*] with *& pry into* written above.
16 *Hamlet*] written above *Village* deleted.
24 *coming*] with *envied* written above and *doubtful* in margin.

Oft did the Harvest to their Sickle yield;   25
Their Furrow oft the stubborn Glebe has broke;
How jocund did they drive their Team a-field!
How bow'd the Woods beneath their sturdy Stroke!

   Let not Ambition mock their useful Toil,
Their rustic Joys & Destiny obscure: 30
Nor Grandeur hear with a disdainful Smile
The short & simple Annals of the Poor.

The Boast of Heraldry the Pomp of Power,
And all, that Beauty, all that Wealth, e'er gave
Awaits alike th' inevitable Hour.   35
The Paths of Glory lead but to the Grave.

   Forgive, ye Proud, th' involuntary Fault,
If Memory to these no Trophies raise,
Where thro' the long-drawn Ile, & fretted Vault
The pealing Anthem swells the Note of Praise.   40

   Can storied Urn, or animated Bust,
Back to its Mansion call the fleeting Breath?
Can Honour's voice awake the silent dust,
Or Flattery sooth the dull cold Ear of Death?

1. Perhaps in this neglected Spot is laid   45
   Some Heart, once pregnant with celestial Fire,
   Hands, that the Reins of Empire might have sway'd,
   Or waked to Ecstasy the living Lyre:

4.   Some Village Cato   with dauntless Breast
   The little Tyrant of his Fields withstood;   50
   Some mute inglorious Tully here may rest;
   Some Caesar, guiltless of his Country's Blood.

2.   But Knowledge to their eyes her ample Page,
   Rich with the Spoils of Time, did ne'er unroll:
   Chill Penury had damp'd their noble Rage,   55
   And froze the genial Current of the Soul.

29 *useful*] underlined with *homely* in margin.
43 *awake*] with *provoke* in margin.
49 A word, presumably *that*, is lost through the fraying of the paper at a crease.
55 *had damp'd*] with *depress'd repress'd* written above.

3. Full many a Gem of purest Ray serene
   The dark unfathom'd Caves of Ocean bear!
   Full many a Flower is born to blush unseen
   And wast its Sweetness on the desert Air!   60

Th' Applause of listening Senates to command,
The Threats of Pain & Ruin to despise,
To scatter Plenty o'er a smiling Land
And read their Hist'ry in a Nation's Eyes

Their Fate forbad: nor circumscribed alone   65
Their struggling Virtues, but their Crimes confined;
Forbad to wade thro' Slaughter to a Throne,
And shut the Gates of Mercy on Mankind

The struggleing Pangs of conscious Truth to hide,
To quench the Blushes of ingenuous Shame,   70
And at the Shrine of Luxury & Pride
With Incense hallowd in the Muse's Flame.

The thoughtless World to Majesty may bow
Exalt the brave, & idolize Success
But more to Innocence their Safety owe   75
Than Power & Genius e'er conspired to bless

And thou, who mindful of the unhonour'd Dead
Dost in these Notes their artless Tale relate
By Night & lonely Contemplation led
To linger in the gloomy Walks of Fate   80

Hark how the sacred Calm, that broods around
Bids ev'ry fierce tumultuous Passion cease
In still small Accents whisp'ring from the Ground
A grateful Earnest of eternal Peace

65 *Fate*] with *Lot* written above.
66 *struggling*] with *growing* written above.
67 *Forbad*] altered from *Forbid*.
71 *at*] with *Crown* written above.
72 *With*] written above *Burn* deleted.
78 *their*] the *y* of *thy* is deleted and *eir* written above.

⎧ No more with Reason & thyself at Strife   85
⎪ Give anxious Cares & endless Wishes room
⎨ But thro' the cool sequester'd Vale of Life
⎩ Pursue the silent Tenour of thy Doom.

Far from the madding Crowd's ignoble Strife;
Their sober Wishes never knew to stray: 90
Along the cool sequester'd Vale of Life
They kept the silent Tenour of their Way.

Yet even these Bones from Insult to protect
Some frail Memorial still erected nigh
With uncouth Rhime, & shapeless Sculpture deckt   95
Implores the passing Tribute of a Sigh.

Their Name, their Years, spelt by th' unletter'd Muse
The Place of Fame, & Epitaph supply,
And many a holy Text around she strews
That teach the rustic Moralist to die.   100

For who to dumb Forgetfulness a Prey
This pleasing anxious Being e'er resign'd;
Left the warm Precincts of the chearful Day,
Nor cast one longing lingring Look behind?

On some fond Breast the parting Soul relies,   105
Some pious Drops the closing Eye requires:
Even from the Tomb the Voice of Nature cries,
And buried Ashes glow with Social Fires

For Thee, who mindful &c: as above.

If chance that e'er some pensive Spirit more,   110
By sympathetic Musings here delay'd,
With vain, tho' kind, Enquiry shall explore
Thy once-loved Haunt, this long-deserted Shade.

Haply some hoary headed Swain shall say,
Oft have we seen him at the Peep of Dawn   115
With hasty Footsteps brush the Dews away
On the high Brow of yonder hanging Lawn

92 *silent*] with *noiseless* written above.
95 *With*] Written above *In* deleted.

Him have we seen the Green-wood Side along,
While o'er the Heath we hied, our Labours done,
Oft as the Woodlark piped her farewell Song   120
With whistful Eyes pursue the setting Sun.

Oft at the Foot of yonder hoary Beech
That wreathes its old fantastic Roots so high
His listless Length at Noontide would he stretch,
And pore upon the Brook that babbles by.   125

With Gestures quaint now smileing as in Scorn,
Mutt'ring his fond Conceits he would he rove:
Now drooping, woeful wan, as one forlorn,
Or crazed with Care, or cross'd in hopeless Love.

One Morn we miss'd him on th' customd Hill,   130
By the Heath and at his fav'rite Tree.
Another came, nor yet beside the Rill,
Nor up'the Lawn, nor at the Wood was he.

The next with Dirges meet in sad Array
Slow thro the Church-way Path we saw him born   135
Approach & read, for thou can'st read the Lay
Wrote on the Stone beneath that ancient Thorn

122 *hoary*] with *spreading* written above and *nodding* in margin.
127 *fond Conceits*] with *wayward fancies* written above.
   he would he] *wont to* is deleted, *loved* written above and deleted and
   finally *would he* written above.
128 *Now ... wan,*] Originally *Now woeful wan, he droop'd* with *drooping,*
   written above and *he droop'd* deleted.
130 *customd*] the *ac* of *accustomd* is deleted.
131 *By the*] with *Along the* written above.
   Heath] *side* is written after *Heath* and deleted.
   at] with *Near* written above.
133 *at*] with *by* written above.
   After this line is written and deleted *There scatter'd oft, the earliest*
135 *thro*] with *by* written above.
137 *Wrote*] with *Graved carved* written above.
   that] with *yon* written above.

There scatter'd oft the earliest of y^c Year
By Hands unseen are frequent Vi'lets found
The Robin loves to build & warble there,   140
And little Footsteps lightly print the Ground.

Here rests his Head upon the Lap of Earth
A Youth to Fortune & to Fame unknown
Fair Science frown'd not on his humble birth
And Melancholy mark'd him for her own   145

Large was his Bounty & his Heart sincere;
Heaven did a Recompence as largely send.
He gave to Mis'ry all he had, a Tear.
He gained from Heav'n, twas all he wish'd, a Friend

No farther seek his Merits to disclose,   150
Nor seek to draw them from their dread Abode
(His Frailties there in trembling Hope repose)
The Bosom of his Father & his God.

138 *Year*] written above *Spring* deleted.
139 *frequent*] with *Showers of* written above.
140 *Robin*] with *Redbreast* written above.
142–53 Written along the outer margin at right angles to the other stanzas.
151 *seek*] with *think* written above.

POEMS
OF
WILLIAM COLLINS

LIST OF COLLINS'S POEMS

1721   25 December. Born at Chichester, son of William Collins, a hatter, Mayor of the town in 1714 and 1721. His elder sisters are Elizabeth (b. 1704) and Anne (b. 1705).

1725–33   Educated probably at the Prebendal School, Chichester.

1733   30 September. Death of his father.

1734   23 February. Admitted as Scholar at Winchester School. Contemporaries include Joseph Warton, James Hampton, and John Mulso.

1739   October. His *Sonnet* published in the *Gentleman's Magazine*. Writes his *Persian Eclogues* at this period.

1740   Placed first on list of Scholars for New College, but no vacancy occurs.

        22 March. Matriculates at Queen's College, Oxford.

1741   29 July. Elected Demy of Magdalen College, where his cousin William Payne is a Fellow. Joseph Warton and another friend, Gilbert White, are at Oriel.

1742   January. His *Persian Eclogues* published by J. Roberts.

1743   18 November. Graduates B.A.

        December. His *Verses . . . to Sir Thomas Hanmer* published by M. Cooper.

1744   9 May. Revised edition of the *Epistle to Hanmer* published by M. Cooper and R. Dodsley, including the *Song from Cymbelyne*. Probably in London by this date.

        3 July. Death of his mother. Her will leaving her property to her three children not proved until 12 August 1745.

        18 July. Letter from Mulso to Gilbert White describes Collins in London as 'entirely an Author' and refers to his 'Subscriptions' (see December).

        17 September. By this date has applied to the Duke of Richmond for a living and has been offered a curacy at Birdham. Dissuaded from accepting it by John Hardham, tobacconist and under-treasurer at Drury Lane Theatre.

        8 October. By this date is lodging with Miss Bundy at the corner of King's Square Court, Soho.

        December. His proposed *History of the Revival of Learning* mentioned in *A Literary Journal* in Dublin.

1745   At this period his friends include Johnson, Armstrong, and the actors Quin, Garrick, Foote, and Davies. Plans a tragedy, undertakes a translation of Aristotle's *Poetics* with commentary and engages to supply articles for the *Biographia Britannica*: none of these projects is known to have been executed. Gilbert White describes him at this period as 'spending his time in all the dissipation of Ranelagh, Vauxhall, and the playhouses'.

        13 March. Will of his uncle, Charles Collins, proved, leaving him property in Chichester.

        11 May. Battle of Fontenoy. Writes his *Ode to a Lady* before the end of the month.

17 September. Mulso tells White that Collins 'has been some Time return'd from Flanders', is intending to take orders and wants an army chaplaincy. Collins may have been motivated by the landing of the Young Pretender in Scotland in July to visit his uncle Colonel Martin, then in Flanders, for advice about his career.

1746   16 April. Battle of Culloden.

23 April. Letter from John Gilbert Cooper to Dodsley refers to Collins as 'that wandering Knight'.

c. 20 May. Meets Joseph Warton at Guildford Races and plans a joint volume of their *Odes*, eventually abandoned.

28 May. His encounter with a bailiff mentioned by Mulso. At some point during the next few months probably removes to Richmond.

7 June. His *Ode to a Lady* published in *The Museum*, edited by Mark Akenside and published by Dodsley.

1 August. Mulso has received a letter from Collins in Antwerp, describing his travels through Holland and his plan to 'set out for the army', presumably to meet Colonel Martin once more, who has left Scotland for Flanders at about this time.

10 October. Sells property at Chichester, on which he had raised money by a mortgage in April.

4 December. Joseph Warton's *Odes on Various Subjects* published by Dodsley.

20 December. Collins's *Odes on Several Descriptive and Allegoric Subjects*, dated 1747, published by A. Millar in an edition of 1000 copies. Later destroys the unsold copies.

1747   By this period living at Richmond and friendly with James Thomson and John Ragsdale.

1 May. Joins with his sisters to sell his father's old premises and other property in Chichester.

10 November. Writes to J. G. Cooper about their projected *Clarendon Review*, never published.

1748   7 April. Johnson's Preface to *The Preceptor* refers to a commentary on Aristotle's *Poetics*, presumably Collins's, as 'soon to be published'.

27 August. Death of James Thomson at Richmond.

December. Three poems published in 2nd edition of Dodsley's *Collection*.

1749   19 April. His uncle, Colonel Martin, makes his will and dies a week later, leaving Collins one-third of his property, estimated by some sources as £2000.

June. His *Ode Occasion'd by the Death of Mr Thomson* published by R. Manby and H. S. Cox.

October. His *Song from Cymbelyne* reprinted in the *Gentleman's Magazine* as 'Elegiac Song'.

1749-50   c. December–January. Writes his *Ode to a Friend*, presented to John Home (published in 1788 as *Ode on the Popular Superstitions of the Highlands*).

1750   Seen in London at this period by Thomas Warton, still planning his *History of the Revival of Learning* (of which only the preliminary dissertation was ever written) and the *Clarendon Review*.

February–March. His *Epistle to the Editor of Fairfax his Translation of Tasso* advertised but not published by Manby and Cox.

2 July. *The Passions*, set to music by William Hayes, performed at Encaenia at Oxford and printed as a pamphlet.

15 October. Elizabeth Collins marries Lieut. Nathaniel Tanner.

8 November. Writes to William Hayes from Chichester (where he may have been living permanently for some time), referring to a revised version of *The Passions* and *Lines on the Music of the Grecian Theatre*.

1751   Easter. Seriously ill, according to Thomas Warton.

9 June. Missing letter from Chichester mentioned by Warton.

1751–54   According to Ragsdale, travels in France and visits Bath in an attempt to regain health. Johnson mentions meeting him at Islington after his return to England.

1753   May. *The Union*, edited by T. Warton, published at Oxford, contains *Ode to Evening* and *Ode on Thomson*.

1754   According to Ragsdale is removed by his sister from McDonald's madhouse at Chelsea. Visits Oxford for a month, lodging opposite Christ Church and is seen there by Gilbert White. His sister Elizabeth Tanner dies in the early summer.

September. Visited by the Wartons at Chichester, where he is living in the Cathedral Cloisters with his sister Anne. Shows them several fragmentary MS. poems.

1755   28 January. His sister Anne marries Lieut. Hugh Sempill; after his death she will marry Thomas Durnford, Rector of Bramdean and Vicar of Harting.

March. His *Epistle to Hanmer* printed in Dodsley's *Collection of Poems*, vol. iv.

1757   His *Oriental* [*Persian*] *Eclogues* reprinted by J. Payne.

1759   12 June. Dies at Chichester and is buried in St Andrew's Church three days later.

POEMS

1. Sonnet

[First printed in the *Gentleman's Magazine*, ix. 545, in October 1739, signed 'Delicatulus'. The attribution was made by Joseph Warton, who was at Winchester with Collins at the time and who contributed a poem to the same number.(John Wooll, *Memoirs of Joseph Warton*, 1806, p. 107 n.).]

When *Phœbe* form'd a wanton smile,
    My soul! it reach'd not here!
Strange, that thy peace, thou trembler, flies
    Before a rising tear!

From midst the drops, my love is born,   5
    That o'er those eyelids rove:
Thus issued from a teeming wave
    The fabled queen of love.

2. Persian Eclogues

Joseph Warton inscribed the copy of the *Persian Eclogues* in the Dyce Library, South Kensington, 'By Mr Collins, (written at Winchester School)'. If taken literally, this statement would mean that the *Eclogues* were written not later than March 1740, when Collins left Winchester. Warton repeated the statement in 1797 (*Works of Pope*, i. 61 n.), where he added that Collins 'had been just reading that volume of Salmon's Modern History, which described Persia; which determined him to lay the scene of these pieces [there], as being productive of new images and sentiments'. Thomas Salmon's *Modern History* (31 vols., 1725–38) had been reprinted in three quarto volumes in April 1739.

    Collins was at Oxford when the *Eclogues* were published in January 1742. The Dyce copy contains a number of autograph corrections by Collins himself. Warton has noted on the back of the title-page that 'Mr Collins gave me this Copy with his own Hands when I & my Brother visited Him for the Last Time at Chichester', a visit which occurred in September 1754. When the poems were reprinted as *Oriental Eclogues* in January 1757 most of

Collins's corrections had been made, but there are a number of other changes which do not appear in the Dyce copy and for which Warton may have been responsible. For this reason the text followed here is that of 1742 as corrected by Collins himself, with variants recorded from 1757.

The motto in 1742 was from Cicero, *Pro Archia Poeta*, vii. 16: *Quod si non hic tantas fructus ostenderetur, et si ex his studiis delectatis sola peteretur; tamen, ut opinor, hanc animi remissionem humanissimam ac liberalissimam judicaretis* ('But let us for a moment waive these solid advantages; let us assume that entertainment is the sole end of reading; even so I think you would hold that no mental relaxation is so broadening to the sympathies or so enlightening to the understanding'). In the Dyce copy Collins substituted a line from Virgil, *Georgics*, i. 250, which appeared (slightly altered) on the title-page in 1757: *ubi primus equis Oriens adflavit anhelis* ('and when on us the rising sun first breathed with panting steeds').]

THE PREFACE

It is with the Writings of Mankind, in some Measure, as with their Complexions or their Dress, each Nation hath a Peculiarity in all these, to distinguish it from the rest of the World.

The Gravity of the *Spaniard*, and the Levity of the *Frenchman*, are as evident in all their Productions as in their Persons themselves; and the   5 Stile of my Countrymen is as naturally Strong and Nervous, as that of an *Arabian* or *Persian* is rich and figurative.

There is an Elegancy and Wildness of Thought which recommends all their Compositions; and our Genius's are as much too cold for the Entertainment of such Sentiments, as our Climate is for their Fruits and   10 Spices. If any of these Beauties are to be found in the following *Eclogues*, I hope my Reader will consider them as an Argument of their being Original. I received them at the Hands of a Merchant, who had made it his Business to enrich himself with the Learning, as well as the Silks and Carpets of the *Persians*. The little Information I could gather concern-   15 ing their Author, was, That his Name was *Mahamed*, and that he was a Native of *Tauris*.

It was in that City that he died of a Distemper fatal in those Parts, whilst he was engag'd in celebrating the Victories of his favourite Monarch, *the Great Abbas*. As to the *Eclogues* themselves, they give a   20 very just View of the Miseries and Inconveniences, as well as the Felicities that attend one of the finest Countries in the East.

The Time of the Writing them was probably in the Beginning of *Sha Sultan Hosseyn*'s Reign, the Successor of *Sefi* or *Solyman* the Second.

Whatever Defects, as, I doubt not, there will be many, fall under the   25 Reader's Observation, I hope his Candour will incline him to make the following Reflections:

That the Works of *Orientals* contain many Peculiarities, and that thro' Defect of Language few *European* Translators can do them Justice.

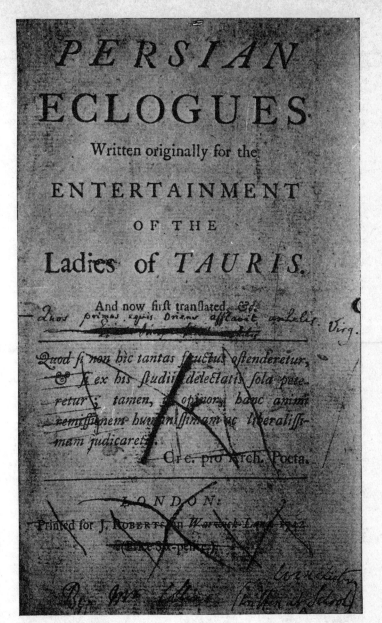

PERSIAN ECLOGUES.

Written originally for the

ENTERTAINMENT

OF THE

Ladies of *TAURIS*.

And now first translated. *&c.*

Quos primus equis Oriens afflavit anhelis

Virg.

Quod si non hic tantas fructus ostenderetur,
& ex his studiis delectatis sola peteretur; tamen, ut opinor, hanc animi remissionem humanissimam ac liberalissimam judicaretis.

Cic. pro Arch. Poeta.

LONDON:

Printed for J. ROBERTS in Warwick-Lane. 1742.

(Price Six-pence.)

Title-page of the *Persian Eclogues* as corrected by Collins.

ECLOGUE THE FIRST

SELIM; *or, the Shepherd's Moral.*
SCENE, *a Valley near* Bagdat.
· TIME, *the* MORNING.

Ye *Persian* Maids, attend your Poet's Lays,
And hear how Shepherds pass their golden Days:
Not all are blest, whom Fortune's Hand sustains
With Wealth in Courts, nor all that haunt the Plains:
Well may your Hearts believe the Truths I tell;   5
'Tis Virtue makes the Bliss, where'er we dwell.

Thus *Selim* sung, by sacred Truth inspir'd;
No Praise the Youth, but her's alone desir'd:
Wise in himself, his meaning Songs convey'd
Informing Morals to the Shepherd Maid,   10
Or taught the Swains that surest Bliss to find,
What Groves nor Streams bestow, a virtuous Mind.

When sweet and od'rous, like an Eastern Bride,
The radiant Morn resum'd her orient Pride,
When wanton Gales, along the Valleys play,   15
Breathe on each Flow'r, and bear their Sweets away:
By *Tigris'* wand'ring Waves he sate, and sung
This useful Lesson for the Fair and Young.

Ye *Persian* Dames, he said, to you belong,
Well may they please, the Morals of my Song;   20
No fairer Maids, I trust, than you are found,
Grac'd with soft Arts, the peopled World around!
The Morn that lights you to your Loves supplies
Each gentler Ray delicious to your Eyes:
For you those Flow'rs her fragrant Hands bestow,   25
And yours the Love that Kings delight to know.
Yet think not these, all beauteous as they are,
The best kind Blessings Heav'n can grant the Fair!
Who trust alone in Beauty's feeble Ray,
* *Balsora's* Pearls have more of Worth, than they;   30
Drawn from the Deep, they sparkle to the Sight,
And all-unconscious shoot a lust'rous Light:

---

* The Gulph of that Name, famous for the Pearl-fishery.

Such are the Maids, and such the Charms they boast,
By Sense unaided, or to Virtue lost.
Self-flattering Sex! your Hearts believe in vain   35
That Love shall blind, when once he fires the Swain;
Or hope a Lover by your Faults to win,
As Spots on Ermin beautify the Skin:
Who seeks secure to rule, be first her Care
Each softer Virtue that adorns the Fair,   40
Each tender Passion Man delights to find,
The lov'd Perfections of a female Mind.

    Blest were the Days, when Wisdom held her Reign,
And Shepherds sought her on the silent Plain,
With Truth she wedded in the secret Grove,   45
The fair-eyed Truth, and Daughters bless'd their Love.

    O haste, fair Maids, ye Virtues come away,
Sweet Peace and Plenty lead you on your way!
The balmy Shrub, for you shall love our Shore,
By *Ind'* excell'd or *Araby* no more.   50

    Lost to our Fields, for so the Fates ordain,
The dear Deserters shall return again.
O come, thou Modesty, as they decree,
The Rose may then improve her Blush by Thee.
Here make thy Court amidst our rural Scene,   55
And Shepherd-Girls shall own Thee for their Queen.
With Thee be Chastity, of all afraid,
Distrusting all, a wise suspicious Maid;
But Man the most; not more the Mountain Doe
Holds the swift Falcon for her deadly Foe.   60
Cold is her Breast, like Flow'rs that drink the Dew,
A silken Veil conceals her from the View.
No wild Desires amidst thy Train be known,
But Faith, whose Heart is fix'd on one alone:
Desponding Meekness with her down-cast Eyes,   65
And friendly Pity full of tender Sighs;
And Love the last: By these your Hearts approve,
These are the Virtues that must lead to Love.

    Thus sung the Swain, and Eastern Legends say,
The Maids of *Bagdat* verify'd the Lay: 70
Dear to the Plains, the Virtues came along,
The Shepherds lov'd, and *Selim* bless'd his Song.

ECLOGUE THE SECOND

HASSAN; *or, the Camel-driver.*
SCENE, *the Desart.*
TIME, Mid-day.

In silent Horror o'er the Desart-Waste
The Driver *Hassan* with his Camels past.
One Cruise of Water on his Back he bore,
And his light Scrip contain'd a scanty Store:
A Fan of painted Feathers in his Hand,   5
To guard his shaded Face from scorching Sand.
The sultry Sun had gain'd the middle Sky,
And not a Tree, and not an Herb was nigh.
The Beasts, with Pain, their dusty Way pursue,
Shrill roar'd the Winds, and dreary was the View!   10
With desp'rate Sorrow wild th' affrighted Man
Thrice sigh'd, thrice strook his Breast, and thus began:
   Sad was the Hour, and luckless was the Day,
When first from Schiraz' *Walls I bent my Way.*

   Ah! little thought I of the blasting Wind,   15
The Thirst or pinching Hunger that I find!
Bethink thee, *Hassan*, where shall Thirst assuage,
When fails this Cruise, his unrelenting Rage?
Soon shall this Scrip its precious Load resign,
Then what but Tears and Hunger shall be thine?   20

   Ye mute Companions of my Toils, that bear
In all my Griefs a more than equal Share!
Here, where no Springs, in Murmurs break away,
Or Moss-crown'd Fountains mitigate the Day:
In vain ye hope the green Delights to know,   25
Which Plains more blest, or verdant Vales bestow.
Here Rocks alone, and tasteless Sands are found,
And faint and sickly Winds for ever howl around.
   Sad was the Hour, and luckless was the Day,
When first from Schiraz' *Walls I bent my Way.*   30

   Curst be the Gold and Silver which persuade
Weak Men to follow far-fatiguing Trade.
The Lilly-Peace outshines the silver Store,
And Life is dearer than the golden Ore.

Yet Money tempts us o'er the Desart brown,   35
To ev'ry distant Mart, and wealthy Town:
Full oft we tempt the Land, and oft the Sea,
And are we only yet repay'd by Thee?
Ah! why was Ruin so attractive made,
Or why fond Man so easily betray'd?   40
Why heed we not, whilst mad we haste along,
The gentle Voice of Peace, or Pleasure's Song?
Or wherefore think the flow'ry Mountain's Side,
The Fountain's Murmurs, and the Valley's Pride,
Why think we these less pleasing to behold,   45
Than dreary Desarts, if they lead to Gold?
    Sad was the Hour, and luckless was the Day,
    When first from Schiraz' *Walls I bent my Way.*

    O cease, my Fears! all frantic as I go,
When Thought creates unnumber'd Scenes of Woe,   50
What if the Lion in his Rage I meet!
Oft in the Dust I view his printed Feet:
And fearful! oft, when Day's declining Light
Yields her pale Empire to the Mourner Night,
By Hunger rous'd, he scours the groaning Plain,   55
Gaunt Wolves and sullen Tygers in his Train:
Before them Death with Shrieks directs their Way,
Fills the wild Yell, and leads them to their Prey.
    Sad was the Hour, and luckless was the Day,
    When first from Schiraz' *Walls I bent my Way.*   60

    At that dead Hour the silent Asp shall creep,
If ought of rest I find, upon my Sleep:
Or some swoln Serpent twist his Scales around,
And wake to Anguish with a burning Wound.
Thrice happy they, the wise contented Poor,   65
From Lust of Wealth, and Dread of Death secure;
They tempt no Desarts, and no Griefs they find;
Peace rules the Day, where Reason rules the Mind.
    Sad was the Hour, and luckless was the Day,
    When first from Schiraz' *Walls I bent my Way.*   70

    O hapless Youth! for she thy Love hath won,
The tender *Zara*, will be most undone!
Big swell'd my Heart, and own'd the pow'rful Maid,
When fast she dropt her Tears, as thus she said;

"Farewel the Youth whom Sighs could not detain,   75
"Whom *Zara*'s breaking Heart implor'd in vain;
"Yet as thou go'st, may ev'ry Blast arise,
"Weak and unfelt as these rejected Sighs!
"Safe o'er the Wild, no Perils mayst thou see,
"No Griefs endure, nor weep, false Youth, like me."   80
O let me safely to the Fair return,
Say with a Kiss, she must not, shall not mourn.
Go teach my Heart, to lose its painful Fears,
Recall'd by Wisdom's Voice, and *Zara*'s Tears.

He said, and call'd on Heav'n to bless the Day,   85
When back to *Schiraz*' Walls he bent his Way.

ECLOGUE THE THIRD

ABRA; *or, the* Georgian *Sultana.*
SCENE, *a Forest.*
TIME, *the* EVENING.

In *Georgia*'s Land, where *Tefflis*' Tow'rs are seen,
In distant View along the level Green,
While Ev'ning Dews enrich the glitt'ring Glade,
And the tall Forests cast a longer Shade,
Amidst the Maids of *Zagen*'s peaceful Grove,   5
Emyra sung the pleasing Cares of Love.

Of *Abra* first began the tender Strain,
Who led her Youth, with Flocks upon the Plain:
At Morn she came those willing Flocks to lead,
Where Lillies rear them in the wat'ry Mead;   10
From early Dawn the live-long Hours she told,
'Till late at silent Eve she penn'd the Fold.
Deep in the Grove beneath the secret Shade,
A various Wreath of od'rous Flow'rs she made:
*Gay-motley'd Pinks and sweet Junquils she chose,   15
The Violet-blue, that on the Moss-bank grows;
All-sweet to Sense, the flaunting Rose was there;
The finish'd Chaplet well-adorn'd her Hair.

---

* That these Flowers are found in very great Abundance in some of the Provinces of
Persia; see the *Modern History* of the ingenious Mr. *Salmon* [3rd. edn., 1739, I. 392].

Great *Abbas* chanc'd that fated Morn to stray,
By Love conducted from the Chace away;   20
Among the vocal Vales he heard her Song,
And sought the Vales and echoing Groves among:
At length he found, and woo'd the rural Maid,
She knew the Monarch, and with Fear obey'd.
 Be ev'ry Youth like Royal Abbas *mov'd,*   25
 And ev'ry Georgian *Maid like* Abra *lov'd.*

The Royal Lover bore her from the Plain,
Yet still her Crook and bleating Flock remain:
Oft as she went, she backward turn'd her View,
And bad that Crook, and bleating Flock Adieu.   30
Fair happy Maid! to other Scenes remove,
To richer Scenes of golden Pow'r and Love!
Go leave the simple Pipe, and Shepherd's Strain,
With Love delight thee, and with *Abbas* reign.
 Be ev'ry Youth like Royal Abbas *mov'd,*   35
 And ev'ry Georgian *Maid like* Abra *lov'd.*

Yet midst the Blaze of Courts she fix'd her Love,
On the cool Fountain, or the shady Grove;
Still with the Shepherd's Innocence her Mind
To the sweet Vale, and flow'ry Mead inclin'd,   40
And oft as Spring renew'd the Plains with Flow'rs,
Breath'd his soft Gales, and led the fragrant Hours,
With sure Return she sought the sylvan Scene,
The breezy Mountains, and the Forests green.
Her Maids around her mov'd, a duteous Band!   45
Each bore a Crook all-rural in her Hand:
Some simple Lay, of Flocks and Herds they sung,
With Joy the Mountain, and the Forest rung.
 Be ev'ry Youth like Royal Abbas *mov'd,*
 And ev'ry Georgian *Maid like* Abra *lov'd.*   50

And oft the Royal Lover left the Care,
And Thorns of State, attendant on the Fair:
Oft to the Shades and low-roof'd Cots retir'd,
Or sought the Vale where first his Heart was fir'd;·
A Russet Mantle, like a Swain, he wore,   55
And thought of Crowns and busy Courts no more.
 Be ev'ry Youth like Royal Abbas *mov'd,*
 And ev'ry Georgian *Maid like* Abra *lov'd.*

Blest was the Life, that Royal *Abbas* led:
Sweet was his Love, and innocent his Bed.   60
What if in Wealth the noble Maid excel;
The simple Shepherd Girl can love as well.
Let those who rule on *Persia*'s jewell'd Throne,
Be fam'd for Love, and gentlest Love alone:
Or wreath, like *Abbas*, full of fair Renown,   65
The Lover's Myrtle, with the Warrior's Crown.

Oh happy Days! the Maids around her say,
Oh haste, profuse of Blessings, haste away!
Be ev'ry Youth, like Royal Abbas, *mov'd;*
And ev'ry Georgian *Maid, like* Abra, *lov'd.*   70

ECLOGUE THE FOURTH

A GIB *and* SECANDER; *or, the Fugitives.*
SCENE, *a Mountain in* Circassia.
TIME, MIDNIGHT.

In fair *Circassia*, where to Love inclin'd,
Each Swain was blest, for ev'ry Maid was kind!
At that still Hour, when awful Midnight reigns,
And none, but Wretches, haunt the twilight Plains;
What Time the Moon had hung her Lamp on high,   5
And past in Radiance, thro' the cloudless Sky:
Sad o'er the Dews, two Brother Shepherds fled,
Where wild'ring Fear and desp'rate Sorrow led.
Fast as they prest their Flight, behind them lay
Wide ravag'd Plains, and Valleys stole away.   10
Along the Mountain's bending Sides they ran,
Till faint and weak *Secander* thus began.

SECANDER

O stay thee, *Agib*, for my Feet deny,
No longer friendly to my Life, to fly.
Friend of my Heart, O turn thee and survey,   15
Trace our sad Flight thro' all its length of Way!
And first review that long-extended Plain,
And yon wide Groves, already past with Pain!
Yon ragged Cliff, whose dang'rous Path we try'd,
And last this lofty Mountain's weary Side!   20

AGIB

Weak as thou art, yet hapless must thou know
The Toils of Flight, or some severer Woe!
Still as I haste, the *Tartar* shouts behind,
And Shrieks and Sorrows load the sad'ning Wind:
In rage of Heart, with Ruin in his Hand,   25
He blasts our Harvests, and deforms our Land.
Yon Citron Grove, whence first in Fear we came,
Droops its fair Honours to the conqu'ring Flame:
Far fly the Swains, like us, in deep Despair,
And leave to ruffian Bands their fleecy Care.   30

SECANDER

Unhappy Land, whose Blessings tempt the Sword,
In vain, unheard, thou call'st thy *Persian* Lord!
In vain, thou court'st him, helpless to thine Aid,
To shield the Shepherd, and protect the Maid,
Far off in thoughtless Indolence resign'd,   35
Soft Dreams of Love and Pleasure sooth his Mind:
'Midst fair *Sultanas* lost in idle Joy,
No Wars alarm him, and no Fears annoy.

AGIB

Yet these green Hills, in Summer's sultry Heat,
Have lent the Monarch oft a cool Retreat,   40
Sweet to the Sight is *Zabran*'s flow'ry Plain,
And once by Maids and Shepherds lov'd in vain!
No more the Virgins shall delight to rove,
By *Sargis*' Banks, or *Irwan*'s shady Grove:
On *Tarkie*'s Mountain catch the cooling Gale,   45
Or breathe the Sweets of *Aly*'s flow'ry Vale:
Fair Scenes! but, ah no more with Peace possest,
With Ease alluring, and with Plenty blest.
No more the Shepherds whit'ning Tents appear,
Nor the kind Products of a bounteous Year;   50
No more the Date with snowy Blossoms crown'd,
But Ruin spreads her baleful Fires around.

SECANDER

In vain *Circassia* boasts her spicy Groves,
For ever fam'd for pure and happy Loves:
In vain she boasts her fairest of the Fair,   55
Their Eyes' blue languish, and their golden Hair!

Those Eyes in Tears, their fruitless Grief must send,
Those Hairs the *Tartar*'s cruel Hand shall rend.

AGIB

  Ye *Georgian* Swains that piteous learn from far
Circassia's Ruin, and the Waste of War: 60
Some weightier Arms than Crooks and Staves prepare,
To shield your Harvests, and defend your Fair:
The *Turk* and *Tartar* like Designs pursue,
Fix'd to destroy, and stedfast to undo.
Wild as his Land, in native Deserts bred,   65
By Lust incited, or by Malice led,
The Villain-*Arab*, as he prowls for Prey,
Oft marks with Blood and wasting Flames the Way;
Yet none so cruel as the *Tartar* Foe,
To Death inur'd, and nurst in Scenes of Woe.   70

  He said, when loud along the Vale was heard
A shriller Shriek, and nearer Fires appear'd:
Th' affrighted Shepherds thro' the Dews of Night
Wide o'er the Moon-light Hills, renew'd their Flight.

3. *An Epistle: Addrest to Sir Thomas Hanmer on his Edition of Shakespear's Works*

[The first edition, entitled *Verses Humbly Address'd to Sir Thomas Hanmer. On his Edition of Shakespear's Works. By a Gentleman of Oxford*, is dated at the end 'Oxford, Dec.3. 1743', and was published in London later that month by M. Cooper. Its occasion was the imminent appearance of Hanmer's elaborate edition of Shakespeare in six quarto volumes, published in 1744 at the Clarendon Press, Oxford. A second and extensively revised edition of Collins's poem was published on 9 May 1744 by M. Cooper and Robert Dodsley, the poet's name appearing on the title-page for the first time and his 'Song from *Cymbelyne*' being added. The poem was reduced from 160 to 148 lines, six passages were substantially revised and two notes were added. The main effect of the changes at the beginning of the poem was to omit the original celebration of the University of Oxford's connection with the edition of Shakespeare and to reduce the compliments to Hanmer. The changes may suggest that Collins had in the interim left Oxford in disgust, perhaps after failing to obtain a Fellowship, and had given up hope of obtaining patronage from Hanmer. The main concerns of the poem—the progress of drama from Ancient Greece to Shakespeare's England, and the relationship of poetry and painting—are accordingly clearer in the 1744 edition, the text followed here, with variants from 1743 recorded in the textual notes. Some of Collins's smaller changes appear to have been intended to avoid verbal repetition and to reduce echoes of Pope in the 1743 text.

Collins begins by referring, with considerable exaggeration, to the neglect of Shakespeare before Hanmer (1–16). His account of the development of drama moves from Euripides and Sophocles, to Roman Comedy, and to the Middle Ages and the Revival of Learning in Italy (17–44), especially under Pope Julius II and Cosimo de Medici (37–8). Collins refers vaguely in lines 40–2 to Provençal troubadours, who had in fact flourished in Italy since the thirteenth century. Shakespeare eventually unites '*Tuscan* Fancy, and *Athenian* Strength', although Jonson and Fletcher mark a decline (45–66). The achievements of Corneille and Racine in France (comparable to Maro, i.e. Virgil) are acknowledged (67–74) before the poet returns to Shakespeare's peculiar powers: the depiction of truth and the 'manners' in the history plays, in particular *Henry V* and *Richard III* (75–92); his 'fancy' in *A Midsummer Night's Dream* and *The Tempest* (93–100); and his capacity to inspire the painter, with particular reference to scenes from *Julius Caesar* and *Coriolanus* (101–32). The poet finally asserts that Hanmer's edition, which will so inspire the 'Sister Arts', is comparable to the early collecting and arrangement in Athens of the scattered works of Homer (133–48).]

SIR
While born to bring the Muse's happier Days,
A Patriot's Hand protects a Poet's Lays:
While nurst by you she sees her Myrtles bloom,
Green and unwither'd o'er his honour'd Tomb:
Excuse her Doubts, if yet she fears to tell 5
What secret Transports in her Bosom swell:
With conscious Awe she hears the Critic's Fame,
And blushing hides her Wreath at *Shakespear*'s Name.
Hard was the Lot those injur'd Strains endur'd,
Unown'd by Science, and by Years obscur'd: 10
Fair Fancy wept; and echoing Sighs confest
A fixt Despair in ev'ry tuneful Breast.
Not with more Grief th' afflicted Swains appear
When wintry Winds deform the plenteous Year:
When ling'ring Frosts the ruin'd Seats invade 15
Where Peace resorted, and the Graces play'd.

Each rising Art by just Gradation moves,
Toil builds on Toil, and Age on Age improves.

The Muse alone unequal dealt her Rage,
And grac'd with noblest Pomp her earliest Stage.   20
Preserv'd thro' Time, the speaking Scenes impart
Each changeful Wish of *Phædra*'s tortur'd Heart:
Or paint the Curse, that mark'd the * *Theban*'s Reign,
A Bed incestuous, and a Father slain.
With kind Concern our pitying Eyes o'erflow,   25
Trace the sad Tale, and own another's Woe.

To *Rome* remov'd, with Wit secure to please,
The *Comic* Sisters kept their native Ease.
With jealous Fear declining *Greece* beheld
Her own *Menander*'s Art almost excell'd!   30
But ev'ry Muse essay'd to raise in vain
Some labour'd Rival of her *Tragic* Strain;
Ilissus' Laurels, tho' transferr'd with Toil,
Droop'd their fair Leaves, nor knew th' unfriendly Soil.

As Arts expir'd, resistless Dulness rose;   35
Goths, *Priests*, or *Vandals*, - - - - all were Learning's Foes.
Till † *Julius* first recall'd each exil'd Maid,
And *Cosmo* own'd them in th' *Etrurian* Shade:
Then deeply skill'd in Love's engaging Theme,
The soft *Provencial* pass'd to *Arno*'s Stream: 40
With graceful Ease the wanton Lyre he strung,
Sweet flow'd the Lays - - - - but Love was all he sung.
The gay Description could not fail to move;
For, led by Nature, all are Friends to Love.

But Heav'n, still various in its Works, decreed   45
The perfect Boast of Time should last succeed.
The beauteous Union must appear at length,
Of *Tuscan* Fancy, and *Athenian* Strength:
One greater Muse *Eliza*'s Reign adorn,
And ev'n a *Shakespear* to her Fame be born!   50

Yet ah! so bright her Morning's op'ning Ray,
In vain our *Britain* hop'd an equal Day!
No second Growth the Western Isle could bear,
At once exhausted with too rich a Year.

---

* The *Oedipus of Sophocles*.
† *Julius* the Second [Pope, 1503–13], the immediate Predecessor of *Leo* the Tenth.

Too nicely *Johnson* knew the Critic's Part;   55
Nature in him was almost lost in Art.
Of softer Mold the gentle *Fletcher* came,
The next in Order, as the next in Name.
With pleas'd Attention 'midst his Scenes we find
Each glowing Thought, that warms the Female Mind;   60
Each melting Sigh, and ev'ry tender Tear,
The Lover's Wishes and the Virgin's Fear.
His * ev'ry strain the *Smiles* and *Graces* own;
But stronger *Shakespear* felt for *Man* alone:
Drawn by his Pen, our ruder Passions stand   65
Th' unrival'd Picture of his early Hand.

   † With gradual Steps, and slow, exacter *France*
Saw Art's fair Empire o'er her Shores advance:
By length of Toil, a bright Perfection knew,
Correctly bold, and just in all she drew.   70
Till late *Corneille*, with ‡ *Lucan*'s spirit fir'd,
Breath'd the free Strain, as *Rome* and He inspir'd:
And classic Judgment gain'd to sweet *Racine*
The temp'rate Strength of *Maro*'s chaster Line.

   But wilder far the *British* Laurel spread,   75
And Wreaths less artful crown our Poet's Head.
Yet He alone to ev'ry Scene could give
Th' Historian's Truth, and bid the Manners live.
Wak'd at his Call I view, with glad Surprize,
Majestic Forms of mighty Monarchs rise.   80
There *Henry*'s Trumpets spread their loud Alarms,
And laurel'd Conquest waits her Hero's Arms.
Here gentler *Edward* claims a pitying Sigh,
Scarce born to Honours, and so soon to die!
Yet shall thy Throne, unhappy Infant, bring   85
No Beam of Comfort to the guilty King?

---

   * Their Characters are thus distinguish'd by Mr. *Dryden* [Preface to *Troilus and Cressida*].
   † About the Time of *Shakespear*, the Poet [Alexandre] *Hardy* [*c*. 1569–1632] was in great Repute in *France*. He wrote, according to *Fontenelle*, six hundred Plays. The *French* Poets after him applied themselves in general to the correct Improvement of the Stage, which was almost totally disregarded by those of our own Country, *Johnson* excepted.
   ‡ The favourite Author of the Elder *Corneille*.

The *Time shall come, when *Glo'ster*'s Heart shall bleed
In Life's last Hours, with Horror of the Deed:
When dreary Visions shall at last present
Thy vengeful Image, in the midnight Tent: 90
Thy Hand unseen the secret Death shall bear,
Blunt the weak Sword, and break th' oppressive Spear.

    Where'er we turn, by Fancy charm'd, we find
Some sweet Illusion of the cheated Mind.
Oft, wild of Wing, she calls the Soul to rove   95
With humbler Nature, in the rural Grove;
Where Swains contented own the quiet Scene,
And twilight Fairies tread the circled Green:
Drest by her Hand, the Woods and Vallies smile,
And Spring diffusive decks th' *enchanted Isle*.   100

    O more than all in pow'rful Genius blest,
Come, take thine Empire o'er the willing Breast!
Whate'er the Wounds this youthful Heart shall feel,
Thy Songs support me, and thy Morals heal!
There ev'ry Thought the Poet's Warmth may raise,   105
There native Music dwells in all the Lays.
O might some Verse with happiest Skill persuade
Expressive Picture to adopt thine Aid!
What wond'rous Draughts might rise from ev'ry Page!
What other *Raphaels* Charm a distant Age!   110

    Methinks ev'n now I view some free Design,
Where breathing Nature lives in ev'ry Line:
Chast and subdu'd the modest Lights decay,
Steal into Shade, and mildly melt away.
- - - - And see, where †*Anthony* in Tears approv'd,   115
Guards the pale Relicks of the Chief he lov'd:
O'er the cold Corse the Warrior seems to bend,
Deep sunk in Grief, and mourns his murther'd Friend!
Still as they press, he calls on all around,
Lifts the torn Robe, and points the bleeding Wound.   120

---

* Tempus erit Turno, magno cum optaverit emptum
  Intactum Pallanta, &c.

                                    [*Aeneid*, X. 503-04].

† See the Tragedy of *Julius Cæsar* [III. iii]

  But * who is he, whose Brows exalted bear
A Wrath impatient, and a fiercer Air?
Awake to all that injur'd Worth can feel,
On his own *Rome* he turns th'avenging Steel.
Yet shall not War's insatiate Fury fall,   125
(So Heav'n ordains it) on the destin'd Wall.
See the fond Mother 'midst the plaintive Train
Hung on his Knees, and prostrate on the Plain!
Touch'd to the Soul, in vain he strives to hide
The Son's Affection, in the *Roman*'s Pride: 130
O'er all the Man conflicting Passions rise,
Rage grasps the Sword, while *Pity* melts the Eyes.

  Thus, gen'rous Critic, as thy Bard inspires,
The Sister Arts shall nurse their drooping Fires;
Each from his Scenes her Stores alternate bring,   135
Blend the fair Tints, or wake the vocal String:
Those *Sibyl*-Leaves, the Sport of ev'ry Wind,
(For Poets ever were a careless Kind)
By thee dispos'd, no farther Toil demand,
But, just to Nature, own thy forming Hand.   140

  So spread o'er *Greece*, th' harmonious Whole unknown,
Ev'n *Homer*'s Numbers charm'd by Parts alone.
Their own *Ulysses* scarce had wander'd more,
By Winds and Water cast on ev'ry Shore:
When, rais'd by Fate, some former *Hanmer* join'd   145
Each beauteous Image of the boundless Mind:
And bad, like Thee, his *Athens* ever claim,
A fond Alliance with the Poet's Name.

---

* *Coriolanus* [V. iii]. See Mr. *Spence*'s Dialogues on the *Odyssey* [1726, p. 84].

4. *A Song from Shakespear's Cymbelyne*

Sung by Guiderus and Arviragus over Fidele, suppos'd to be Dead

See page 278 of the 7th Vol. of THEOBALD'S *Edition of* SHAKESPEAR.

[First published in the second edition of Collins's *Epistle to Hanmer* on 9 May 1744. In October 1749 it was reprinted as 'Elegiac Song' in the *Gentleman's Magazine*, xix. 466–7, with a number of changes apparently made by the editor Edward Cave, and therefore without textual authority. Dodsley restored the 1744 text, which is followed here, in his *Collection of Poems*, iv. 71–2, in 1755.

Collins's reference to Theobald's Shakespeare (2nd edition, 1740) directed the reader to *Cymbeline*, IV. ii, in particular to the well-known dirge over Imogen, the supposed Fidele, 'Fear no more the heat o' th' sun'.]

I

To fair FIDELE's grassy Tomb
 Soft Maids, and Village Hinds shall bring
Each op'ning Sweet, of earliest Bloom,
 And rifle all the breathing Spring.

II

No wailing Ghost shall dare appear   5
 To vex with Shrieks this quiet Grove:
But Shepherd Lads assemble here,
 And melting Virgins own their Love.

III

No wither'd Witch shall here be seen,
 No Goblins lead their nightly Crew: 10
The Female Fays shall haunt the Green,
 And dress thy Grave with pearly Dew!

IV

The Redbreast oft at Ev'ning Hours
 Shall kindly lend his little Aid:
With hoary Moss, and gather'd Flow'rs,   15
 To deck the Ground where thou art laid.

V

When howling Winds, and beating Rain,
 In Tempests shake the sylvan Cell:
Or midst the Chace on ev'ry Plain,
 The tender Thought on thee shall dwell.   20

VI

Each lonely Scene shall thee restore,
 For thee the Tear be duly shed:
Belov'd, till Life could charm no more;
 And mourn'd, till Pity's self be dead.

5. *Song. The Sentiments Borrowed from Shakespeare*

[First published in the *Gentleman's Magazine*, lviii (pt. i). 155, in February
1788, with a letter signed 'C—T—O', apparently by Henry Headley, a
friend of Thomas Warton. The poem was reprinted a few days later in the
Public Advertiser, 7 March 1788. The attribution to Collins may be
cautiously accepted. It was added to his poems in the 1790 edition of
Johnson's *English Poets*, vol. liii, and has appeared in all subsequent editions.
In 1858 W. Moy Thomas referred to a MS. of the poem (not in Collins's
hand), which has now disappeared, inscribed, 'Written by Collins when at
Winchester School. From a Manuscript'. There is no other evidence for
dating the poem, which may best be associated with Collins's other imitation
of Shakespeare. Although there are repeated echoes of Ophelia's mad-scene
in *Hamlet*, IV. v, they are blended with similar phrases from David Mallet's
popular ballad *William and Margaret*. The text is that of the *Gentleman's
Magazine*.]

Young Damon of the vale is dead,
 Ye lowland hamlets moan:
A dewy turf lies o'er his head,
 And at his feet a stone.

His shroud, which death's cold damps destroy,   5
 Of snow-white threads was made:
All mourn'd to see so sweet a boy
 In earth for ever laid.

Pale pansies o'er his corpse were plac'd,
 Which, pluck'd before their time,   10
Bestrew'd the boy like him to waste,
 And wither in their prime.

But will he ne'er return, whose tongue
 Could tune the rural lay?
Ah, no! his bell of peace is rung,   15
 His lips are cold as clay.

They bore him out at twilight hour,
    The youth who lov'd so well:
Ah me! how many a true-love shower
    Of kind remembrance fell!   20

Each maid was woe—but Lucy chief,
    Her grief o'er all was tried,
Within his grave she dropp'd in grief,
    And o'er her lov'd-one died.

6. *Written on a Paper, Which Contained a Piece of Bride Cake Given to the Author by a Lady*

[First published, with an attribution to 'the late Mr Collins', in the *Gentleman's Magazine*, xxxv. 231, in May 1765, with no other explanation of its provenance. In spite of the appearance of Langhorne's edition of Collins in the preceding March, the poet's reputation was hardly enough at this period to provide a motive for forgery and the attribution may be accepted. The poem was reprinted in Pearch's *Collection of Poems*, ii. 46–7, in 1768 and collected in Johnson's *English Poets*, vol. xlix. The text is that of the *Gentleman's Magazine*.]

Ye curious hands, that, hid from vulgar eyes,
    By search profane shall find this hallow'd cake,
With virtue's awe forbear the sacred prize,
    Nor dare a theft for love and pity's sake!

This precious relick, form'd by magick pow'r,   5
    Beneath her shepherd's haunted pillow laid,
Was meant by love to charm the silent hour,
    The secret present of a matchless maid.

The *Cypryan* queen, at hymen's fond request,
    Each nice ingredient chose with happiest art;   10
Fears, sighs, and wishes of th' enamoured breast,
    And pains that please, are mixt in every part.

With rosy hand the spicy fruit she brought
    From *Paphian* hills, and fair *Cythera*'s isle;
And tempered sweet with these the melting thought,   15
    The kiss ambrosial and the yielding smile.

Ambiguous looks, that scorn and yet relent,
    Denials mild, and firm unalter'd truth,
Reluctant pride, and amorous faint consent,
    And meeting ardors and exulting youth.   20

Sleep, wayward God! hath sworn while these remain,
    With flattering dreams to dry his nightly tear,
And chearful *Hope*, so oft invok'd in vain,
    With fairy songs shall soothe his pensive ear.

If bound by vows to friendship's gentle side,   25
    And fond of soul, thou hop'st an equal grace,
If youth or maid thy joys and griefs divide,
    O much intreated leave this fatal place.

Sweet *Peace*, who long hath shunn'd my plaintive day,
    Consents at length to bring me short delight,   30
Thy careless steps may scare her doves away,
    And grief with raven note usurp the night.

O D E S

ON SEVERAL
Descriptive and *Allegoric*
S U B J E C T S.

By WILLIAM COLLINS.

————Ειην
Ευρησιεπης αναγεισθαι
Προσφορος εν Μοισᾶν Διφρω˙
Τολμα δε και αμφιλαφης Δυναμις
Εσποιτο.———   Πινδαρ, Ολυμπ. Θ.

LONDON:
Printed for A. MILLAR, in the *Strand*.
M.DCC.XLVII.
(Price One Shilling.)

Title-page of Collins's *Odes*.

Odes on Several Descriptive and Allegoric Subjects

[Collins originally intended to publish his *Odes* in one volume with those of his friend Joseph Warton, according to a letter written by Warton in the early summer of 1746 (J. Wooll, *Memoirs of Joseph Warton*, 1806, pp.14–15 n.). Warton's *Odes on Various Subjects* were in fact published by Dodsley on 4 December 1746 and Collins's *Odes* by Andrew Millar on 20 December 1746 (with 1747 on the title-page). The short 'Advertisement' prefixed to Warton's volume expresses views with which Collins almost certainly sympathised:

The Public has been so much accustom'd of late to didactic Poetry alone, and Essays on moral Subjects, that any work where the imagination is much indulged, will perhaps not be relished or regarded. The author therefore of these pieces is in some pain least certain austere critics should think them too fanciful and descriptive. But as he is convinced that the fashion of moralizing in verse has been carried too far, and as he looks upon Invention and Imagination to be the chief faculties of a Poet, so he will be happy if the following Odes may be look'd upon as an attempt to bring back Poetry into its right Channel.

Collins made no such theoretical statement, but his title-page has an epigraph from Pindar, *Olympian Odes*, ix. 80–3: 'Would I could find me words, as I move onward as a bearer of good gifts in the Muse's car; would I might be attended by Daring and by all-embracing Power.'

All the *Odes* appear to have been written after Collins's arrival in London in 1744, most of them probably in 1746. Because no firm dating is possible, the poems are printed here in Collins's own sequence. Errata noted in 1746 have been silently corrected.]

7. *Ode to Pity*

[This and the following *Ode* may be connected with a translation and commentary on Aristotle's *Poetics*, which Collins projected in 1745 and 1746, since they deal with the two emotions involved in the process of tragic catharsis. Ilissus (line 14) is the river flowing to the south of Athens, where Euripides spent most of his life. At line 20 Collins refers to Thomas Otway (1652–85), the poet and playwright, who like himself was a native of Sussex, a Wykehamist, and an Oxonian.]

> O Thou, the Friend of Man assign'd,
> With balmy Hands his Wounds to bind,
>   And charm his frantic Woe:
> When first *Distress* with Dagger keen
> Broke forth to waste his destin'd Scene,   5
>   His wild unsated Foe!

2

By *Pella*'s *Bard, a magic Name,
By all the Griefs his Thought could frame,
   Receive my humble Rite:
Long, *Pity*, let the Nations view   10
Thy sky-worn Robes of tend'rest Blue,
   And Eyes of dewy Light!

3

But wherefore need I wander wide
To old *Ilissus*' distant Side,
   Deserted Stream, and mute?   15
Wild *Arun* † too has heard thy Strains,
And Echo, 'midst my native Plains,
   Been sooth'd by *Pity*'s Lute.

4

There first the Wren thy Myrtles shed
On gentlest *Otway*'s infant Head,   20
   To Him thy Cell was shown;
And while He sung the Female Heart,
With Youth's soft Notes unspoil'd by Art,
   Thy Turtles mix'd their own.

5

Come, *Pity*, come, by Fancy's Aid,   25
Ev'n now my Thoughts, relenting Maid,
   Thy Temple's Pride design:
Its Southern Site, its Truth compleat
Shall raise a wild Enthusiast Heat,
   In all who view the Shrine.   30

---

  * *Euripides*, of whom *Aristotle* pronounces, on a Comparison of him with *Sophocles*, That he was the greater Master of the tender Passions, ἦν τραγικώτερος [*Poetics*, XIII. 10].
  † The River *Arun* runs by the Village in *Sussex*, where *Otway* had his Birth.

6

There Picture's Toils shall well relate,
How Chance, or hard involving Fate,
   O'er mortal Bliss prevail:
The Buskin'd Muse shall near her stand,
And sighing prompt her tender Hand,   35
   With each disastrous Tale.

7

There let me oft, retir'd by Day,
In Dreams of Passion melt away,
   Allow'd with Thee to dwell:
There waste the mournful Lamp of Night,   40
Till, Virgin, Thou again delight
   To hear a *British* Shell!

8. *Ode to Fear*

[The Epode (26–45) once more reflects Collins's interest in Greek tragedy.
Aeschylus fought against the Persians at Marathon in 490 B.C. (31). Although
Sophocles lived in Athens, he was often associated with Hybla, a city in
Sicily famous for its honey, because of the sweetness of his verse (35). The
setting of his *Oedipus at Colonus* is a grove dedicated to the Eumenides or
Furies (37).]

Thou, to whom the World unknown
With all its shadowy Shapes is shown;
Who see'st appall'd th' unreal Scene,
While Fancy lifts the Veil between:
   Ah *Fear!* Ah frantic *Fear!*   5
   I see, I see Thee near.
I know thy hurried Step, thy haggard Eye!
Like Thee I start, like Thee disorder'd fly,
For lo what *Monsters* in thy Train appear!
Danger, whose Limbs of Giant Mold   10
What mortal Eye can fix'd behold?
Who stalks his Round, an hideous Form,
Howling amidst the Midnight Storm,
Or throws him on the ridgy Steep
Of some loose hanging Rock to sleep: 15

And with him thousand Phantoms join'd,
Who prompt to Deeds accurs'd the Mind:
And those, the Fiends, who near allied,
O'er Nature's Wounds, and Wrecks preside;
Whilst *Vengeance*, in the lurid Air,   20
Lifts her red Arm, expos'd and bare:
On whom that rav'ning *Brood of Fate,
Who lap the Blood of Sorrow, wait;
Who, *Fear*, this ghastly Train can see,
And look not madly wild, like Thee?   25

EPODE

In earliest *Grece* to Thee with partial Choice,
    The Grief-full Muse addrest her infant Tongue;
The Maids and Matrons, on her awful Voice,
    Silent and pale in wild Amazement hung.

Yet He the Bard †who first invok'd thy Name,   30
    Disdain'd in *Marathon* its Pow'r to feel:
For not alone he nurs'd the Poet's flame,
    But reach'd from Virtue's Hand the Patriot's Steel.

But who is He whom later Garlands grace,
    Who left a-while o'er *Hybla*'s Dews to rove,   35
With trembling Eyes thy dreary Steps to trace,
    Where Thou and *Furies* shar'd the baleful Grove?

Wrapt in thy cloudy Veil th' *Incestuous Queen* ‡
    Sigh'd the sad Call § her Son and Husband hear'd,
When once alone it broke the silent Scene,   40
    And He the Wretch of *Thebes* no more appear'd.

---

* Alluding to the Κύνας ἀφύκτους of *Sophocles*. See the ELECTRA [1385–88].
† *Æschylus*.
‡ *Jocasta*
§   οὐδ' ἔτ' ὠρώρει βοή,
  ῏Ην μὲν σιωπή, φθέγμα δ' ἐξαίφνης τινὸς
  Θώϋξεν αὐτόν, ὥστε πάντας ὀρθίας
  Στῆσαι φόβῳ δείσαντας ἐξαίφνης τρίχας.
                    See the Œdip[us at] Colon[us] of *Sophocles* [1622–25].
  [But when they had made an end of wailing, and the sound went up no more, there
was a stillness; and suddenly a voice of one who cried aloud to him, so that the hair of
all stood up on their heads for sudden fear, and they were afraid.]

O *Fear*, I know Thee by my throbbing Heart,
  Thy with'ring Pow'r inspir'd each mournful Line,
Tho' gentle *Pity* claim her mingled Part,
  Yet all the Thunders of the Scene are thine!   45

ANTISTROPHE

Thou who such weary Lengths hast past,
Where wilt thou rest, mad Nymph, at last?
Say, wilt thou shroud in haunted Cell,
Where gloomy *Rape* and *Murder* dwell?
Or in some hollow'd Seat,   50
'Gainst which the big Waves beat,
Hear drowning Sea-men's Cries in Tempests brought!
Dark Pow'r, with shudd'ring meek submitted Thought
Be mine, to read the Visions old,
Which thy awak'ning Bards have told: 55
And lest thou meet my blasted View,
Hold each strange Tale devoutly true;
Ne'er be I found, by Thee o'eraw'd,
In that thrice-hallow'd Eve abroad,
When Ghosts, as Cottage-Maids believe,   60
Their pebbled Beds permitted leave,
And *Gobblins* haunt from Fire, or Fen,
Or Mine, or Flood, the Walks of Men!
  O Thou whose Spirit most possest
The sacred Seat of *Shakespear*'s Breast!   65
By all that from thy Prophet broke,
In thy Divine Emotions spoke:
Hither again thy Fury deal,
Teach me but once like Him to feel:
His *Cypress Wreath* my Meed decree,   70
And I, O *Fear*, will dwell with *Thee!*

9. *Ode to Simplicity*

[For Hybla (14) see the headnote to *Ode to Fear* (page 139). Cephisus (19) is the river flowing to the west of Athens. At line 35 Collins refers to the encouragement of poetry under Augustus.]

I

O Thou by *Nature* taught,
To breathe her genuine Thought,
In Numbers warmly pure, and sweetly strong:
Who first on Mountains wild,
In *Fancy* loveliest Child,   5
Thy Babe, or *Pleasure*'s, nurs'd the Pow'rs of Song!

2

Thou, who with Hermit Heart
Disdain'st the Wealth of Art,
And Gauds, and pageant Weeds, and trailing Pall:
But com'st a decent Maid   10
In *Attic* Robe array'd,
O chaste unboastful Nymph, to Thee I call!

3

By all the honey'd Store
On *Hybla*'s Thymy Shore,
By all her Blooms, and mingled Murmurs dear,   15
By Her *, whose Love-lorn Woe
In Ev'ning Musings slow
Sooth'd sweetly sad *Electra*'s Poet's Ear:

4

By old *Cephisus* deep,
Who spread his wavy Sweep   20
In warbled Wand'rings round thy green Retreat,
On whose enamel'd Side
When holy *Freedom* died
No equal Haunt allur'd thy future Feet.

* The ἀηδών, or Nightingale, for which *Sophocles* seems to have entertain'd a peculiar Fondness.

5

O Sister meek of Truth,   25
To my admiring Youth,
Thy sober Aid and native Charms infuse!
The Flow'rs that sweetest breathe,
Tho' Beauty cull'd the Wreath,
Still ask thy Hand to range their order'd Hues.   30

6

While *Rome* could none esteem
But Virtue's Patriot Theme,
You lov'd her Hills, and led her Laureate Band:
But staid to sing alone
To one distinguish'd Throne,   35
And turn'd thy Face, and fled her alter'd Land.

7

No more, in Hall or Bow'r,
The Passions own thy Pow'r,
Love, only Love her forceless Numbers mean:
For Thou hast left her Shrine,   40
Nor Olive more, nor Vine,
Shall gain thy Feet to bless the servile Scene.

8

Tho' Taste, tho' Genius bless,
To some divine Excess,
Faints the cold Work till Thou inspire the whole;   45
What each, what all supply,
May court, may charm our Eye,
Thou, only Thou can'st raise the meeting Soul!

9

Of These let others ask,
To aid some mighty Task,   50
I only seek to find thy temp'rate Vale:
Where oft my Reed might sound
To Maids and Shepherds round,
And all thy Sons, O *Nature*, learn my Tale.

10. *Ode on the Poetical Character*

[In lines 1–16 Collins refers to the episode in Spenser's *Faerie Queene* in which various ladies compete for Florimel's girdle, which only the chaste can wear. For Collins, true poetic power is similarly rare. The girdle of Venus was often called 'cestus' (19). The 'Enthusiast' (29) is Fancy or Imagination (from 17): Collins is exploring the analogy between God's creation of the world and the poet's act of imaginative creation. At line 46 'tarsel' is the tercel or male hawk. The reference to Edmund Waller (69), an initiator of the Augustan poetic mode, emphasizes Collins's declaration of allegiance to the poetic line of Spenser and Milton.]

> As once, if not with light Regard,
> I read aright that gifted Bard,
> (Him whose School above the rest
> His Loveliest *Elfin* Queen has blest.)
> One, only One, unrival'd Fair*,   5
> Might hope the magic Girdle wear,
> At solemn Turney hung on high,
> The Wish of each love-darting Eye;
> Lo! to each other Nymph in turn applied,
>   As if, in Air unseen, some hov'ring Hand,   10
> Some chaste and Angel-Friend to Virgin-Fame,
>   With whisper'd Spell had burst the starting Band,
> It left unblest her loath'd dishonour'd Side;
>   Happier hopeless Fair, if never
>   Her baffled Hand with vain Endeavour   15
> Had touch'd that fatal Zone to her denied!
> Young *Fancy* thus, to me Divinest Name,
>   To whom, prepar'd and bath'd in Heav'n,
>   The Cest of amplest Pow'r is giv'n:
> To few the God-like Gift assigns,   20
>   To gird their blest prophetic Loins,
> And gaze her Visions wild, and feel unmix'd her Flame!
>
>   2
> The Band, as Fairy Legends say,
> Was wove on that creating Day,
> When He, who call'd with Thought to Birth   25
> Yon tented Sky, this laughing Earth,

---

* *Florimel.* See *Spenser* Leg. 4th. [*Faerie Queene*, IV. iv–v].

And drest with Springs, and Forests tall,
And pour'd the Main engirting all,
Long by the lov'd *Enthusiast* woo'd,
Himself in some Diviner Mood, 30
Retiring, sate with her alone,
And plac'd her on his Saphire Throne,
The whiles, the vaulted Shrine around,
Seraphic Wires were heard to sound,
Now sublimest Triumph swelling, 35
Now on Love and Mercy dwelling;
And she, from out the veiling Cloud,
Breath'd her magic Notes aloud:
And Thou, Thou rich-hair'd Youth of Morn,
And all thy subject Life was born! 40
The dang'rous Passions kept aloof,
Far from the sainted growing Woof:
But near it sate Ecstatic *Wonder*,
List'ning the deep applauding Thunder:
And *Truth*, in sunny Vest array'd, 45
By whose the Tarsel's Eyes were made;
All the shad'wy Tribes of *Mind*,
In braided Dance their Murmurs join'd,
And all the bright uncounted *Pow'rs*,
Who feed on Heav'n's ambrosial Flow'rs. 50
Where is the Bard, whose Soul can now
Its high presuming Hopes avow?
Where He who thinks, with Rapture blind,
This hallow'd Work for Him design'd?

3
High on some Cliff, to Heav'n up-pil'd, 55
Of rude Access, of Prospect wild,
Where, tangled round the jealous Steep,
Strange Shades o'erbrow the Valleys deep,
And holy *Genii* guard the Rock,
Its Gloomes embrown, its Springs unlock, 60
While on its rich ambitious Head,
An *Eden*, like his own, lies spread:
I view that Oak, the fancied Glades among,
    By which as *Milton* lay, His Ev'ning Ear,
From many a Cloud that drop'd Ethereal Dew, 65
    Nigh spher'd in Heav'n its native Strains could hear:

On which that ancient Trump he reach'd was hung;
  Thither oft his Glory greeting,
  From *Waller*'s Myrtle Shades retreating,
With many a Vow from Hope's aspiring Tongue,   70
My trembling Feet his guiding Steps pursue;
  In vain—Such Bliss to One alone,
  Of all the Sons of Soul was known,
  And Heav'n, and *Fancy*, kindred Pow'rs,
  Have now o'erturn'd th' inspiring Bow'rs,   75
Or curtain'd close such Scene from ev'ry future View.

11. *Ode, Written in the Beginning of the Year 1746*

[Collins's title might seem to allude to the Battle of Falkirk on 17 January 1746, when the English forces were defeated by the Young Pretender; but when the poem was reprinted in Dodsley's *Collection of Poems*, 2nd edition, 1748, i. 330, it followed the *Ode to a Lady*, 'Written May, 1745', and was stated to have been 'Written in the same Year'. If he were responsible for this change of date, Collins may have come to prefer to give the impression that his poem celebrated British soldiers who had died fighting the French during 1745. The present poem seems to contain a reworking of lines 7–20 of the first version of the *Ode to a Lady*, although Collins's revision of the earlier poem for the *Odes* seems in turn to have been influenced by certain details in the *Ode, Written in . . . 1746*.]

  How sleep the Brave, who sink to Rest,
  By all their Country's Wishes blest!
  When *Spring*, with dewy Fingers cold,
  Returns to deck their hallow'd Mold,
  She there shall dress a sweeter Sod,   5
  Than *Fancy*'s Feet have ever trod.

2

  By Fairy Hands their Knell is rung,
  By Forms unseen their Dirge is sung;
  There *Honour* comes, a Pilgrim grey,
  To bless the Turf that wraps their Clay,   10
  And *Freedom* shall a-while repair,
  To dwell a weeping Hermit there!

12. *Ode to Mercy*

[The *Ode* may be connected with the trial of the three Jacobite noblemen, the Earls of Kilmarnock and Cromartie and Lord Balmerino, who were sentenced to death on 1 August 1746. There was widespread discussion during the summer of the proper punishment for their supposed 'treason' in participating in the Jacobite invasion and mercy was urged from various quarters, with which Collins may have been identified. 'Salvage' (21) is an archaic form of 'savage'.]

STROPHE

O Thou, who sit'st a smiling Bride
By *Valour*'s arm'd and awful Side,
Gentlest of Sky-born Forms, and best ador'd:
Who oft with Songs, divine to hear,
Win'st from his fatal Grasp the Spear,   5
And hid'st in Wreaths of Flow'rs his bloodless Sword!
Thou who, amidst the deathful Field,
By Godlike Chiefs alone beheld,
Oft with thy Bosom bare art found,
Pleading for him the Youth who sinks to Ground: 10
See, *Mercy*, see, with pure and loaded Hands,
Before thy Shrine my Country's Genius stands,
And decks thy Altar still, tho' pierc'd with many a Wound!

ANTISTROPHE

When he whom ev'n our Joys provoke,
The *Fiend of Nature* join'd his Yoke,   15
And rush'd in Wrath to make our Isle his Prey;
Thy Form, from out thy sweet Abode,
O'ertook Him on his blasted Road,
And stop'd his Wheels, and look'd his Rage away.
I see recoil his sable Steeds,   20
That bore Him swift to Salvage Deeds,
Thy tender melting Eyes they own;
O Maid, for all thy Love to *Britain* shown,
Where *Justice* bars her Iron Tow'r,
To Thee we build a roseate Bow'r,   25
Thou, Thou shalt rule our Queen, and share our Monarch's
Throne!

13. *Ode to Liberty*

[The reference in line 49 to Genoa's 'bleeding State' is probably an allusion to the allied attack on Genoa during the campaign against the French in Italy, and suggests that the poem was written in the autumn of 1746. It rests on the widespread eighteenth-century belief in the connection between political liberty and the arts. The poem begins by locating Liberty in Ancient Greece and describing the Fall of Rome (1–25). The survival of Liberty in Italy is depicted in Florence, San Marino, Venice, and Genoa and, later, in Switzerland and Holland (26–63). Britain's 'divorce' from the Continent makes her the last abode of Liberty (64–88). Liberty's Druid-temple in Britain mixes Grecian and Gothic styles (89–128). The poet finally hopes that Liberty will be joined with Peace in Britain, alluding to the recent Jacobite invasion and the war with France (129–44).

The poem referred to in line 7 is preserved in Athenaus' *Deipnosophistae*, although the attribution to Alcaeus is mistaken. Harmodius and Aristogeiton conspired to kill Hippius and Hipparchus, the tyrants of Athens, and were revered, as in this well-known poem, as champions of liberty. Collins omits six lines from the poem, which fully translated reads:

'In a myrtle-branch I will carry my sword, as did Harmodius and Aristogeiton, when they slew the tyrant and made Athens a city of equal rights.

'Dearest Harmodius, thou art not dead, I ween, but they say that thou art in the Islands of the Blest, where swift-footed Achilles lives, and, they say, the brave son of Tydeus, Diomed.

'In a myrtle-branch I will carry my sword, as did Harmodius and Aristogeiton, when at the Feast of Athena they slew the tyrant Hipparchus.

'Ever shall your fame live in the earth, dearest Harmodius and Aristogeiton, for that ye slew the tyrant, and made Athens a city of equal rights.'

At line 15 Collins quotes Callimachus, *Hymn to Demeter*: 'Nay, nay, let us not speak of that which brought the tear to Demeter.' Line 58 refers to the attempt of the Duke of Alva, the Spanish general sent by Philip II, to crush the Protestant revolt in the Netherlands in 1567. 'Orcas' (72) is the most northerly promontory of Scotland opposite the Orkneys.]

STROPHE

Who shall awake the *Spartan* Fife,
And call in solemn Sounds to Life,
The Youths, whose Locks divinely spreading,
 Like vernal Hyacinths in sullen Hue,
At once the Breath of Fear and Virtue shedding,   5
 Applauding *Freedom* lov'd of old to view?

What New *Alcæus*,* Fancy-blest,
Shall sing the Sword, in Myrtles drest,
  At *Wisdom*'s Shrine a-while its Flame concealing,
(What Place so fit to seal a Deed renown'd?) 10
  Till she her brightest Lightnings round revealing,
It leap'd in Glory forth, and dealt her prompted Wound!
    O Goddess, in that feeling Hour,
  When most its Sounds would court thy Ears,
    Let not my Shell's misguided Pow'r†, 15
  E'er draw thy sad, thy mindful Tears.

No, *Freedom*, no, I will not tell,
How *Rome*, before thy weeping Face,
With heaviest Sound, a Giant-statue, fell,
Push'd by a wild and artless Race, 20
From off its wide ambitious Base,
When Time his Northern Sons of Spoil awoke,
  And all the blended Work of Strength and Grace,
    With many a rude repeated Stroke,
And many a barb'rous Yell, to thousand Fragments broke. 25

EPODE

Yet ev'n, where'er the least appear'd,
Th' admiring World thy Hand rever'd;
Still 'midst the scatter'd States around,
Some Remnants of Her Strength were found;
They saw by what escap'd the Storm, 30
How wond'rous rose her perfect Form;
How in the great the labour'd Whole,
Each mighty Master pour'd his Soul!

---

* Alluding to that beautiful Fragment of *Alcæus* [in Athenaus, *Deipnosophistae*, XV. 695].

    Ἐν μύρτου κλαδὶ τὸ ξίφος φορήσω,
   "Ωσπερ Ἁρμόδιος καὶ Ἀριστογείτων.
   Φίλταθ' Ἁρμόδι', οὔπω τέθνηκας,
   Νήσοις δ' ἐν Μακάρων σέ φασιν εἶναι.
   Ἐν μύρτου κλαδὶ τὸ ξίφος φορήσω,
   "Ωσπερ Ἁρμόδιος καὶ Ἀριστογείτων,
   "Οτ' Ἀθηναίης ἐν θυσίαις
   "Ανδρα τύραννον Ἵππαρχον ἐκαινέτην.
   Ἀεὶ σφῶν κλέος ἔσσεται κατ' αἶαν,
   Φίλταθ' Ἁρμόδι', καὶ Ἀριστογείτων.

† Μὴ μὴ ταῦτα λέγωμες, ἃ δάκρυον ἤγαγε Δηοῖ.
  Callimach. Ὕμνος εἰς Δήμητρα [17].

For sunny *Florence*, Seat of Art,
Beneath her Vines preserv'd a part,   35
Till They*, whom Science lov'd to name,
(O who could fear it?) quench'd her Flame.
And lo, an humbler Relick laid
In jealous *Pisa*'s Olive Shade!
See small *Marino* † joins the Theme,   40
Tho' least, not last in thy Esteem:
Strike, louder strike th' ennobling Strings
To those ‡, whose Merchant Sons were Kings;
To him §, who deck'd with pearly Pride,
In *Adria* weds his green-hair'd Bride;   45
Hail Port of Glory, Wealth, and Pleasure,
Ne'er let me change this *Lydian* Measure:
Nor e'er her former Pride relate,
To sad *Liguria*'s ‖ bleeding State.
Ah no! more pleas'd thy Haunts I seek,   50
On wild *Helvetia*'s ¶ Mountains bleak:
(Where, when the favor'd of thy Choice,
The daring Archer heard thy Voice;
Forth from his Eyrie rous'd in Dread,
The rav'ning *Eagle* northward fled.)   55
Or dwell in willow'd Meads more near,
With Those** to whom thy Stork is dear:
Those whom the Rod of *Alva* bruis'd,
Whose Crown a *British* Queen ††refus'd!
The Magic works, Thou feel'st the Strains,   60
One holier Name alone remains;
The perfect Spell shall then avail,
Hail Nymph, ador'd by *Britain*, Hail!

ANTISTROPHE

Beyond the Measure vast of Thought,
The Works, the Wizzard *Time* has wrought!   65

* The Family of the *Medici*.   † The little Republic of *San Marino*.
‡ The *Venetians*.   § The Doge of Venice.   ‖ *Genoa*.   ¶ *Switzerland*.
** The *Dutch*, amongst whom there are very severe Penalties for those who are
convicted of killing this Bird. They are kept tame in almost all their Towns, and
particularly at the *Hague*, of the Arms of which they make a Part. The common People
of *Holland* are said to entertain a superstitious Sentiment, That if the whole Species of
them should become extinct, they should lose their Liberties.
     †† Queen *Elizabeth*.

The *Gaul*, 'tis held of antique Story,
Saw *Britain* link'd to his now adverse Strand*,
  No Sea between, nor Cliff sublime and hoary,
He pass'd with unwet Feet thro' all our Land.
    To the blown *Baltic* then, they say,   70
    The wild Waves found another way,
Where *Orcas* howls, his wolfish Mountains rounding,
  Till all the banded West at once 'gan rise,
A wide wild Storm ev'n Nature's self confounding,
  With'ring her Giant Sons with strange uncouth Surprise. 75
      This pillar'd Earth so firm and wide,
        By Winds and inward Labors torn,
      In Thunders dread was push'd aside,
        And down the should'ring Billows born.
And see, like Gems, her laughing Train,   80
  The little Isles on ev'ry side,
Mona †, once hid from those who search the Main,
  Where thousand Elfin Shapes abide,
And *Wight* who checks the west'ring Tide,
  For Thee consenting Heav'n has each bestow'd,   85
A fair Attendant on her sov'reign Pride:
  To Thee this blest Divorce she ow'd,
For thou hast made her Vales thy lov'd, thy last Abode!

SECOND EPODE

Then too, 'tis said, an hoary Pile,
'Midst the green Navel of our Isle,   90
Thy Shrine in some religious Wood,
O Soul-enforcing Goddess stood!
There oft the painted Native's Feet,
Were wont thy Form celestial meet:

---

* This Tradition is mention'd by several of our old Historians. Some Naturalists too have endeavour'd to support the Probability of the Fact, by Arguments drawn from the correspondent Disposition of the two opposite Coasts. I don't remember that any Poetical Use has been hitherto made of it.

  † There is a Tradition in the Isle of *Man*, that a Mermaid becoming enamour'd of a young Man of extraordinary Beauty, took an Opportunity of meeting him one day as he walked on the Shore, and open'd her Passion to him, but was receiv'd with a Coldness, occasion'd by his Horror and Surprize at her Appearance. This however was so misconstrued by the Sea-Lady, that in revenge for his Treatment of her, she punish'd the whole Island, by covering it with a Mist, so that all who attempted to carry on any Commerce with it, either never arriv'd at it, but wander'd up and down the Sea, or were on a sudden wreck'd upon its Cliffs.

Tho' now with hopeless Toil we trace   95
Time's backward Rolls, to find its place;
Whether the fiery-tressed *Dane*,
Or *Roman*'s self o'erturn'd the Fane,
Or in what Heav'n-left Age it fell,
'Twere hard for modern Song to tell.   100
Yet still, if Truth those Beams infuse,
Which guide at once, and charm the Muse,
Beyond yon braided Clouds that lie,
Paving the light-embroider'd Sky:
Amidst the bright pavilion'd Plains,   105
The beauteous *Model* still remains.
There happier than in Islands blest,
Or Bow'rs by Spring or *Hebe* drest,
The Chiefs who fill our *Albion*'s Story,
In warlike Weeds, retir'd in Glory,   110
Hear their consorted *Druids* sing
Their Triumphs to th' immortal String.
  How may the Poet now unfold
What never Tongue or Numbers told?
How learn delighted, and amaz'd,   115
What Hands unknown that Fabric rais'd?
Ev'n now before his favor'd Eyes,
In *Gothic* Pride it seems to rise!
Yet *Græcia*'s graceful Orders join,
Majestic thro' the mix'd Design;   120
The secret Builder knew to chuse,
Each sphere-found Gem of richest Hues:
Whate'er Heav'n's purer Mold contains,
When nearer Suns emblaze its Veins;
There on the Walls the *Patriot*'s Sight,   125
May ever hang with fresh Delight,
And, grav'd with some Prophetic Rage,
Read *Albion*'s Fame thro' ev'ry Age.
  Ye Forms Divine, ye Laureate Band,
That near her inmost Altar stand!   130
Now sooth Her, to her blissful Train
Blithe *Concord*'s social Form to gain:
Concord, whose Myrtle Wand can steep
Ev'n *Anger*'s blood-shot Eyes in Sleep:
Before whose breathing Bosom's Balm,   135
Rage drops his Steel, and Storms grow calm;

Her let our Sires and Matrons hoar
Welcome to *Britain*'s ravag'd Shore,
Our Youths, enamour'd of the Fair,
Play with the Tangles of her Hair,   140
Till in one loud applauding Sound,
The Nations shout to Her around,
O how supremely art thou blest,
Thou, Lady, Thou shalt rule the West!

14. *Ode, to a Lady on the Death of Colonel Ross in the Action of Fontenoy*

[The *Ode* was first printed anonymously in *The Museum: Or, The Literary and Historical Register*, i. 215–17, on 7 June 1746. In this periodical (edited by Mark Akenside and published by Dodsley) the poem was entitled 'Ode to a Lady, On the Death of Col. Charles Ross, in the Action at Fontenoy. Written May, 1745'. The battle had taken place on 11 May 1745. Captain (not Colonel) Charles Ross (1721–45), son of Lord Ross of Balnagown and M.P. for the County of Ross, was probably not known personally to Collins. In the *Odes* the title was slightly altered and two new stanzas (lines 37–48) were added as a compliment to William, Duke of Cumberland, the hero of Culloden, who was widely expected at the time to return to Flanders to avenge the defeat at Fontenoy. In the 2nd edition of Dodsley's *Collection*, i. 327–9, in 1748, the added stanzas were removed (perhaps because of Cumberland's defeat at Laeffelt in July 1747) and further revision took place. Further variants from a MS. were recorded by Thomas Warton (see Nathan Drake, *The Gleaner*, 1811, iv. 477), who also identified the lady addressed by Collins as Elizabeth Goddard of Harting in Sussex (see line 58). In 1746 Joseph Warton had also identified the recipient of the *Ode* as Miss Goddard and as a close friend of Ross (Wooll, *Memoirs of Joseph Warton*, 1806, pp. 14–15 n.). It is by no means clear, however, that Miss Goddard was herself an inhabitant of Harting. The text followed here is that of the *Odes* of 1746; variants are recorded from the *Museum*, Dodsley's *Collection*, and the MS. seen by Warton.]

I

While, lost to all his former Mirth,
Britannia's Genius bends to Earth,
    And mourns the fatal Day:
While stain'd with Blood he strives to tear
Unseemly from his Sea-green Hair   5
    The Wreaths of chearful *May:*

2

The Thoughts which musing Pity pays,
And fond Remembrance loves to raise,
  Your faithful Hours attend:
Still Fancy to Herself unkind,   10
Awakes to Grief the soften'd Mind,
  And points the bleeding Friend.

3

By rapid *Scheld*'s descending Wave
His Country's Vows shall bless the Grave,
  Where'er the Youth is laid: 15
That sacred Spot the Village Hind
With ev'ry sweetest Turf shall bind,
  And Peace protect the Shade.

4

Blest Youth, regardful of thy Doom,
Aërial Hands shall build thy Tomb,   20
  With shadowy Trophies crown'd:
Whilst *Honor* bath'd in Tears shall rove
To sigh thy Name thro' ev'ry Grove,
  And call his Heros round.

5

The warlike Dead of ev'ry Age,   25
Who fill the fair recording Page,
  Shall leave their sainted Rest:
And, half-reclining on his Spear,
Each wond'ring Chief by turns appear,
  To hail the blooming Guest.   30

6

Old *Edward*'s Sons, unknown to yield,
Shall croud from *Cressy*'s laurell'd Field,
  And gaze with fix'd Delight:
Again for *Britain*'s Wrongs they feel,
Again they snatch the gleamy Steel,   35
  And wish th' avenging Fight.

7

But lo where, sunk in deep Despair,
Her Garments torn, her Bosom bare,
 Impatient *Freedom* lies!
Her matted Tresses madly spread,   40
To ev'ry Sod, which wraps the Dead,
 She turns her joyless Eyes.

8

Ne'er shall she leave that lowly Ground,
Till Notes of Triumph bursting round
 Proclaim her Reign restor'd: 45
Till *William* seek the sad Retreat,
And bleeding at her sacred Feet,
 Present the sated Sword.

9

If, weak to sooth so soft an Heart,
These pictur'd Glories nought impart,   50
 To dry thy constant Tear:
If yet, in Sorrow's distant Eye,
Expos'd and pale thou see'st him lie,
 Wild War insulting near:

10

Where'er from Time Thou court'st Relief,   55
The Muse shall still, with social Grief,
 Her gentlest Promise keep:
Ev'n humble *Harting*'s cottag'd Vale
Shall learn the sad repeated Tale,
 And bid her Shepherds weep.   60

15. *Ode to Evening*

[After its appearance in the *Odes* of 1746, this poem was reprinted with some revision in the 2nd edition of Dodsley's *Collection*, i. 331–2, and these alterations have been adopted in the present text (except that in line 32 'it's' has been corrected to 'its'). It was later reprinted in Thomas Warton's *The Union: Or Select Scots and English Poems* (1753).]

If ought of Oaten Stop, or Pastoral Song,
May hope, chaste *Eve*, to sooth thy modest Ear,
   Like thy own solemn Springs,
   Thy Springs, and dying Gales,
O *Nymph* reserv'd, while now the bright-hair'd Sun   5
Sits in yon western Tent, whose cloudy Skirts,
   With Brede ethereal wove,
   O'erhang his wavy Bed:
Now Air is hush'd, save where the weak-ey'd Bat,
With short shrill Shriek flits by on leathern Wing,   10
   Or where the Beetle winds
   His small but sullen Horn,
As oft he rises 'midst the twilight Path,
Against the Pilgrim born in heedless Hum:
   Now teach me, *Maid* compos'd,   15
   To breathe some soften'd Strain,
Whose Numbers stealing thro' thy darkning Vale,
May not unseemly with its Stillness suit,
   As musing slow, I hail
   Thy genial lov'd Return!   20
For when thy folding Star arising shews
His paly Circlet, at his warning Lamp
   The fragrant *Hours*, and *Elves*
   Who slept in Flow'rs the Day,
And many a *Nymph* who wreaths her Brows with Sedge, 25
And sheds the fresh'ning Dew, and lovelier still,
   The *Pensive Pleasures* sweet
   Prepare thy shadowy Car.
Then lead, calm *Vot'ress*, where some sheety Lake
Cheers the lone Heath, or some time-hallow'd Pile,   30
   Or up-land Fallows grey
   Reflect its last cool Gleam.
But when chill blustring Winds, or driving Rain,
Forbid my willing Feet, be mine the Hut,
   That from the Mountain's Side,   35

Views Wilds, and swelling Floods,
And Hamlets brown, and dim-discover'd Spires,
And hears their simple Bell, and marks o'er all
  Thy Dewy Fingers draw
  The gradual dusky Veil.   40
While *Spring* shall pour his Show'rs, as oft he wont,
And bathe thy breathing Tresses, meekest *Eve!*
  While *Summer* loves to sport,
  Beneath thy ling'ring Light:
While sallow *Autumn* fills thy Lap with Leaves,   45
Or *Winter* yelling thro' the troublous Air,
  Affrights thy shrinking Train,
  And rudely rends thy Robes.
So long sure-found beneath the Sylvan Shed,
Shall *Fancy*, *Friendship*, *Science*, rose-lip'd *Health*,   50
  Thy gentlest Influence own,
  And hymn thy fav'rite Name!

16. *Ode to Peace*

[Probably written in the summer or autumn of 1746 when the powers
involved in the War of the Spanish Succession were negotiating a peace.]

I

O Thou, who bad'st thy Turtles bear
Swift from his Grasp thy golden Hair,
  And sought'st thy native Skies:
When *War*, by Vultures drawn from far,
To *Britain* bent his Iron Car,   5
  And bad his Storms arise!

2

Tir'd of his rude tyrannic Sway,
Our Youth shall fix some festive Day,
  His sullen Shrines to burn:
But Thou who hear'st the turning Spheres,   10
What Sounds may charm thy partial Ears,
  And gain thy blest Return!

3

O *Peace*, thy injur'd Robes up-bind,
O rise, and leave not one behind
 Of all thy beamy Train: 15
The *British* Lion, Goddess sweet,
Lies stretch'd on Earth to kiss thy Feet,
 And own thy holier Reign.

4

Let others court thy transient Smile,
But come to grace thy western Isle,   20
 By warlike *Honour* led!
And, while around her Ports rejoice,
While all her Sons adore thy Choice,
 With Him for ever wed!

17. *The Manners. An Ode*

[This poem has often been interpreted as a literal farewell to academic
studies, in which case it would date from early 1744 when Collins left Oxford
for London. The *Ode* does not demand so literal a reading, however, as it
proposes only a turning away from philosophical studies to the study of
humanity and to an art which reflects nature and describes human manners,
notably to Cervantes (line 63) or Le Sage (line 67). Collins's lines on Le
Sage, even if written in the mistaken belief that he had died in 1745, point to
a later date of composition than has often been suggested. Collins's emphasis
on the story of Blanche from *Gil Blas* may be due to the fact that it had
provided the basis for James Thomson's tragedy *Tancred and Sigismunda*,
first performed in March 1745.]

Farewell, for clearer Ken design'd,
The dim-discover'd Tracts of Mind:
Truths which, from Action's Paths retir'd,
My silent Search in vain requir'd!
No more my Sail that Deep explores,   5
No more I search those magic Shores,
What Regions part the World of Soul,
Or whence thy Streams, *Opinion*, roll:
If e'er I round such Fairy Field,
Some Pow'r impart the Spear and Shield,   10
At which the Wizzard *Passions* fly,
By which the Giant *Follies* die!

Farewell the Porch, whose Roof is seen,
Arch'd with th' enlivening Olive's Green:
Where *Science*, prank'd in tissued Vest,   15
By *Reason*, *Pride*, and *Fancy* drest,
Comes like a Bride so trim array'd,
To wed with *Doubt* in *Plato*'s Shade!
 Youth of the quick uncheated Sight,
Thy Walks, *Observance*, more invite!   20
O Thou, who lov'st that ampler Range,
Where Life's wide Prospects round thee change,
And with her mingling Sons ally'd,
Throw'st the prattling Page aside:
To me in Converse sweet impart,   25
To read in Man the native Heart,
To learn, where Science sure is found,
From Nature as she lives around:
And gazing oft her Mirror true,
By turns each shifting Image view!   30
Till meddling *Art*'s officious Lore,
Reverse the Lessons taught before,
Alluring from a safer Rule,
To dream in her enchanted School;
Thou Heav'n, whate'er of Great we boast,   35
Hast blest this social Science most.
 Retiring hence to thoughtful Cell,
As *Fancy* breathes her potent Spell,
Not vain she finds the charmful Task,
In Pageant quaint, in motley Mask,   40
Behold before her musing Eyes,
The countless *Manners* round her rise;
While ever varying as they pass,
To some *Contempt* applies her Glass:
With these the *white-rob'd Maids* combine,   45
And those the laughing *Satyrs* join!
But who is He whom now she views,
In Robe of wild contending Hues?
Thou by the Passions nurs'd, I greet
The comic Sock that binds thy Feet!   50
O *Humour*, Thou whose Name is known
To *Britain*'s favor'd Isle alone:
Me too amidst thy Band admit,
There where the young-eyed healthful *Wit*,

(Whose Jewels in his crisped Hair   55
Are plac'd each other's Beams to share,
Whom no Delights from Thee divide)
In Laughter loos'd attends thy Side!
    By old *Miletus* * who so long
Has ceas'd his Love-inwoven Song: 60
By all you taught the *Tuscan* Maids,
In chang'd *Italia*'s modern Shades:
By Him †, whose *Knight*'s distinguish'd Name
Refin'd a Nation's Lust of Fame;
Whose Tales ev'n now, with Echos sweet,   65
Castilia's *Moorish* Hills repeat:
Or Him ‡, whom *Seine*'s blue Nymphs deplore,
In watchet Weeds on *Gallia*'s Shore,
Who drew the sad *Sicilian* Maid,
By Virtues in her Sire betray'd: 70
    O Nature boon, from whom proceed
Each forceful Thought, each prompted Deed;
If but from Thee I hope to feel,
On all my Heart imprint thy Seal!
Let some retreating Cynic find,   75
Those oft-turn'd Scrolls I leave behind,
The *Sports* and I this Hour agree,
To rove thy Scene-full World with Thee!

---

* Alluding to the *Milesian* Tales, some of the earliest Romances.
† *Cervantes.*
‡ Monsieur *Le Sage*, Author of the incomparable Adventures of *Gil Blas de Santillane*, who died in *Paris* in the Year 1745 [actually 1747].

18. *The Passions. An Ode for Music*

[As its title suggests, the *Ode* was written with a musical setting in mind and it was eventually performed to a setting by William Hayes, Professor of Music in the University, at Encaenia at Oxford on 2 July 1750. Hayes's score is in the Bodleian Library and reveals that Collins's poem was interrupted at line 93 and followed by 21 lines added by the Earl of Litchfield, the Chancellor of the University. This text was printed at the time in pamphlet form, was reprinted without date for another performance at Winchester, and again at Gloucester in 1760.]

When Music, Heav'nly Maid, was young,
While yet in early *Greece* she sung,
The Passions oft to hear her Shell,
Throng'd around her magic Cell,
Exulting, trembling, raging, fainting,   5
Possest beyond the Muse's Painting;
By turns they felt the glowing Mind,
Disturb'd, delighted, rais'd, refin'd.
Till once, 'tis said, when all were fir'd,
Fill'd with Fury, rapt, inspir'd,   10
From the supporting Myrtles round,
They snatch'd her Instruments of Sound,
And as they oft had heard a-part
Sweet Lessons of her forceful Art,
Each, for Madness rul'd the Hour,   15
Would prove his own expressive Pow'r.

First *Fear* his Hand, its Skill to try,
   Amid the Chords bewilder'd laid,
And back recoil'd he knew not why,
   Ev'n at the Sound himself had made.   20

Next *Anger* rush'd, his Eyes on fire,
   In Lightnings own'd his secret Stings,
In one rude Clash he struck the Lyre,
   And swept with hurried Hand the Strings.

With woful Measures wan *Despair*   25
   Low sullen Sounds his Grief beguil'd,
A solemn, strange, and mingled Air,
   'Twas sad by Fits, by Starts 'twas wild.

But thou, *O Hope*, with Eyes so fair,
  What was thy delightful Measure?   30
Still it whisper'd promis'd Pleasure,
  And bad the lovely Scenes at distance hail!
Still would Her Touch the Strain prolong,
  And from the Rocks, the Woods, the Vale,
She call'd on Echo still thro' all the Song;   35
  And where Her sweetest Theme She chose,
  A soft responsive Voice was heard at ev'ry Close,
And *Hope* enchanted smil'd, and wav'd Her golden Hair.

And longer had She sung,—but with a Frown,
  Revenge impatient rose,   40
He threw his blood-stain'd Sword in Thunder down,
    And with a with'ring Look,
  The War-denouncing Trumpet took,
And blew a Blast so loud and dread,
Were ne'er Prophetic Sounds so full of Woe.   45
    And ever and anon he beat
    The doubling Drum with furious Heat;
  And tho' sometimes each dreary Pause between,
    Dejected *Pity* at his Side,
    Her Soul-subduing Voice applied,   50
  Yet still He kept his wild unalter'd Mien,
While each strain'd Ball of Sight seem'd bursting from his Head.

·Thy Numbers, *Jealousy*, to nought were fix'd,
    Sad Proof of thy distressful State,
  Of diff'ring Themes the veering Song was mix'd,   55
    And now it courted *Love*, now raving call'd on *Hate*.

With Eyes up-rais'd, as one inspir'd,
Pale *Melancholy* sate retir'd,
And from her wild sequester'd Seat,
In Notes by Distance made more sweet,   60
Pour'd thro' the mellow *Horn* her pensive Soul:
  And dashing soft from Rocks around,
  Bubbling Runnels join'd the Sound;
Thro' Glades and Glooms the mingled Measure stole,
  Or o'er some haunted Stream with fond Delay,   65
    Round an holy Calm diffusing,
    Love of Peace, and lonely Musing,
  In hollow Murmurs died away.

But O how alter'd was its sprightlier Tone!
When *Chearfulness*, a Nymph of healthiest Hue,   70
  Her Bow a-cross her Shoulder flung,
  Her Buskins gem'd with Morning Dew,
Blew an inspiring Air, that Dale and Thicket rung,
    The Hunter's Call to *Faun* and *Dryad* known!
    The Oak-crown'd *Sisters*, and their chast-eye'd *Queen*,   75
    Satyrs and sylvan Boys were seen,
    Peeping from forth their Alleys green;
Brown *Exercise* rejoic'd to hear,
  And *Sport* leapt up, and seiz'd his Beechen Spear.

Last came *Joy*'s Ecstatic Trial,   80
He with viny Crown advancing,
  First to the lively Pipe his Hand addrest,
But soon he saw the brisk awak'ning Viol,
    Whose sweet entrancing Voice he lov'd the best.
    They would have thought who heard the Strain,   85
    They saw in *Tempe*'s Vale her native Maids,
    Amidst the festal sounding Shades,
To some unwearied Minstrel dancing,
  While as his flying Fingers kiss'd the Strings,
  LOVE fram'd with *Mirth*, a gay fantastic Round,   90
  Loose were Her Tresses seen, her Zone unbound,
  And HE amidst his frolic Play,
As if he would the charming Air repay,
Shook thousand Odours from his dewy Wings.

O *Music*, Sphere-descended Maid,   95
Friend of Pleasure, *Wisdom*'s Aid,
Why, Goddess, why to us deny'd?
Lay'st Thou thy antient Lyre aside?
As in that lov'd *Athenian* Bow'r,
You learn'd an all-commanding Pow'r,   100
Thy mimic Soul, O Nymph endear'd,
Can well recall what then it heard.
Where is thy native simple Heart,
Devote to Virtue, Fancy, Art?
Arise as in that elder Time,   105
Warm, Energic, Chaste, Sublime!
Thy Wonders in that God-like Age,
Fill thy recording *Sister*'s Page—

'Tis said, and I believe the Tale,
Thy humblest *Reed* could more prevail,   110
Had more of Strength, diviner Rage,
Than all which charms this laggard Age,
Ev'n all at once together found,
Cæcilia's mingled World of Sound—
O bid our vain Endeavors cease,   115
Revive the just Designs of *Greece*,
Return in all thy simple State!
Confirm the Tales Her Sons relate!

19. *Ode Occasion'd by the Death of Mr Thomson*

[James Thomson, author of *The Seasons* and *The Castle of Indolence*, died at
Richmond on 27 August 1748. Collins's *Ode* was first published as a folio
pamphlet in June 1749. He himself had been living at Richmond and
friendly with Thomson since 1747. The poem is dedicated to George
Lyttelton, later 1st Baron Lyttelton (1709–73), politician and patron of a
number of well-known literary men of the day, including Thomson. The *Ode*
was reprinted in Warton's *The Union* (1753), *The Art of Poetry on a New
Plan* (1762) and Patrick Murdoch's edition of Thomson's *Works* (1762). The
epigraph is from Virgil, *Eclogues*, v. 74–5 and 52: 'These rites shall be thine
for ever, both when we pay our yearly vows to the Nymphs, and when we
purify our fields' and 'Me, too, Daphnis loved'. The text is that of 1749.
Immediately above the poem, the title appears as 'ODE ON THE DEATH
of Mr. *THOMSON*'.]

*Hæc tibi semper erunt, & cum solennia Vota
Reddemus Nymphis, & cum lustrabimus Agros.*

+ — ———— *Amavit nos quoque Daphnis.*
                          VIRG. Bucol. Eclog. v.

To George Lyttleton, Esq; this Ode is inscrib'd by the Author.

ADVERTISEMENT

The Scene of the following STANZAS is suppos'd to lie on the *Thames* near *Richmond*.

1

In yonder Grave a DRUID lies
    Where slowly winds the stealing Wave!
The *Year*'s best Sweets shall duteous rise
    To deck *it's* POET's sylvan Grave!

2

In yon deep Bed of whisp'ring Reeds   5
    His airy Harp * shall now be laid,
That He, whose Heart in Sorrow bleeds
    May love thro' Life the soothing Shade.

3

Then Maids and Youths shall linger here,
    And while it's Sounds at distance swell,   10
Shall sadly seem in Pity's Ear
    To hear the WOODLAND PILGRIM's Knell.

4

REMEMBRANCE oft shall haunt the Shore
    When THAMES in Summer-wreaths is drest,
And oft suspend the dashing Oar   15
    To bid his gentle Spirit rest!

* The Harp of *Æolus*, of which see a Description in the *Castle of Indolence* [by Thomson, 1748, I. xl–xli].

5

And oft as EASE and HEALTH retire
    To breezy Lawn, or Forest deep,
The Friend shall view yon whit'ning Spire*,
    And 'mid the varied Landscape weep.   20

6

But Thou, who own'st that Earthy Bed,
    Ah! what will ev'ry Dirge avail?
Or Tears, which LOVE and PITY shed
    That mourn beneath the gliding Sail!

7

Yet lives there one, whose heedless Eye   25
    Shall scorn thy pale Shrine glimm'ring near?
With Him, Sweet Bard, may FANCY die,
    And JOY desert the blooming Year.

8

But thou, lorn STREAM, whose sullen Tide
    No sedge-crown'd SISTERS now attend,   30
Now waft me from the green Hill's Side
    Whose cold Turf hides the buried FRIEND!

9

And see, the Fairy Valleys fade,
    Dun *Night* has veil'd the solemn View!
—Yet once again, Dear parted SHADE   35
    Meek NATURE's CHILD again adieu!

10

The genial Meads assign'd to bless
    Thy Life, shall mourn thy early Doom,
Their Hinds, and Shepherd-Girls shall dress
    With simple Hands thy rural Tomb.   40

11

Long, long, thy Stone and pointed Clay
    Shall melt the musing BRITON's Eyes,
O! VALES, and WILD WOODS, shall HE say
    In yonder Grave YOUR DRUID lies!

* *Richmond*-Church.

20. [*An Ode on the Popular Superstitions of the Highlands of Scotland, Considered as the Subject of Poetry*]

[The poem was written between November 1749 and early 1750, during the visit to London of John Home (1722–1808), a Scottish clergyman and later a celebrated dramatist, to whom the poem was addressed and presented. Collins had met him through Thomas Barrow, who is referred to in lines 5–8. The Warton brothers saw a MS. of the poem when they visited Collins at Chichester in 1754 (see Nathan Drake, *The Gleaner*, 1811, iv. 475–8), a recollection mentioned by Johnson in his biography of Collins in the *Lives of the Poets* in 1781. Johnson's reference to the missing MS. led to its rediscovery by Alexander Carlyle, a friend of Home, and its publication in March 1788 in the *Transactions of the Royal Society of Edinburgh*, I. ii. 63–75. One leaf of the MS., containing stanza 5 and half of stanza 6, was missing, and this gap, and some smaller ones, were filled by Henry Mackenzie and Carlyle. In May 1788 another text, claiming to be the complete poem as seen by the Wartons in 1754, was published in London by J. Bell. Although it was often reprinted in the nineteenth century, the interpolations in this text are now recognized to be spurious. Collins's own MS. was finally rediscovered in Scotland in 1967 by Miss C. Lamont, who transcribed it in an article in the *Review of English Studies*, N.S. xix. 137–47, in May 1968.

Collins's main sources for the poem were Martin Martin's *Description of the Western Islands of Scotland* (1703) and *A Voyage to St Kilda* (1698): a new edition of this second work had been published in 1749. Collins may well have obtained information about certain superstitions from conversation with Home himself, especially about the 'kaelpie' (100–37), the water-demon which delighted in drowning travellers. More literary allusions are to *Macbeth* (176–82), Tasso's *Gerusalemme Liberata* and Edward Fairfax's translation of it (1600; 4th edition, 1749) (188–203); and to Ben Jonson's visit to William Drummond of Hawthornden near Edinburgh in 1619 (211–12).

The title by which the poem has been known for almost two centuries has been retained. The MS. is entitled only 'Ode to a Friend on his Return &c'. The text of the MS. has been followed here, but light punctuation has been added (usually at the end of the line) to supplement Collins's own, which is erratic or non-existent. Collins's sometimes inconsistent indentation of lines has been preserved. Variants are recorded from the *Transactions* of 1788, although the interpolations of Mackenzie and Carlyle have been omitted.]

1

H[ome], Thou return'st from Thames, whose Naiads long
  Have seen Thee ling'ring with a fond delay
  'Mid those soft Friends, whose hearts some future day
Shall melt perhaps to hear thy Tragic Song.
Go not unmindfull of that cordial Youth   5
  Whom long endear'd thou leav'st by Lavant's side;
Together let us wish Him lasting truth
  And Joy untainted with his destin'd Bride.
Go! nor regardless, while these Numbers boast
  My short-liv'd bliss, forget my social Name   10
But think far-off how on the Southern coast
  I met thy Friendship with an equal Flame!
Fresh to that soil thou turn'st, whose ev'ry Vale
  Shall prompt the Poet, and his Song demand;
    To Thee thy copious Subjects ne'er shall fail;   15
  Thou need'st but take the Pencil to thy Hand
And paint what all believe who own thy Genial Land.

2

There must Thou wake perforce thy Doric Quill:
  'Tis Fancy's Land to which thou set'st thy Feet
  Where still, tis said, the Fairy People meet   20
Beneath Each birken Shade, on mead or Hill.
  There Each Trim Lass that Skims the milky store
  To the Swart Tribes their creamy Bowl allots,
By Night They sip it round the cottage Door
While Airy Minstrels warble jocund notes.   25
  There ev'ry Herd by sad experience knows
    How wing'd with fate their Elph-shot arrows fly
When the Sick Ewe her summer food foregoes
  Or stretch'd on Earth the Heart-smit Heifers lie!
Such Airy Beings awe th'untutor'd Swain;   30
  Nor Thou, tho learn'd, his homelier thoughts neglect,
Let thy sweet Muse the rural faith sustain;
  These are the Themes of simple sure Effect
That add New conquests to her boundless reign
And fill with double force her heart commanding Strain.   35

3

Ev'n yet preserv'd how often may'st thou hear,
   Where to the Pole the Boreal Mountains run,
   Taught by the Father to his list'ning Son
Strange lays whose pow'r had charm'd a Spenser's Ear.
   At Ev'ry Pause, before thy Mind possest,   40
Old Runic Bards shall seem to rise around
   With uncouth Lyres, in many-colour'd Vest,
   Their Matted Hair with boughs fantastic crown'd:
Whether Thou bidst the well-taught Hind repeat
   The Choral Dirge that mourns some Chieftain brave,   45
When Ev'ry Shrieking Maid her bosom beat
   And strew'd with choicest herbs his scented Grave,
Or whether sitting in the Shepherd's Shiel*
   Thou hear'st some Sounding Tale of War's alarms,
When at the Bugle's call with fire and steel   50
   The Sturdy Clans pour'd forth their bonny Swarms
And hostile Brothers met to prove each Other's Arms.

4

'Tis thine to Sing how framing hideous Spells
   In Sky's lone Isle the Gifted Wizzard Seer,
Lodg'd in the Wintry cave with   55
Or in the depth of Ust's dark forrests dwells;
   How They whose Sight such dreary dreams engross
      With their own Visions oft astonishd droop,
When o'er the watry strath or quaggy Moss
   They see the gliding Ghosts unbodied troop.   60
Or if in Sports or on the festive Green
   Their   glance some fated Youth descry,
Who now perhaps in lusty Vigour seen
   And rosy health shall soon lamented die.
For them the viewless Forms of Air obey,   65
   Their bidding heed, and at their beck repair;
They know what Spirit brews the stormfull day
   And heartless oft like moody Madness stare
To see the Phantom train their secret work prepare!

5
[Missing]

---

* a Kind of Hut built ev'ry summer for the convenience of milking the Cattle

[6]

[8 lines missing]

What tho far off from some dark dell espied   95
    His glimm'ring Mazes cheer th'excursive sight,
Yet turn ye Wandrers turn your steps aside
    Nor chuse the Guidance of that faithless light!
For watchfull lurking mid th' unrustling Reed
    At those mirk hours the wily Monster lies   100
And listens oft to hear the passing Steed
    And frequent round him rolls his sullen Eyes,
If Chance his Savage wrath may some weak wretch surprise.

7

Ah luckless Swain, oer All Unblest indeed!
    Whom late bewilder'd in the dank dark Fen,   105
Far from his Flocks and smoaking Hamlet then!
    To that sad spot his
On Him enrag'd the Fiend in Angry mood
    Shall never look with Pity's kind concern,
But Instant Furious rouse the whelming Flood,   110
O'er its drown'd Banks forbidding All return.
Or if He meditate his wish'd Escape
    To some dim Hill that seems uprising near,
To his faint Eye the Grim and Griesly Shape
    'In all its Terrors clad shall wild appear.   115
Mean time the Watry Surge shall round him rise,
    Pour'd sudden forth from evry swelling source.
What now remains but Tears and hopeless sighs?
    His Fear-shook limbs have lost their Youthly force
And down the waves He floats a Pale and breathless Corse.   120

8

For Him in vain his anxious Wife shall wait
    Or wander forth to meet him on his way;
    For Him in vain at Tofall of the Day
His Bairns shall linger at the unclosing Gate.
Ah neer shall He return—Alone if Night   125
    Her travell'd limbs in broken slumbers steep,
With Dropping Willows drest his Mournfull Sprite
    Shall visit sad perhaps her silent Sleep;

Then He perhaps with moist and watry hand
   Shall fondly seem to press her shuddring cheek, 130
And with his blue swoln face before her stand
   And Shivring cold these piteous accents speak:
   'Pursue Dear Wife, thy daily toils pursue
   'At Dawn, or dusk Industrious as before,
   'Nor e'er of Me one hapless thought renew 135
   'While I lie weltring on the Osier'd Shore,
   'Drown'd by the Kaelpie's wrath nor eer shall aid thee more.'

9

Unbounded is thy range, with varied style
   Thy Muse may, like those feath'ry tribes which spring
From their Rude Rocks, extend her skirting wing 140
   Round the Moist Marge of each cold Hebrid Isle
To that hoar Pile which still its ruin shows,
   In whose small vaults a Pigmie-Folk is found,
Whose Bones the Delver with his Spade up-throws
   And culls them wondring from the hallow'd Ground! 145
Or thither, where beneath the show'ry west
   The Mighty Kings of three fair Realms are laid,
Once Foes perhaps, together now they rest,
   No Slaves revere them, and no Wars invade:
Yet frequent now at Midnight's solemn hour 150
   The Rifted Mounds their yawning cells unfold
And forth the Monarchs stalk with sovreign Pow'r
In pageant Robes, and wreath'd with sheeny Gold,
And on their twilight tombs Aerial council hold.

10

But O o'er all forget not Kilda's race 155
   On Whose bleak rocks which brave the wasting tides
   Fair Nature's Daughter Virtue yet Abides!
Go just, as They, their blameless Manners trace!
   Then to my Ear transmit some gentle Song
   Of Those whose Lives are yet sincere and plain, 160
Their bounded walks the ragged Cliffs Along
   And all their Prospect but the wintry main.
With sparing Temp'rance at the needfull Time
   They drain the Sainted Spring, or Hunger-prest
Along th'Atlantic Rock undreading climb 165
   And of its Eggs despoil the Solan's nest.

Thus blest in primal Innocence they live
   Sufficed and happy with that frugal fare
Which Tastefull Toil and hourly Danger [g]ive.
   Hard is their Shallow Soil,   and ba[re]   170
Nor Ever Vernal Bee was heard to mu[rmur] there!

11

Nor needst Thou blush that such false Themes [en]gage
   Thy gentle Mind of fairer stores possest,
For not Alone they touch the Village Breast,
But fill'd in Elder Time th'Historic page.   175
   There Shakespeare's Self with evry Garland crown'd
In Musing hour his Wayward Sisters found
   And with their terrors drest the magic Scene!
[Fro]m them He sung, when mid his bold design,
   Before the Scot afflicted and aghast,   180
[Th]e Shadowy Kings of Banquo's fated line
   Thro' the dark cave in gleamy Pageant past.
Proceed nor quit the tales which simply told
   Could once so well my Answering Bosom pierce;
Proceed, in forcefull sounds and Colours bold   185
   The Native Legends of thy Land rehearse,
To such adapt thy Lyre, and suit thy pow'rfull Verse.

12

In Scenes like these which, daring to depart
   From sober Truth, are still to Nature true
   And call forth fresh delights to Fancy's view,   190
Th'Heroic Muse employ'd her Tasso's Art!
How have I trembled, when at Tancred's stroke
   Its gushing Blood, the gaping Cypress pour'd,
When Each live Plant with Mortal accents spoke
   And the wild Blast up-heav'd the vanish'd Sword.   195
How have I sate, where pip'd the pensive Wind,
   To hear His harp by British Fairfax strung,
Prevailing Poet, whose undoubting Mind
   Believ'd the Magic Wonders which He sung!
Hence at Each Sound Imagination glows,   200
Hence his warm lay with softest Sweetness flows,
   Melting it flows, pure, num'rous, strong and clear,
And fills th'impassion'd heart, and lulls th'Harmonious Ear.

13

All Hail Ye Scenes that oer my soul prevail,
 Ye   Firths and Lakes, which far away   205
 Are by smooth Annan fill'd, or past'ral Tay,
Or Don's Romantic Springs, at distance hail!
 The Time shall come, when I perhaps may tread
 Your lowly Glens oerhung with spreading Broom,
Or o'er your Stretching Heaths by Fancy led,   210
Then will I dress once more the faded Bow'r
 Where Johnson sate in Drummond's* Shade,
Or crop from Tiviot's dale Each
 And mourn on Yarrow Banks
Mean time Ye Pow'rs, that on the plains which bore 215
 The Cordial Youth, on Lothian's plains attend,
Where'er he dwell, on Hill or lowly Muir,
 To Him I lose, your kind protection lend
And touch'd with Love, like Mine, preserve my Absent Friend.

---

* [William] Drummond of Hawthornden See Heads of a Conversation &c. [in
Drummond's *Works*, Edinburgh, 1711, pp. 224–7].

DRAFTS AND FRAGMENTS

[These ten incomplete drafts of poems, together with a poem only partly in Collins's handwriting, were discovered among the Warton papers in the Library of Trinity College, Oxford, and first printed as *Drafts and Fragments of Verse*, edited by J. S. Cunningham, in 1956. Collins may have given them to Joseph Warton in September 1754, when he and his brother visited the poet at Chichester and saw various MS. poems. They are presumably the 'few fragments of some other odes [by Collins], but too loose and imperfect for publication, yet containing traces of high imagery', which Thomas Warton stated in about 1783 were in the possession of his brother Joseph (see Nathan Drake, *The Gleaner*, 1811, iv. 477–8).

The fragments cannot be definitely dated, but stylistic evidence (especially the strong influence of Pope) and other indications suggest that most of them were written after Collins arrived in London in 1744 and before he wrote the poetry published in his *Odes* in December 1746. The exception is the 'Lines on the Music of the Grecian Theatre', which appears to date from the autumn of 1750.

A fully annotated, modernized, and punctuated text of these poems is given in my edition of *The Poems of Gray, Collins and Goldsmith* (1969), pp. 523–56. The following text is a transcription of the MSS. without editorial interference. Collins's deletions and corrections are recorded in the textual notes. Because of the difficulty of dating the poems, which are written on loose sheets of paper, the sequence in which they appear (which is not that of Cunningham's edition) is to some extent arbitrary.]

21. [*Lines on Restoration Drama*]

[It is natural to connect this discussion of post-Restoration drama with the *Epistle to Hanmer*, which surveyed drama up to Shakespeare. The influence of Pope also suggests a date of 1743–44.]

> Yet this wild pomp so much in vain pursued,
> The Courtly Davenant in our Thames renew'd.
> For who can trace thro' Time's oer-clouded maze
> The dawning stage of old Eliza's days?
> What Critic search its rise, or Changes know,   5
> With all the Force of Hollingshead or Stow?
> Yet all may gain, from many a worthless page,
> Some lights of Charles and his Luxurious age.
> Then, Thanks to those! who sent him forth to roam
> Or equal Weakness! brought the Monarch home!   10
> The Taste of France, her Manners and her Stile
> (The Fool's gay Models) delug'd all our Isle;

Those courtly Wits which spoke the Nation's voice
In Paris learn'd their judgment and their choice
Vain were the Thoughts, which Nature's Passions speak, 15
Thy woes Monimia [*] Impotent and weak!
Vain all the Truth of just Dramatic Tales!
Nought pleas'd Augustus, but what pleasd Versailles!
His Hand of Powr outstretch'd with princely care
From his low state uprais'd th'instructive Play'r 20
And ev'n in Palaces, for never age
Was grac'd like Richlieus, plac'd his regal stage
To Those Proud Halls where Burgundy had vied
With all his Gallic Peers in Princely pride
The Muse succeeded like some Splendid Heir 25
And plac'd her Chiefs and favor'd Heroes there!

2

And could that Theatre, believe you, trust
To those weak Guides—the Decent and the just?
Ah no! could ought delight that modish Pit?
Twas but the Froth, and Foppery of Wit. 30
True Nature ceas'd; and in her Place, were seen
That Pride of Pantomime, the rich Machine—

3

There, when some God, or Spirit pois'd in Air,
Surpris'd the scented Beau, or masking Fair
Think! with what Thunder, in so just a cause, 35
The Mob of Coxcombs swelld their loud applause!
These Witlings heeded Nature, less than they
That rule thy taste, the Critics of to day:
Yet All could talk how *Betterton* was drest
And gave that Queen their Praise, who curtsied Best. 40
Thus Folly lasted long at Truth's expense
Spite of Just Nature, or reluctant sense—
Ask you what broke at last her Idle reign?
Wits Easy Villan could not laugh in vain.—

---

* Otway despis'd as a Writer while Dav'nant was in repute

22. [*Lines of Composite Authorship*]

[Lines 1–24 are written in an unknown hand, the remaining lines in Collins's autograph. Concerned with the cost of theatrical production and scenery, the poem may date from 1744–5, when Collins himself entertained theatrical ambitions.]

But why you'll Say to me this   Song
Can these proud Aims to private Life belong
Fair instances your Verse unbidden brings
Th'ambitious names of Ministers and Kings
Am I that Statesman whom a Realm obeys   5
What ready Tributes will my Mandate raise
Or like the Pontiff can my Word command
Exacted Sums from every Pliant Land
That all of which the Men of Leisure Read
This Tast and Splendor must from me proceed   10
Tell me if Wits reprove or Fortune frown
Where is my Hope but in th'uncertain Town
Yet e'er you urge weigh well the mighty Task
Behold what Sums one Poet's Drama's Ask
When Shakespear shifts the place so oft to View   15
Must each Gay Scene be beautifull and new
Come you who Trade in Ornament appear
Come Join your Aids thro' all the busy Year
Plan Build and Paint thro' each laborious Day
And let us once produce this finish'd play   20
Yes the proud Cost allows some short Suspence
I grant the Terrors of that Word Expence
Did Tast at once for full perfection call
That sole Objection might determine all
But such just Elegance not gain'd at Ease   25
Scarce wishd and seen, may come by slow degrees
To day   may one fair Grace restore
And some kind Season add one Beauty more
And with these aims of Elegant desire
The Critic's Unities, tis sure, conspire   30
And tho' no scenes suffice to deck the wild
     round their works on whom the Muse has smild
Some Scenes may still the fair design admit
Chast Scenes which Addison or Phillips writ.

Is but our just delight in one increast   35
Tis something gain'd to Decency at least:
And what thy Judgement first by Nature plann'd
May find completion from some future Hand.
          &c
The Pomp

23. [*Lines Addressed to James Harris*]

[Joseph Warton has inscribed the MS., 'This addrest by *Collins* to Mr.
Harris of Sarum.' Collins's lines refer to *Three Treatises. The First
Concerning Art. The Second Concerning Music, Painting, and Poetry. The
Third Concerning Happiness*, by James Harris (1709–80) of Salisbury. This
work was published in May 1744, which may indicate the approximate date
of composition. The 'Art' referred to in line 1 is music: the lines begin one-
third down the page, and Collins probably intended to return later to the
opening of the poem.]

These would I sing—O Art for ever dear
Whose Charms so oft have caught my raptur'd Ear
O teach me Thou, if my unpolish'd lays
Are all too rude to speak thy gentle praise
O teach me softer sounds of sweeter kind   5

Then let the Muse and Picture Each contend
This plan her Tale, and that her Colours blend
With me tho' both their kindred charms combine
No Pow'r shall emulate or equal thine!   10

And Thou the Gentlest Patron born to grace
And add new Brightness ev'n to Ashley's race
Intent like Him in Plato's polish'd style   15
To fix fair Science in our careless Isle
Whether thro' Wilton's Pictur'd halls you stray
Or o'er some speaking Marble waste the day
Or weigh each Sound its various pow'r to learn
Come Son of Harmony O hither turn!   20
Led by thy hand *Philosophy* will deign
To own me meanest of her votive train

O I will listen, as thy lips impart
Why all my soul obeys her pow'rfull Art
Why at her bidding or by strange surprise   25
Or wak'd by fond degrees my Passions rise
How well-form'd Reed's my sure attention gain
And what the Lyre's well-measur'd strings contain
The Mighty Masters too unprais'd so long
Shall not be lost, if Thou assist my Song,   30
They who with Pindars in one Age bestowd
Cloath'd the sweet words which in their numbers flowd
And Rome's and Adria's Sons—if Thou but strive
To guard their Names, shall in my Verse survive

24. [*Lines Addressed to Jacob Tonson*]

[These lines appear to date from the period of Collins's first arrival in London in 1744 and may reflect his efforts to establish himself in literary circles there. They are addressed almost certainly to Jacob Tonson (d. 1767), great-nephew of Jacob Tonson (1656?–1736), the founder of the famous publishing business and the 'Jovial Jacob' of line 2. Collins reminds Tonson of what his family owed to such poets as Waller and Cowley whose works it had published. Lines 3–4 refer to the portraits of the Whig Kit-Cat Club, which had been housed in the elder Tonson's home at Barn Elms in Surrey and which were still in his descendant's possession.]

While You perhaps exclude the wintry gloom
In Jovial Jacob's academic Room
There pleas'd by turns in breathing paint to trace
The Wits gay Air or Poet's genial Face
Say happy Tonson, Say, what Great Design   5
(For warmest Gratitude must sure be thine)
What due return employs thy musing Heart
For all the Happiness their works impart
What taste directed monument which They
Might own with Smiles, and Thou with Honour pay?   10
    Evn from the Days when Courtly Waller sung
And tun'd with polish'd sounds our barbrous tongue
Eer yet the Verse to full perfection brought
With nicer Music cloath'd the Poet's thought
The Muse whose Song bespoke securest Fame   15
Made fair Alliance with thy favor'd Name

Dealt from thy press the Maid of Elder Days
Lisp'd the soft Lines to Sacharissa's praise
Or the gay Youth for livelier Spirits known
By Cowleys pointed thought improv'd his own   20
Evn All the Easy Sons of Song who gain'd
A Poets Name when Charles and Pleasure reign'd
All from thy Race a lasting praise deriv'd
Not by Their toil the careless Bards surviv'd
You wisely sav'd the Race who   gay   25
But sought to wear the Mirtles of a day
At soft Barn Elms (Let evry Critic join)
You more than all Enjoy Each flowing line
Your's is the price whate'er their merits claim
Heir of their Verse and Guardian of their Fame!   30

                                   move
                         Luxury and Love

25. [*Lines Addressed to a Fastidious Critic*]

[Line 16 refers to Roger de Piles's *The Principles of Painting . . . To which is Added, The Balance of Painting*, translated into English in May 1743.]

Yes, Tis but Angelo's or Shakespear's Name
The Striking Beauties are in each the same
The s

Were Horace Dumb, who knows Ev'n Fresnoy's Art   5
Might guide the Muse in some   Part
Or Searchfull Vinci, who his Precepts drew
For Tuscan Pencils, form the Poet too!

                                                  10

From these fair Arts,
Obtain some fair Ef
Nor fear to talk of Numbers or of Oil
Tho' not quite form'd like Addison or Boyle
Defect in Each abound and more, you say   15
Than Sage Despiles instructs us how to weigh

Defects which glanc'd on those who finely feel
All Thornhills Colours would in vain conceal
Or all the Golden Lines howeer they flow
Thro' each soft Drama of unfruitfull Rowe   20
These too you sometimes praise to Censure loth
But fix the Name of Mannerist on both
And should my Friend, who knew not Anna's age
So nicely judge the Canvas or the Page?
Still should his thought on some old Model plac'd   25
Reject the Briton with so nice a taste?
From each some forcefull Character demand
            but peculiar to his happy hand?
Some Sovreign Mark of Genius all his own

                                                     30
Ah where on Thames shall Gentle Dodsley find
The Verse contriv'd for so correct a Mind?
Or how shall Hayman trembling as you gaze
Obtain one breath of such unwilling praise?
Go Then in all unsatisfied complain   35
Of Time's Mistake in Waller's desprate strain [*]
For Ah untimely cam'st Thou forth Indeed
With whom Originals Alone succeed!
Go as Thou wilt, require the bliss denied
To call back Art and live e'er Carlo died   40
But O in Song the Public voice obey
There let Each Author   his   day
Abroad be Candid, reason as You will
And live at home a Chast Athenian still!
    For each correct design the Critic Kind   45
Look back thro' Age to Homer's godlike Mind
But Blackhall's self might doubt if all of Art
Were Self produced in one exhaustless Heart

[*] Waller to a very young Lady:
                Why came I so untimely forth
                Into a world wch wanting thee
                        [To My Young Lady Lucy Sidney, st. ii]

26. [*Lines Addressed to a Friend about to visit Italy*]

[The marked influence of Pope points to an early period of Collins's years in London. Joseph Warton also has an 'Ode to a Gentleman upon his Travels thro' Italy' in his *Odes* (1746) and Collins may have been addressing the same person.]

On each new scene the Sons of   Vertú
Shall give fresh Objects to thy   view
Bring the grav'd Gem or offer as you pass
Th'Imperial Medal, and historic Brass
Then o'er its narrow surface mayst thou trace   5
The genuine Spirit of some Hero's face
Or see minutely touch'd the powrfull charms
Of some proud Fair that set whole realms in arms
The Patriot's Story with his look compare
And know the Poet by his genial air   10

Nor, for they boast no pure Augustan vein
Reject her Poets with a cold disdain
O Think in what sweet lays how sweetly strong   15
Our Fairfax warbles Tasso's forcefull Song,
How Spenser too, whose lays you oft resume
Wove their Gay   in his fantastic loom
That Cynthio prompted oft ev'n Shakespear's flame
And Milton valued ev'n Marino's name!   20

27. [*Stanzas on a Female Painter*]

[In this poem Collins combines his interest in painting with spasmodic imitation of Pope's *Elegy to the Memory of an Unfortunate Lady*. The poem is written on two leaves: lines 1–12 on page 1, with the verso blank; lines 13–28 on page 3, with lines 29–36 written vertically at the side (perhaps a later addition); and lines 37 ff. on page 4. 'Lavinia' (13–16) is Lavinia Fontana (1552–1614), a successful Italian portrait painter. 'Tintoretta' (20–4) is Marietta, the daughter of Tintoretto.]

The Moon with dewy lustre bright
  Her mild Æthereal radiance gave
On Paly Cloisters gleam'd her light
  Or trembled o'er th'unresting wave

T'was Midnight's hour—   5

Long o'er the Spires and Glimmring Tow'rs
   The whispring Flood, and silv'ry sky   10
As One whom Musing Grief devours
   She glanc'd by turns her silent Eye!

Like Hers, The Fair Lavinias hand
   Once mix'd the Pallet's varied store
Blest Maid whom once Italia's Land   15
   In years of better Glory bore!

     [*space for another stanza 17–20*]

Like Her, O Death, O ruthless Powr
   O Grief of Heart remember'd well
In lovely Youth's untimely hour
   Like Her soft Tintoretta fell

Ev'n She, whose Science Philip sought   25
   To share his throne an envied Bride
Like Thee deplor'd, Ah fatal Thought
   By ev'ry Art lamented died

Thy Draught where Love his hand employ'd
   Shall only please a shortliv'd day   30
And timeless like thy self destroyd
   In Each revolving year decay.

Yet soft and melting flow'd thy line
   As Ev'ry Grace had lent her aid
Bid each mild light unglaring shine   35
   And soft imbrown'd each melting shade

And when thy tints, ah fruitless Care
   With softest skill compounded lay
The Flaunting Bow'rs where Spring repairs
   Were not more bloomy sweet than They!   40

The Child of Them who now adore
　　Thy tender tints and godlike Flame
Pass some few years on Adrias shore
　　Shall only know thy gentle Name

Or when his Eyes shall strive in vain   45
　　Thy Fairy Pencil's stroke to trace
The Faded Draught shall scarce retain
　　Some Lifeless line or mangled Grace

28. ['*Ye Genii who in secret state*']

[The later stanzas have been seen as an early version of the *Ode to Evening*.
The painters mentioned by Collins are: Claude Lorraine (1600–82) in lines
25–8; Jacob van Ruisdael or Rysdael (*c.* 1629–82) in lines 31–2; and Salvator
Rosa (1615–73) in lines 33–40.]

Ye Genii who in secret state
　　Far from the wheaten field
At some throng'd Citie's antique Gate
　　Your unseen sceptres wield

Ye Pow'rs that such high Office share   5
　　Oer all the restless Earth
Who see Each day descend with care
　　Or lost in senseless Mirth

Take Them who know not how to prize
　　The walks to Wisdom dear   10
The Gradual Fruits and varying skies
　　That paint the gradual Year

Take all that to the silent Sod
　　Prefer the sounding street
And Let your echoing squares be trod   15
　　By their unresting feet

But me by　　　　　Springlets laid
　　That thro' the Woodland chide
Let Elms and Oaks that lent their Shade
　　To hoary Druids hide   20

Let me where'er wild Nature leads
    My sight Enamour'd look
And chuse my hymning Pipe from Reeds
    That roughen oer the Brook

Some times when Morning oer Plain   25
    Her radiant Mantle throws
I'll mark the Clouds where sweet Lorrain
    His orient Colours chose

Or when the Sun to Noon tide climbs
    I'll hide me from his view   30
By such green Plats and chearful Limes
    As   Rysdael drew

Then on some Heath all wild and bare
    With more delight Ill stand
Than He who sees with wondring air   35
    The Works of Rosa's hand

There where some Rocks deep Cavern gapes
    Or in some tawny dell
Ill seem to see the Wizzard Shapes
    That from his Pencill fell   40

But when Soft Evning o'er the Plain
    Her gleamy Mantle throws
I'll mark the Clouds whence sweet Lorraine
    His   Colours chose

Or from the Vale I'll lift my sight   45
    To some
Where e'er the Sun withdraws his light
    The dying Lustre falls

Such   will I keep
    Till   50
The modest Moon again shall Peep
    Above some Eastern Hill

All Tints that ever Picture us'd
    Are lifeless dull and mean

To paint her dewy Light diffus'd   55

What Art can paint the modest ray
  So sober chaste and cool
As round yon Cliffs it seems to play
  Or skirts yon glimmring Pool?   60

The tender gleam her Orb affords
  No Poet can declare
Altho' he chuse the softest words
  That e'er were sigh'd in air.

29. *To Simplicity*

[An early version of the *Ode to Simplicity*, which is more, however, than a mere revision of this poem.]

I

O Fancy, Alter'd Maid
Who now too long betrayd
To Toys and Pageant wed'st thy cheated Heart
  Yet once with Chastest thought
  Far nobler triumphs sought   5
Thrice Gentle Guide of each exalted Art!

2

Too

No more, sweet Maid, th'enfeebling dreams prolong
  Return sweet Maid at length   10
  In all thy Ancient strength
And bid our Britain hear thy Græcian Song

3

For Thee of loveliest Name
That Land shall ever claim
And laid an Infant on her favor'd shore   15
  Soft Bees of Hybla's vale
  To Age attests the tale
To feed thy Youth   their s   storé

4

From that   hour
Thou knewst the gentle pow'r   20
To charm her Matrons chaste, and virtuous Youth
For Wisdom learn'd to please
By thy persuasive Ease
And Simplest Sweetness more ennobled Truth.

5

Nor modest Picture less   25
Declin'd the wild Excess
Which frequent now distracts her wild design
The Modest Graces laid
Each soft unboastfull shade
While Feeling Nature drew th'impassion'd line!   30

6

O Chaste Unboastfull Guide
O'er all my Heart preside
And 'midst my Cave in breathing Marble wrought
In sober Musing near
With Attic Robe appear   35
And charm my sight and prompt my temprate thought

7

And when soft Maids and Swains
Reward my Native Strains
With flow'rs that chastest bloom and sweetest breathe
I loveliest Nymph Divine   40
Will own the merits thine
And round thy temples bind the modest wreath

30. ['*No longer ask me Gentle Friends*']

[Since Collins alludes once again to a village in Sussex (lines 25–8 presumably refer to Otway's birthplace at Trotton, or to Woolbedding, where his father became Vicar), this poem has been linked by some scholars with the *Ode to a Lady*, written in May 1745. Assertions that 'Delia' is likewise the unidentified Elizabeth Goddard addressed in the *Ode to a Lady* should be treated cautiously. The poetess complimented in lines 49–56 is probably Elizabeth Carter (1717–1806), who wrote poems on the subjects mentioned, which Collins might have seen by about 1746. (For a full discussion of these matters see my *Poems of Gray, Collins and Goldsmith*, 1969, pp. 548–56.)]

I

No longer ask me Gentle Friends
    Why heaves my constant Sigh?
Or why my Eye for ever bends
    To yon fair Eastern Sky
Why view the Clouds that onward roll?   5
    Ah who can Fate command
While here I sit, my wandring Soul
    Is in a distant land.

2

Did Ye not hear of Delias Name?
    When on a fatal day   10
O'er Yonder Northern Hills she came
    And brought an Earlier May.
Or if the Month her bloomy store
    By gentle Custom brought
She ne'er was half so sweet before   15
    To my delighted thought

3

She found me in my Southern vale
    All in her converse blest
My   Heart began to fail
    Within my youngling Breast   20
I thought when as her
    To me of lowly Birth
There liv'd not ought so good and kind
    On all the smiling Earth

4

To Resnel's Banks, again to greet   25
    Her Gentle Eyes I strayd
Where once a Bard with Infant Feet
    Among the Willows play'd
His tender thoughts subdue the Fair
    And melt the Soft and Young   30
But mine I know were softer there
    Than ever Poet sung.

5

I shew'd her there the Songs of One
    Who done to Death by Pride
Tho' Virtue's Friend, and Fancy's Son   35
    In Love unpitied died
I hop'd when to that Shepherd's Truth
    Her Pity should attend
She would not leave another Youth
    To meet his luckless end.   40

6

Now tell me you who hear me sing
    and prompt the tender Theme
How far is *Lavant's little Spring
    From Medway's mightier stream!
Confin'd within my Native dells   45
    The world I little know
But in some Tufted Mead she dwells
    Where'er those waters flow.

7

There too resorts a Maid renown'd
    For framing Ditties sweet   50
I heard her lips
    Her gentle lays repeat
They told how sweetly in her Bow'r
    A Greenwood Nymph complain'd
Of Melancholy's gloomy Pow'r   55
    And joys from Wisdom gain'd

* Dic quibus in terris &c. [Virgil, *Eclogues*, III. 104–07].

8

Sweet sung that Muse, and fair befall
  Her Life whose happy Art
What other Bards might envy All
  Can touch my Laura's Heart   60
Sweet Oaten Reeds for her I'll make
  And Chaplets for her Hair
If She for Friendly Pitys sake
  Will whisper Damon there.

9 and last—

Her strain shall dim if ought succeeds   65
  From my applauding tongue
Whateer within her Native Meads
  The Tuneful Thirsis sung
Less to my Love shall He be Dear
  Altho He earliest paid   70
Full many a soft and tender tear
  To luckless Collin's Shade!

31. [*Lines on the Music of the Grecian Theatre*]

[The description of the fragment as 'Recitative Accompanied' indicates that
it is part of an ode for music. It is presumably all that was written of a poem
mentioned by Collins in a letter of 8 November 1750 to Dr William Hayes,
Professor of Music at Oxford, who had set *The Passions* to music in the
preceding summer. Collins offered Hayes another ode 'on a nobler subject
. . . the *Music of the Grecian Theatre*; in which I have, I hope naturally,
introduced the various characters with which the chorus was concerned, as
Œdipus, Medea, Electra, Orestes, &c. &c.' Collins added that 'I have chosen
the ancient Tragedies for my models, and only copied the most affecting
passages in them' (W. Seward, *Supplement to the Anecdotes of Some
Distinguished Persons*, 1797, pp. 123-4).]

Recitative Accompanied

When Glorious Ptolomy by Merit rais'd
   Successive sate on Ægypt's radiant Throne
Bright Ptolomy, on whom, while Athens gaz'd
   She almost wish'd the Monarch once Her own
Then Virtue own'd one Royal Heart;   5
   For loathing War, humanely wise
For All the Sacred Sons of Art
   He bad the Dome of Science rise.
The Muses knew the festal day
   And call'd by Pow'r Obsequant came   10
With all their Lyres and Chaplets gay
   They gave the *Fabric its immortal Name
      High oer the rest in Golden Pride
      The Monarch sate, and at his side
      His Fav'rite Bards—His Græcian Quire   15
      Who while the Roofs responsive Rung
      To many a Fife and many a tinkling Lyre
Amid the Shouting Tribes in sweet succession Sung.

---

* The Μουσεῖον [the Museum at Alexandria founded by Ptolemy].

APPENDIX

A Dubious Attribution to Collins

In a section devoted to the 'Lost and Doubtful Poems' which have been attributed to Collins in my edition of *The Poems of Gray, Collins and Goldsmith* (1969), p. 559, I summarized the evidence concerning a poem which was first ascribed to him in the early nineteenth century. In his edition of Collins, 1827, p. 42 *, Dyce discussed a note by Thomas Park, communicated to him by Mitford, about an entry in the 'Register' of recent publications in the *Gentleman's Magazine*, IV. 167, for March 1734:

> 18. On the Royal Nuptials. An Irregular Ode. By Mr *Philips*, price 1 *s.*
> 19. A Poem on the same occasion. By *Wm Collins*. Printed for *J. Roberts*, pr. 6 *d.*

Although Roberts was to publish Collins's *Persian Eclogues* in 1742, it must seem unlikely that the same William Collins should have written such a poem, and have had it published in London, at the age of twelve. Since a William Collier wrote a similar poem, *A Congratulatory Poem on his Majesty's Happy Return to England* in 1732, the most reasonable explanation is that the name was misprinted in the *Gentleman's Magazine*.

I do not consider that these conclusions are affected by the recent identification of what may be the poem in question and publication of the text in facsimile by Charles Ryskamp, 'William Collins's Poem to the Prince of Orange', *Book Collector*, XXI (1972), 40–9. The eight-page pamphlet, *A Poem Humbly Address'd to His Highness The Prince of Orange, and The Princess Royal of Great Britain*, is in fact anonymous and therefore throws no further light on the attribution. Mr Ryskamp is himself cautious about the likelihood that these mediocre lines were written by a precocious boy, although he does not exclude the possibility and cites the Warton MSS. in Trinity College, Oxford, as evidence that Collins and Joseph Warton were writing verses during their early years at Winchester. In fact, none of the recently discovered drafts and fragments of poems by Collins can be confidently dated earlier than 1740. If Collins did write and publish the poem at the age of twelve, it must seem surprising that not one of his schoolfriends remembered this remarkable enterprise, which must have happened shortly after his arrival at Winchester. (Joseph Warton did in fact preserve details about the publication of Collins's *Sonnet* in the *Gentleman's Magazine* in 1739 and about the writing of the *Persian Eclogues* at Winchester.)

Although Mr Ryskamp has provided us with the text of the poem, his article does not add to the evidence for the attribution to Collins, which still rests entirely on the entry in the *Gentleman's Magazine* in 1734. It is merely the title of his article, which is much more confident than anything asserted in the main text, which may mislead students in the future.

TEXTUAL NOTES

1. *Lines Spoken by the Ghost of John Dennis at the Devil Tavern* (page 9)
   18 *Stairs*] A piece of the letter has been cut out and *Stairs* supplied in
   pencil, apparently by Walpole.

2. *Agrippina, a Tragedy* (page 11)
   105–17 In 1775 Mason gave these lines inappropriately to Aceronia, his
   version beginning:

> *Did I not wish to check this dangerous passion,*
> *I might remind my mistress that her nod*
> *Can rouse etc.*

   Tovey conjecturally restored the speech to Agrippina as in 105–6,
   introduced the question mark in 108, and substituted *me* for *you* (110),
   mine for *yours* (112) and *my* for *your* (114).
   117–18 *Ha! by Juno . . . semblance*] Possibly an interpolation by Mason, in
   whose text Agrippina now resumed speaking.
   155 Followed in Mason's text by a couplet given to Aceronia:

> *'Tis time we go, the sun is high advanc'd*
> *And, ere mid-day, Nero will come to Baiae.*

   160 *me*] Followed in Mason's text by an interruption from Aceronia:

> *Why then stays my sovereign,*
> *Where he so soon may—*

3. *Ode on the Spring* (page 18)
   12 *Their broadest brownest shade* Commonplace Book.

   19–20 Commonplace Book, letter to Walpole, and Dodsley have:

> *How low, how indigent the Proud,*
> *How little are the Great.*

   47 *plumage*] *Glories* Yale draft.
   48–50 In the fragmentary Yale draft these lines begin:

> *Thy Sun is set, thy*
> *Thy Youth on hasty*
> *We wanton while*

4. *Ode on a Distant Prospect of Eton College* (page 20)
   7 *Of Grove & Lawn & Mead survey,* Commonplace Book.
   22 *sprightly*] *smileing* Commonplace Book, Eton.
   26 *arm*] *arms* Foulis.
   29 *To chase the Hoop's elusive Speed,* Commonplace Book.
   41–55 The motto from Menander is written in the margin in Commonplace
   Book (see headnote).

55 *how*] *where* Eton.
     'em] *them* Eton, Foulis.
59 *murth'rous*] *griesly* underlined, with *murtherous* in margin in Commonplace Book.
60 *them*] *'em* Commonplace Book, Eton, Foulis.
71 *this*] *That* Commonplace Book, Eton, Foulis.
75 *those*] *These* Commonplace Book.
95 *fate?*] *fate,* Commonplace Book.
97 *flies.*] *flies?* Commonplace Book.

6. *Ode to Adversity* (page 24)
  8 *unpitied and alone*] written above *& Misery not their own* deleted in Commonplace Book.
 32 In margin of Commonplace Book   ἁ γλυκυδακρὺς   [*she who causes sweet tears*].
 42 *Thy milder Influence deign to Impart,* Commonplace Book.

7. *Hymn to Ignorance* (page 26)
  3 *Camus'*] *Camus* Mason transcript.
 17 *Oer all the land Lethæan showers dispense* Mason transcript, with present reading opposite.
 18 *To*] *And* Mason transcript.
 38 Mason transcript adds a further line: *The pondrous Waggon lumberd slowly on* * *

8. *Ode on the Death of a Favourite Cat* (page 27)
Title: *On the Death of Selima, a favourite Cat, who fell into a China-Tub with Gold-fishes in it, & was drown'd.* Commonplace Book; *On a favourite Cat, call'd Selima, that fell* etc, Wharton.
 4–5 Transposed in Dodsley.
  8 *The . . . the*] *Her . . . her* Pery.
 10 *Her*] *The* Dodsley, Foulis.
 13 *'midst*] *'mid* Commonplace Book.
 14 *angel*] *beauteous* Commonplace Book, Dodsley, Foulis.
 24 *averse to*] *a foe to* Dodsley.
 25 *looks*] *Eye* Commonplace Book; *Eyes* Wharton.
 35 *Tom*] *John* Pery.
     Susan] *Harry* Wharton, Dodsley.
 36 *What fav'rite has a friend!* Dodsley.
 40 *tempts*] *strikes* Commonplace Book, Wharton.

9. *The Alliance of Education and Government* (page 28)
  2 *barren*] *flinty* Wharton.
 19 *Tyranny has*] *gloomy Sway have* Wharton.
 21 *blooming*] *vernal* Wharton.
 51 A word, perhaps *Nations*, deleted beneath *Myriads* in Wharton.

55 *Heavens*] *Skies* Wharton.

56 *Scent*] *Catch* Wharton.

106 *distant*] *neighb'ring* Mason (1775).

107 Mason adds: *I find also among these papers a single couplet much too beautiful to be lost, though the place where he meant to introduce it cannot be ascertained; it must, however, have made a part of some description of the effect which the reformation had on our national manners:*

> *When Love could teach a monarch to be wise,*
> *And Gospel-light first dawn'd from BULLEN's Eyes.*

10. *Tophet* (page 33)

Title: *M.ʳ Etough, Rector of Therfeild in Hartfordshire, who had been a dissenting Teacher in a Barn at Debden in Essex, died in August 1757* Pembroke; *M.ʳ Etough of Therfield in Hartfordshire. obiit 1757* Cole; *On Mr. - - -'s being ordained* London Mag.

1 *Such Tophet was—so grin'd the bawling Fiend* Cole, London Mag. (with *grum'd* for *grin'd*); *Thus Tophet look'd, so grinn'd the brawling fiend* Gentleman's Mag.

2 *While frighted Prelates bow'd and called him Friend* Cole, Gentleman's Mag. (with *Whilst* for *While*).

3–4 Found only in Mason's transcript, marked for insertion after 2.

servile] written above *civil* Commonplace Book.

6 *griesly*] *grimly* Gentleman's Mag.

11. *Elegy Written in a Country Church-Yard* (page 33)

1 *parting*] originally *dying*, according to Norton Nicholls (*Correspondence*, iii. 1297).

2 *wind*] *winds* edd 1–7.

7 *droning*] *drony* edd 9–12, Dodsley, Foulis.

8 *And*] *Or* Wharton, Commonplace Book, edd 3–7.

11 *secret*] *sacred* edd 1–2, 4b–8 (noted as erratum by Gray, *Correspondence*, i. 344).

19 *or*] *&* Wharton, Commonplace Book.

20 *rouse*] *wake* edd 1–2, 4b, 6–7.

24 *Or*] *Nor* Wharton, Commonplace Book.

25 *sickle*] *sickles* Wharton.

35 *awaits*] *await* edd 9–12, Dodsley, Mason (1775).

36 *paths . . . lead*] *path . . . leads* Foulis.

37–8 Wharton, Commonplace Book and edd 1–7 have:

> *Forgive, ye Proud, th'involuntary Fault,*
> *If Memory to These no Trophies raise,*

The present reading is underlined in the margin of the Commonplace Book.

47 *rod*] *Reins* Wharton, Commonplace Book (with *Rod* in margin), edd 1–7.

58 *fields*] written above *Lands* deleted in Commonplace Book.
68 *And*] *Or* Wharton, Commonplace Book.
71 *shrine*] *Shrines* Wharton.
82 *elegy*] *Epitaph* Commonplace Book.
92 *And in our Ashes glow their wonted Fires* Wharton (with *Even in our ashes*
   live &c noted), Commonplace Book (with *Ev'n* and *live* in margin);
   Awake, & faithful to her wonted Fires Gray's letter to Walpole, 11
   February 1751 (*Correspondence*, i. 341), edd 1–7.
96 *kindred*] *hidden* ed 1 (noted as erratum by Gray).
105 *smiling*] *frowning* edd 1–2, 6–7 (noted as erratum by Gray).
106 *he would*] *would he* Wharton, Commonplace Book.
109 *on*] *from* Commonplace Book.
116 *the*] *his* Foulis.
   aged] *ancient* deleted and *aged* written above in Commonplace Book.
   An additional stanza appears at this point in the Eton MS., was added at
   the foot of the page in the Commonplace Book (with the note *Omitted in*
   1753) and printed in edd 3–7:

> *There scatter'd oft, the earliest of the Year,*
> *By Hands unseen, are show'rs of Violets found;*
> *The Red-breast loves to build and warble there,*
> *And little Footsteps lightly print the Ground.*

   The EPITAPH] *Epitaph* Wharton, Commonplace Book.

12. *A Long Story* (page 40)
   3 *N:B: the House was built by the Earls of Huntingdon, & came from them*
   to Sr Christopher afterwards Ld Keeper, Hatton, prefer'd by Q. Elizabeth
   for his graceful Person & fine Dancing. note in Garrett.
   5–8 Omitted in Garrett, written in margin for insertion in Commonplace
   Book.
   11. In Commonplace Book the note begins *Sr Christ. Hatton, promoted by*
   etc. and refers to 10.
   Brawls] *an old-fashion'd Dance* note in Garrett.
   20 *you*] *ye* Garrett.
   33 *eyes*] *Looks* Garrett.
   35 *Melissa*] *She had been call'd by that Name in Verse before.* note in Garrett.
   41 *P - - - t*] *Purt* Commonplace Book, Garrett, which has an explanatory
   note: *A Clergyman, Tutor to the Duke of Bridgewater, who had first*
   mention'd me to them, as their Neighbour.
   72 *in*] *near* Garrett.
   73 *(Who will, believe.)*] *who will, may believe.* Commonplace Book, Garrett.
   87 *Great-house*] *So the Country People call it.* note in Garrett.
   91 *prefer'd*] *explain'd* Commonplace Book, Garrett.
   95 *Own'd, that*] *He own'd* Garrett.
   97 *Culprit*] *Prisoner* Garrett.
   100 *from*] *in* Garrett.

103 Styack] *Lady C.^s House-keeper*. note in Garrett.
115 Squib] *Her Groom of the Chambers*. note in Garrett.
116 *could*] *might* Commonplace Book, Garrett.
   Groom] *Her Keeper*. note in Garrett.
120 The same note appears in Commonplace Book; but for *hang'd the week before* Garrett reads *hanged last Week*, suggesting that this MS. dates from about 10 October 1750.
123 *hurt*] *spoil* Garrett.
126 *Yet*] *But* Commonplace Book.
137 *turn'd*] *chang'd* Garrett.
After 140: (*Here 500 Stanzas are lost, the last only remaining.*) Garrett.
143 *That*] *Who* Garrett.

13. *Stanzas to Mr Bentley* (page 45)
   26–8 Mason (1775) supplied the missing rhyme words as follows: *impart/ flows confest/heave the heart*. Langhorne, *Monthly Review* (1775), suggested *convey/there shall rest/steal away*; Mitford suggested *convey/is exprest/dies away*.

14. *The Progress of Poesy* (page 46)
   1 *Awake, my Lyre, my Glory, wake* Commonplace Book, with present reading in margin.
   2 *rapture*] *transport* Commonplace Book, Wharton.
   10 *rowling*] *rushing* Bedingfield.
   11 *Headlong, impetuous,*] *With torrent-rapture* Commonplace Book, Wharton; *Impetuous, headlong*, Bedingfield.
   12 *The rocks,*] *While rocks* Bedingfield.
   23 *dark*] *black* Commonplace Book, Wharton, Bedingfield.
   34 *in*] *the* Commonplace Book, Wharton.
   36 *their*] *the* Wharton.
   52–3 Commonplace Book has:

> *Till o'er the eastern cliffs from far*
> *Hyperion hurls around his glittering shafts of war.*

   These lines have been deleted and the following written in the margin:

> *Till fierce Hyperion from afar*
> *Hurls at their flying rear his glitt'ring shafts of war.*

   In the second line Gray then substituted *on* for *at* and *scatter'd* followed by *shadowy* for *flying*. Wharton reads:

> *Till fierce Hyperion from afar*
> *Pours on their scatter'd rear his glitt'ring shafts of war.*

   57 *shiv'ring ... dull*] *buried ... chill* Commonplace Book, with the present readings in the margin.
   69 *Or*] *And* Commonplace Book.

70–1 *Lab'rinths ... Echoes*] 1757 reads *Lab'rinth's* and *Echo's*, as Gray complained in a letter to Walpole of 10 August 1757 (*Correspondence*, ii. 513), but *Echo's* was not corrected in 1768. Both MSS. read *Echoes*.

76 *deep a solemn*] *a celestial* Commonplace Book, with the present reading in the margin.

93 *Horrour*] *Terror* margin of Commonplace Book, Wharton.

108 *Bright-eyed*] *Full-plumed* Commonplace Book, Wharton.

118–22 Commonplace Book has:

> Yet, when they first were open'd on the day,
> Before his visionary eyes would run
> Such Forms, as glitter in the Muse's ray
> With orient hues unborrow'd of the Sun:
> Yet never can he fear a vulgar fate

In the third line *Shapes* is written in the margin to replace *Forms*. The final version of these lines follows.

15. *The Bard* (page 52)

17–18 Gray wrote to Wharton in August 1755 (*Correspondence*, i. 434): *you may alter that Robed in the Sable, &c, almost in your own words thus*

> With fury pale, & pale with woe,
> Secure of fate, the Poet stood &c:

but the alteration was not made.

29 *Cadwallo's*] *Caswallo's* Bedingfield.

30 *stormy*] *roaring* Bedingfield.

31 *Brave*] *Great* Bedingfield.

43 *They*] *ye* Bedingfield.

Gray wrote against this line in his own copy of the *Odes* (Pierpont Morgan Library): *The double cadence is introduced here not only to give a wild spirit and variety to the Epode; but because it bears some affinity to a peculiar measure in the Welch Prosody, called Gorchest-Beirdh, i.e. the Excellent of the Bards.*

47–8 Gray wrote in his own copy: *The image is taken from an ancient Scaldic Ode, written in the old-Norwegian tongue about A:D:1029* [The Fatal Sisters].

62 Gray told Walpole in a letter of 10 August 1757 (*Correspondence*, i. 513) that *Sorrow's* and *Solitude* should have had capital letters, but the correction was not made in 1768.

63 *Victor*] *Conqueror* Wharton, deleted.

64 *his*] *the* Wharton, deleted.

65 *No ... no*] *What ... what* Wharton, deleted.

69 *in ... born?*] *hover'd in thy noontide ray?* Wharton, deleted.

70 *Morn*] *day* Wharton, deleted.

71–6 Wharton reads:

> *Mirrors of Saxon truth & loyalty,*
> *Your helpless old expiring Master view*
> *They hear not. scarce Religion dares supply*
> *Her mutter'd Requiems, & her holy Dew.*
> *Yet thou, proud Boy, from Pomfret's walls shalt send*
> *A sigh, & envy oft thy happy Grandsire's end.*

These lines have been deleted and the present text written on the back of
the MS. with *in* for *on* in 74.

82 *baleful smile upon*] *smile of horror on* Wharton.

87 *Ye*] *Grim* Wharton, deleted.

90 *holy*] *hallow'd* Wharton.

101 *thus*] *here* Wharton, deleted.

102 *me . . . here*] *your despairing Caradoc* Wharton, deleted.

103 *track*] *clouds* Wharton, deleted.

104 *melt*] *sink* Wharton, deleted.

105 *oh!*] *ah!* Wharton.
    solemn scenes] *scenes of heav'n* Wharton, deleted with present reading
    inserted.

106 *glitt'ring*] *golden* Wharton, deleted.

109–10 Wharton has

> *From Cambria's thousand hills a thousand strains*
> *Triumphant tell aloud, another Arthur reigns.*

with the present reading above.

111–12 Mason has

> *Haughty Knights, & Barons bold*
> *With dazzling helm & horrent spear.*

Wharton has the same reading deleted, with *Youthful* for *Haughty*, and
the present text above.

114 *In*] *Of* Mason.

116 *of the Briton-Line;*] *born of Arthur's line,* Mason.

117 *Her . . . her*] *A . . . an* Wharton, deleted.

123 *calls*] *wakes* Mason.

128 *buskin'd*] *mystic* Mason.

130 *Tyrant of*] *wild, that chills* Mason.

142 In his letter to Mason of 11 June 1757 (*Correspondence*, ii. 504) Gray said
    that the line at first read *Lo! to be free, to die, are mine.* He added *Lo!*
    Liberty & Death are mine as an alternative.

144 *plung'd*] *sunk* Wharton, Mason.

16. *Ode on the Pleasure Arising from Vicissitude* (page 59)

10 *Frisking*] *quaintly* Mason variant.

11 *Forgetful of their*] *Rousd from their long &* Mason variant.

15 *less'ning*] *towering* Mason variant.

17 Mason transcribed the following lines from Gray's pocketbook for 1754
into the Commonplace Book:

> Rise my Soul on wings of fire
> Rise the raptu[r]ous Choir among
> Hark tis Nature strikes the Lyre
> And leads the general Song.

At this point in his reconstructed text of the poem in 1775 Mason
printed these lines with four of his own to complete the stanza. Although
followed by many editors, his insertion of Gray's lines at this point
seems purely conjectural.

17 *sullen*] *darkend* Mason variant.

18 *snowy whirlwind*] *scowling tempest* and *snow in whirlwind* Mason variants.

25 *past*] *black* Mason variant.

49–59 These fragmentary lines are not in Mason's transcript but appear on
the opposite page in the Commonplace Book. In 1775 he attempted to
reconstruct these stanzas.

17. *Epitaph on Mrs Clerke* (page 61)

1 *silent*] *little* Bedingfield.

4 *The peaceful virtues*] *Each peaceful Virtue* Bedingfield.

7–10 Bedingfield has

> To hide her cares her only art,
> Her pleasure pleasures to impart.
> In ling'ring pain, in death resign'd,
> Her latest agony of mind
> Was felt for him, who could not save
> His All from an untimely grave:

13 *secret*] *silent* Bedingfield.

18. *Epitaph on a Child* (page 62)

1 *free'd*] *free* Mitford.

2 *Parent's*] *Parents'* Mitford, Gosse.

6 *Here*] *Now* Gosse.

  his] *the* Mitford.

19. *The Fatal Sisters* (page 62)

4 of Note *Valhalla*] *Valkalla* 1768.

15 *Sword*] *Blade* Wharton.

17–18 Wharton has

> Sangrida, terrific Maid,
> Mista black, and Hilda see

23 *Blade*] *Sword* Wharton.

28 *triumph*] *conquer* Commonplace Book, written above *triumph* deleted.

31 *Gunna & Gondula, spread* Commonplace Book, Wharton.

33 *slaughter*] *havock* Commonplace Book.
44 *shall*] *must* Commonplace Book, Wharton.
45 *his*] *her* Commonplace Book.
50 *blot*] *veil* Wharton.
59 *winding*] *ecchoing* Wharton.
61–3 Wharton has

> Sisters, hence! 'tis time to ride:
> Now your thund'ring faulchion wield,
> Now your sable steed bestride,

and so Commonplace Book but with *faulchions* and *steeds*.

20. *The Descent of Odin* (page 66)
  11 *fruitless*] *ceaseless* Wharton.
  14 *shakes*] *quakes* Wharton.
  23 *accents*] *murmurs* Wharton.
  27 *call*] *voice* Wharton.
  29 *my troubled*] *a weary* Wharton.
  35 *he*] *this* Wharton.
  41 *yon*] *the* Wharton, Commonplace Book.
  42 *yon*] *the* Wharton.
  48 *reach*] *touch* Wharton.
  51 *Once again*] *Prophetess* Wharton.
  52 *Prophetess*] *Once again* Wharton.
  59–60 Wharton has

> Once again my call obey,
> Prophetess, arise and say

  61–2 Transposed in Wharton.
  65 *wond'rous*] *giant* Wharton.
  74 *awake*] *arise* Wharton.
  76 *That*] *Who* Wharton.
  77 *That their flaxen*] *Who their flowing* Wharton.
  79 *Tell me*] *Say from* Wharton.
     sorrows] *sorrow* Commonplace Book.
  83 *The Mightiest of the mighty line* Wharton.
  87 *hence, and*] *Odin,* Wharton.
  90 *has*] *have* Wharton.
  92 *Has reassum'd*] *Reassumes* Wharton.

21. *The Triumphs of Owen* (page 69)
  The following lines appear at the end of the fragment in the Commonplace Book but were not included in 1768. Mason inserted them after line 26 in 1775:

> Check'd by the torrent-tide of blood
> Backward Meinai rolls his flood:

While heap'd his Master's feet around
Prostrate Warriors gnaw the ground.

25. *Sketch of His Own Character* (page 72)
   4 *WIT, HE*] *Wit: for he* Mason variant.
   5 *Post*] In the margin of his transcript Mason has written *first word* Place *wch authenticates these lines*, perhaps a reference to Gray's refusal of the poet Laureateship in 1757. Among later editors, Bradshaw and Whibley read *place*.

26. *Epitaph on Sir William Williams* (page 73)
   5 *uncall'd his maiden-*] *his voluntary* Mason transcript, 1775.
   6 *infant-*] *maiden* Mitford.
   -glory] *honour* Mason transcript, 1775.
   8 *And scorn'd*] *nor brooked* variant in Mason transcript.
   9 *intrepid*] *undaunted* Mason transcript, 1775.
   12 Mason's transcript records two variants:

> *Where bleeding Friendship oer her altar weeps*
> *Where Montagu & bleeding Friendship weep*

   and three lines of a 'Rejected Stanza':

> *Warrior, that readst the melancholly line*
> * * * * * * *
> *Oh be his Genius be his spirit thine*
> *And share his Virtues with a happier fate*

27. *Song* [I] (page 73)
   1 *Midst . . . triumphs*] *With Beauty, with Pleasure surrounded,* Warton.
   2 *And droop*] *To weep* Warton.
   source] *cause* Warton.
   my] *one's* Piozzi.
   3 *look*] *wish* Warton.
   4 *Yet*] *To* Warton.
   6 *Sounds*] *Words* Warton.
   8 *but . . . will*] *and . . . can* Piozzi.

28. *Song* [II] (page 74)
   1 *we parted*] *he left me* Piozzi, European Mag.
   2 *E'er*] *In* European Mag.
   3 *What then means yon op'ning Flowr?* Piozzi; *Ah! what means the opening flower!* European Mag.
   4 *buds . . . deck*] *bud . . . decks* Walpole, Piozzi, European Mag.
   that] *which* Piozzi.
   5–6 Transposed in European Mag.
   7 *green*] *bloom* deleted by Gray, noted by Mitford.
   8 *such*] *this* Walpole.

9 *Western*] *Warmer* deleted by Gray, noted by Mason and Mitford.
skies] *sky* European Mag.

10 Mason and Mitford note that Gray first wrote *Can not prove, that Winter's past?*, later changed to *Can ye* etc. Walpole reads *Speak not always* etc.

12 *Spare the honour*] *Dare not to reproach* deleted by Gray, noted by Mason and Mitford. Mitford notes as a further variant *Dare you to reproach your love.*

29. *The Candidate* (page 75)

2 *pious*] *serious* London Mag.

4 *harmless*] Mason told Walpole in a letter of 2 October 1774 that the epithet was originally *awkward* when he first heard Gray read him the poem.

8 *shame*] *sham* London Mag.

9 *Then he*] *He* Lewis.

10 *my dear*] *I swear* London Mag.

11 *now*] *but* London Post, Gentleman's Mag., London Mag.

13 *But*] *Then* London Post, Gentleman's Mag.
But ... Phyzzy,] *The character! phiz!—then* London Mag.
his life] *and life* London Mag.

14 *can't tell*] *don't know* London Mag.
but] omitted in London Post, Gentleman's Mag.

17 *His lying, and filching,*] *And filching and lying,* London Post, Gentleman's Mag., London Mag.

19 *between*] *betwixt* Lewis, London Mag.

21 *dinner*] *table* London Post, Gentleman's Mag.; *the table* London Mag.
with her] *with a* Lewis, London Post, London Mag.; *and with* Gentleman's Mag.

22 *She*] *And* London Post; *First* London Mag.
and] *then* London Mag.

23 *wenching*] *drinking* Lewis.

25 *Did not*] *Didn't* London Post, London Mag.

27–8 Transposed in London Mag.

27 *read,*] *know* Lewis.

29 *refuse*] *reject* London Post, Gentleman's Mag., London Mag.

30 *and*] *for* London Post, Gentleman's Mag., London Mag.
about] *much of* London Mag.

After 30 (*Speaking to Jemmy*) London Post; *To Jemmy* Gentleman's Mag.

33–4 The couplet is omitted from all the early printed texts, except for the flysheet. It is deleted in Walpole's copy in the Pierpont Morgan Library, the only text which includes the final word. Francis Grose's *Classical Dictionary of the Vulgar Tongue* defines it as 'a term for lying with a woman'. For attempts by Mason and Walpole to supply an alternative final couplet in 1774, see *Walpole Correspondence*, ed. W. S. Lewis and others, 1937–, xxviii. 170–1.

30. *William Shakespeare to Mrs Anne* (page 76)

Title: Mitford notes deleted variants of *Meg* for *Anne*, *Regular* and *Mason* for *Precentor*.

  2 *But*] *And* Murray.
    your] *thy* Murray, Mitford.
    sweet] *dear* Murray.
  5 *canker'd*] *crabbed* Mitford.
  7 *Barristers*] *Baronets* Mitford.
  8 *worst of*] *worse than* Mitford.
  9 *'Tis . . . Master's*] *True, the Precentor's* Murray.
10 *fashion'd fair*] *moulded soft* Murray.
    dovelike] *lowly* Murray, with *dovelike* as an alternative.
12 *sore eyes?*] *Mince Pies?* Mitford.
14 *at*] *in* Mitford.
17–20 These lines followed 8 in Mitford; 17 and 19 are transposed in Murray.
17 *cheesecakes*] *puddings* Murray, altered to *biscuits*.
20 *one's*] *my* Murray.
22 *our*] *thy* Murray, altered to *our*.
    works] *work* Mitford.
23 *earns*] *reaps* Murray.
24 *For . . . puddings,*] *To . . . Cheese cakes,* Mitford.

31. *Invitation to Mason* (page 77)
  1 *Prim Hurd*] *Weddell* Mitford variant.
  6 *in*] *on* Mitford.

32. *On Lord Holland's Seat near Margate, Kent* (page 78)
  1 *each*] *its* Cole.
  2 *took*] *form'd* Cole (with *framed* in margin), Jones.
  3 *some*] *a* Gentleman's Mag., Jones.
  6 *Godwin*] *Goodwin* all other texts.
  8 *dread*] *fear* Gentleman's Mag.
  9 *reign*] *reigns* New Foundling Hospital, Gentleman's Mag.; *reign'd* Cole.
11 *cannot*] *could not* Gentleman's Mag., Jones.
12 *horrors*] *terrors* Gentleman's Mag.
    still] written above a deleted word, perhaps *here*, in Cole.
13 *Now*] *Here* Jones.
14 *Arches and turrets*] *Turrets and arches* Gentleman's Mag., Jones.
15 *palaces . . . his*] *monasteries . . . our* Gentleman's Mag., Jones.
18 *Nor Shelburne's, Calcraft's, Rigby's friendship vain,* New Foundling Hospital; *Nor Calcraft's, Shelburne's, Rigby's Friendship vain,* Cole; *Nor G – – – –'s, nor B – – – –d's promises been vain,* Nichols; *Nor M – – – – –'s, R – – – –'s, B – – – –'s friendship vain,* Jones. Gentleman's Mag. leaves the names blank.
    Calcraft's] *Calcrofts* Wharton.
19 *other*] *better* Jones.
    these] *this* Gentleman's Mag.

bless'd] *crown'd* New Foundling Hospital, Cole; *grac'd* Gentleman's Mag.

20 *ruins that*] *glories which* Gentleman's Mag.; *horrors which* Nichols; *beauties which* Cole, Jones.

21 *beautifyed*] *purify'd* Gentleman's Mag., Jones, Cole (as a marginal alternative).

23 *might*] *should* Gentleman's Mag.; *would* Jones.

35. *Lines on Dr Robert Smith* (page 83)
  2 *won't suffer*] *leaves not* Gosse.
  3 *'Tis not that old Focus himself has got eyes,* Gosse.

36. *Satire on the Heads of Houses* (page 84)
Title: *Lines on the Heads of Houses. Never a barrell better Herring* Mitford.
  2 *I've*] *I* Mitford.
  3 *thy*] *the* Mitford.
  6 *hugely*] *largely* Mitford.
  12 *him*] *these* Mitford.
  13 *As the Master*] *The Master* Mitford.
  15 *So the Master*] *The Master* Mitford.
  20 *his*] *a* Mitford.
  25 *But the Master*] *The Master* Mitford.
  28 *the*] *a* Mitford.
  35 *P.S. —*] Omitted in Mitford.

47. Translation from Propertius, *Elegies*, II.I (page 98)
  10 *those*] *the* West.
  32 *sound*] *sing* West.
  36 *Structures*] *Structure* West.
  38 *Or*] *Nor* West.
  45–6 Written in margin of the Commonplace Book for insertion.
  50 After this line West adds:

> The long-contended World's old Discords cease,
> And Actium's Terrours grace the Pomp of Peace;

  51 *Prows*] *Beaks* West.
  59 *Winds & Seas*] *Seas & Winds* West.
  78 *Door*] *Doors* West.
  81 *Melian's*] *Lemnian's* West, Commonplace Book (but with *Melian's* substituted in margin).
  84 *recall'd*] *restored* West.
  85 *Arts are*] *Skill is* West.
  90 *Or*] *And* West.
  100 *but preserves*] *shall preserve* West.
  102 *retain*] *detain* West; *restrain* Mitford.

COLLINS

2. *Persian Eclogues* (page 115)

THE PREFACE

16 *Mahamed*] A BDALLAH 1757.

20 *Abbas*] 1757 adds a note: *In the Persian tongue, A BBAS signifieth 'the father of the people'.*

23 *the Writing*] *Writing* 1757.

27 *Reflections*] *reflection* 1757.

28 *Orientals*] *Orientials* 1757.

ECLOGUE THE FIRST

8 *Nor praise, but such as Truth bestow'd, desir'd:* 1757.

13 *od'rous . . . an Eastern*] *blushing . . . a virgin* 1757.

17 *wand'ring*] *Wand'rer* 1742, corrected by Collins in Dyce copy and 1757.

19, 21, 25 *you*] *ye* 1742, corrected by Collins in Dyce copy and in 1757.

30–2 1757 has:

> *Boast but the worth* * *Balsora's pearls display;*
> *Drawn from the deep we own their surface bright,*
> *But, dark within, they drink no lust'rous light:*

46 *The fair-eyed Truth*] *Immortal T RUTH* 1757.

49 *you* 1757] *ye* 1742. (Cp. the alterations to 19, 21, 25 above by Collins himself.)

53–4 1757 has:

> *Come thou whose thoughts as limpid springs are clear,*
> *To lead the train, sweet M ODESTY appear:*

69 *Eastern*] *ancient* 1757.

ECLOGUE THE SECOND

1 *Desart-Waste*] *boundless waste* 1757.

29–30 1742 from this point gives only the first 4 words of the refrain, which is given in full in the present text.

83 *O! let me teach my heart to lose its fears,* 1757.

ECLOGUE THE THIRD

4 After this line 1757 adds:

> *What time 'tis sweet o'er fields of rice to stray,*
> *Or scent the breathing maze at setting day;*

15 *Junquils*] *Jonquils* 1757.
Collins's note to this line is cut through in the Dyce copy but was retained in 1757.

35–6 1742 from this point gives only the first 3 words of the refrain, which is given in full in the present text.

ECLOGUE THE FOURTH

49 *Tents*] *Seats* 1742, corrected by Collins in the Dyce copy and in 1757.
51 *Date*] *Dale* 1742, corrected by Collins in the Dyce copy and in 1757.
65 *Deserts*] *desarts* 1757.

3. *An Epistle: Addrest to Sir Thomas Hanmer* (page 126)
  1–6 1743 has:

> *While, own'd by You, with Smiles the Muse surveys,*
> *Th' expected Triumph of her sweetest Lays:*
> *While, stretch'd at Ease, she boasts your Guardian Aid,*
> *Secure, and happy in her sylvan Shade:*
> *Excuse her Fears, who scarce a Verse bestows,*
> *In just Remembrance of the Debt she owes;*

  9–16 1743 has:

> *Long slighted* Fancy, *with a Mother's Care,*
> *Wept o'er his Works, and felt the last Despair.*
> *Torn from her Head, she saw the Roses fall,*
> *By all deserted, tho' admir'd by all.*
> *"And oh! she cry'd, shall Science still resign*
> *"Whate'er is Nature's, and whate'er is mine?*
> *"Shall* Taste *and* Art, *but shew a cold Regard,*
> *"And scornful Pride reject th' unletter'd Bard?*
> *"Ye myrtled Nymphs, who own my gentle Reign,*
> *"Tune the sweet Lyre, and grace my airy Train!*
> *"If, where ye rove, your searching Eyes have known*
> *"One perfect Mind, which Judgment calls its own:*
> *"There ev'ry Breast its fondest Hopes must bend,*
> *"And ev'ry Muse with Tears await her Friend.*
>
> *'Twas then fair* Isis *from her Stream arose,*
> *In kind Compassion of her Sister's Woes.*
> *'Twas then she promis'd to the mourning Maid*
> *Th' immortal Honours, which thy Hands have paid:*
> *"My best-lov'd Son (she said) shall yet restore*
> *"Thy ruin'd Sweets, and Fancy weep no more.*

17 *just*] *slow* 1743.
25 *With kind Concern*] *Line after Line,* 1743.
27 *Wit secure*] *equal Pow'r* 1743.
35–41 1743 has:

> *When* Rome *herself, her envy'd Glories dead,*
> *No more Imperial, stoop'd her conquer'd Head:*
> *Luxuriant* Florence *chose a softer Theme,*
> *While all was Peace, by* Arno's *silver Stream.*
> *With sweeter Notes th'* Etrurian *Vales complain'd,*

> *And Arts reviving told—a* Cosmo *reign'd.*
> *Their wanton Lyres the Bards of* Provence *strung,*

37 The note was added in 1744.
41 *he*] *they* 1743.
45 *various*] *rising* 1743.
63 Smiles] *Loves* 1743.
67 The note was added in 1744.
71–2 1743 has:

> *Till late* Corneille *from Epick* Lucan *brought*
> *The full Expression, and the* Roman *Thought;*

101–10 1743 has:

> *O blest in all that Genius gives to charm,*
> *Whose Morals mend us, and whose Passions warm!*
> *Oft let my Youth attend thy various Page,*
> *Where rich Invention rules th' unbounded Stage.*
> *There ev'ry Scene the Poet's Warmth may raise,*
> *And melting Music find the softest Lays.*
> *O might the Muse with equal Ease persuade,*
> *Expressive Picture, to adopt thine Aid!*
> *Some pow'rful* Raphael *shou'd again appear,*
> *And Arts consenting fix their Empire here.*

111 *free*] *fair* 1743.
113–16 1743 has:

> *Chaste, and subdu'd, the modest Colours lie,*
> *In fair Proportion to th' approving Eye.—*
> *And see, where* † Antony *lamenting stands*
> *In fixt Distress, and spreads his pleading Hands!*

117 *cold*] *pale* 1743.
122 *Wrath*] *Rage* 1743.
123–30 1743 has:

> *Ev'n now, his Thoughts with eager Vengeance doom*
> *The last sad Ruin of ungrateful* Rome.
> *Till, slow-advancing o'er the tented Plain,*
> *In sable Weeds, appear the Kindred-train:*
> *The frantic Mother leads their wild Despair,*
> *Beats her swoln Breast, and rends her silver Hair.*
> *And see he yields! – the Tears unbidden start,*
> *And conscious Nature claims th' unwilling Heart!*

136 Blend] *Spread* 1743.
146 *boundless*] *tuneful* 1743.

7. *Ode to Pity* (page 137)
 31 *Toils*] *toil* Langhorne (1765).

9. *Ode to Simplicity* (page 142)
  6 *or*] *and* Langhorne (1765).
  45 *Faints*] *Faint's* Langhorne (1765).

14. *Ode, to a Lady on the Death of Colonel Ross* (page 153)
Title: *Ode to a Lady, On the Death of Col. Charles Ross, in the Action at*
    Fontenoy. Written May, 1745. Museum, Dodsley.
  4 *stain'd with Blood*] *sunk in grief* Warton.
  19–24 Museum has:

> Ev'n now, regardful of his Doom,
> Applauding Honour *haunts his Tomb,*
>   With shadowy Trophies crown'd:
> Whilst Freedom's Form beside her roves
> Majestic thro' the twilight Groves,
>   And calls her Heroes round.

Warton follows this text with *regardless* for *regardful*. Dodsley (1748)
has:

> O'er him, whose doom thy virtues grieve,
> Aërial forms shall sit at eve
>   And bend the pensive head!
> And, fall'n to save his injur'd land,
> Imperial Honor's awful hand
>   Shall point his lonely bed!

  31 *unknown*] *untaught* Warton.
  37–48 Added in 1746 and omitted in Dodsley (1748); the two stanzas did
    not appear in the MS. seen by Warton.
  49 *If drawn by all a lover's art* Warton.
    an] *a* Museum.
  58 *Harting's*] H———'s Museum.
    cottag'd] *cottage* Dodsley.

15. *Ode to Evening* (page 156)
  2 *May hope, O pensive Eve, to sooth thine Ear* 1746.
  3 *solemn*] *brawling* 1746.
  10 *Shriek*] *shrieks* Dodsley (1751 and later editions).
  24 *Flow'rs*] *Buds* 1746.
  29–32 1746 has:

> Then let me rove some wild and heathy Scene,
> Or find some Ruin 'midst its dreary Dells,
>   Whose Walls more awful nod
>   By thy religious Gleams.

  33 *But when*] *Or if* 1746.
  34 *Forbid*] *Prevent* 1746.
  49 *sure-found . . . Shed*] *regardful of thy quiet Rule* 1746.
  50 *rose-lip'd* Health] *smiling* Peace 1746.

52 *hymn*] *love* 1746.

17. *The Manners. An Ode* (page 158)
23 *mingling*] *mingled* Langhorne (1765).
35–6 *Thou . . . /Hast*] *Tho' . . . /Has* Whibley (1937), an unnecessary emendation urged by H. W. Garrod (1928).
49 *Thou*] *Tho'* Whibley (1937), another emendation proposed by Garrod.

18. *The Passions. An Ode for Music* (page 161)
30 *delightful*] *delighted* Langhorne (1765).

19. *Ode Occasion'd by the Death of Mr Thomson* (page 164)
1 *Grave*] *grove* Poetical Calendar (1763).
21 *Earthy*] *earthly* Langhorne (1765).

20. *An Ode on the Popular Superstitions of the Highlands* (page 167)
6 Scored through in MS. with *Whose* written above *Whom*, but without further substitution. Since Collins intended to revise rather than omit the line, it is retained as in 1788.
25 *Airy*] *viewless* written above and deleted in MS.
44 *repeat*] written above *relate* deleted in MS.
48 Note: *A kind of hut, built for a summer habitation to the herdsmen, when the cattle are sent to graze in distant pastures.* 1788.
51 *The*] written above *They* deleted in MS.
   bonny] *bony* 1788.
56 *depth*] written above *gloom* deleted in MS.
58 *astonishd*] written above *afflicted* deleted in MS.
66 *heed*] written above *mark* deleted in MS.
67 *Spirit*] written above *Fiend* deleted in MS.
95 A leaf, containing stanza 5 and half of stanza 6, was missing when Carlyle rediscovered the MS. The line numbering assumes that 25 lines are missing.
98 *chuse*] *trust* 1788.
100 *mirk*] written above *sad* in MS.
110 *rouse*] *raise* 1788.
111 *Banks*] *bank* 1788.
119 *Youthly*] written over one or two letters of an illegible word in MS.
124 *Bairns*] *babes* 1788.
   unclosing] written above *Cottage* deleted in MS.
127 *Dropping*] written over part of an illegible word, perhaps beginning *Sh*, in MS.
128 *perhaps*] *perchance* 1788.
130 *fondly*] inserted above the line in MS.
   shuddring] written above *cold and shuddring* deleted in MS.
133 *Pursue*] written above *Proceed* deleted in MS.
137 Note: *A name given in Scotland to a supposed spirit of the waters.* 1788.

151 *Rifted*] written above *Yawning* deleted in MS.

161 *ragged*] *rugged* 1788.

168 *Sufficed*] written above *Content* deleted in MS.

169 *give*] first letter torn away in MS., but Carlyle's transcript and 1788 read *give*, perhaps clearly legible then.

170 *bare*] last two letters torn away in MS., but Carlyle could no doubt read *bare*, which is in any case required by the rhyme.

171 *murmur*] so Carlyle and 1788: only the first two letters are visible in MS.

176 Note: *This stanza is more incorrect in its structure than any of the foregoing. There is apparently a line wanting between this and the subsequent one, In Musing hour, &c. The deficient line ought to have rhymed with Scene.* 1788.

179, 181 The tear in the MS. has removed a few letters at the beginning of these lines.

190 *delights*] *delight* 1788.

192–5 Written above the following deleted in MS.:

> *How have I trembled, when at Tancred's side*
> *Like him I stalkd and all his Passions felt*
> *Where Charmd by Ismen thro' the Forrest wide*
> *Barkd in Each Plant a talking Spirit dwelt!*

193 *Its gushing*] written above *The Cypress* deleted in MS.

196 *where*] *when* 1788.

200–3 Written above the following deleted in MS.:

> *Hence with Each Strain*
> *Hence sure to Charm his Early Numbers flow*
> *Tho faithfull sweet, tho' strong, of simple kind.*
> *Hence with Each Theme he bids the bosom glow*
> *While his warm lays an easy passage find*
> *Pour'd thro' Each inmost nerve,*

In the third of these lines *faithfull* is written above *strong yet*.

201 *softest*] *est* is written above *ness* deleted in MS.

203 *and lulls*] written above *and win* in MS., which is not deleted, but the revised grammar requires the singular verb; *and wins* 1788.

205 *Firths*] *friths* 1788.

206 *Are*] Written over *By* in MS.

212 Note: *BEN JOHNSON undertook a journey to Scotland afoot in 1619, to visit the poet DRUMMOND, at his seat of Hawthornden, near Edinburgh. DRUMMOND has preserved in his works, some very curious heads of their conversation.* 1788.

214 *Yarrow*] *Yarrow's* 1788.

219 After this line MS. has *The End*.

21. *Lines on Restoration Drama* (page 175)
Lines 1–18 are written on the recto of a folio leaf with 19–26 on the

verso; 27–32 are headed '2' and written vertically in the margin of the recto; 33–44, headed '3', are written upside down on the verso.

1 *pomp*] written over *scene*.

2 *Thames*] written above *Isle* deleted.

6 The names of the two historians are starred in the MS. but the footnote clearly refers to 16.

13 *Those courtly*] written above *That Court of* deleted.

14 *In . . . learn'd their*] written above *From . . . took its* deleted.

22 *plac'd*] written over *built*.

39 *talk*] written above *tell* deleted.

41 *Thus Folly*] written above *Such Follies* deleted.
  long at] written above *till* deleted.

22. *Lines of Composite Authorship* (page 177)

7 *can*] after *will* deleted.

15 *place*] written above *scene* deleted.

19 *each*] after *every* deleted.

26 *Scarce*] written above *Just* deleted.

29 Written above *With these amendments, what some yet admire* deleted.

31 *no . . . deck*] written above *your Arts can not attend* deleted.

32 Written above *whom The Muse by Art untutor'd smild:* deleted (the first word has been torn away).

37 *thy*] *my* 1956.

23. *Lines Addressed to James Harris* (page 178)

3 *teach me*] written above *Scorn not* deleted.

5 *O teach*] *O Smile* deleted above.

6 Left blank.

9 *With . . . both*] *Ev'n these would I resign* deleted above.

10 After this line Collins has deleted:

> *Ye too who living own'd her genial rule*
> *The Sons and Daughters of her happy school*

Collins left a blank in the text after the cancelled couplet.

15 *Intent*] written above *Whether* deleted.

16 *To fix*] written above *Few form* deleted.

20 *Son of Harmony*] written above *Sweet Philosopher* deleted.

21 Philosophy] written by Collins in a larger hand and here italicized.

22 *own*] after *take* and *aid* deleted.

23 *as thy lips impart*] written above *will thy tongue reveals* deleted (1956 reads *well*, but Collins seems to have written *will* as a mistake for *while*), with *as* above *when* deleted.

26 *wak'd*] written above *gradual* deleted.

30 *assist*] written above *inspire* deleted.

24. *Lines Addressed to Jacob Tonson* (page 179)

1 *exclude . . . gloom*] written above *ev'n now your hours consume* deleted,

with an earlier version also deleted: *When oft in ease at lov'd Barn Elms you trace*

8 *Happiness*] written over *Pleas[ure]*

9 *What taste*] written over *Some tastefu[l]*

10 *Might*] written above *May* deleted.

11 *Evn from*] written over *From those*
   Courtly] written over *Poli[shed]*

13 *yet the Verse to*] written above *yet the chaste Expression* deleted.

17 *Maid of Elder Days*] written above *Distant Lovers Eyes* deleted.

19 *for*] written over *by*

24 *by Their toil*] written above *from Themselves* deleted.

27 *At soft*] written over *Else had*

31–2 Collins left these lines blank except for the concluding words.

25. *Lines Addressed to a Fastidious Critic* (page 180)

   3–4 Collins wrote no more of 3 and left 4 blank, no doubt intending to complete the couplet later.

   7 *Precepts*] written over *Lessons*

   11 *which trust our Critic Friends*] deleted after *Arts*.

   12 Left blank after *Ef[?fects]*

   28 In the first part of the line a word, perhaps *bold*, is written over another, perhaps *But*

   30 Left blank.

   31 *on Thames*] written above *Eugenia where* deleted.

   35 *Then*] written over *Rather*

   47 *Blackhall*] Probably an error for *Blackwell*. Thomas Blackwell published an *Enquiry into the Life and Writings of Homer* (1735).

26. *Lines Addressed to a Friend about to visit Italy* (page 182)

   5 *o'er*] after *bending* deleted.
     narrow] written above *little* deleted.

   8 *whole realms*] written above *the world* deleted.

   9 *Patriot's*] written above *Sage's* deleted.
     Story] written over *Writing*
     look] written above *form* deleted.

   10 After this line, two lines left blank.

   15 *O Think*] written above *Remember* deleted.

   17 *too*] written above *oft* deleted.

   18 *in*] after *Colours* deleted.

   19 *That Cynthio*] *How Shakespear's* deleted above.

27. *Stanzas on a Female Painter* (page 182)

   1 *lustre*] written above *radiance* deleted.

   2 *radiance*] written above *lustre* deleted.

   5 Apart from these words the stanza is left blank.

   17–20 Collins left a blank space for another stanza.

21 *Like*] written over *The*
28 *By*] after *Adorn'd with* deleted.
29 *Thy . . . his*] written above *Yet thy sweet draught* and *Gentle* deleted.
36 *soft imbrown'd*] written above *softly shed* deleted.
37 *when*] written over *thy* deleted.
46. *Fairy*] written above *Mingling* deleted.
After 48 Collins left space for two more stanzas of which he wrote only the
    first (49) and last (56) lines: *What tho' thy touch, belov'd of Art* deleted,
    and *And but thy Grave be all forgot*

28. 'Ye Genii who in secret state' (page 184)
    5 *Take all who for the* deleted above.
    7 *day*] written over *Sun*
    25 *the* is accidentally omitted before *Plain* (cp. 41).
    29 *to*] written over *at*
    33 *all . . . bare*] written above *of all unseen* deleted.
    34 *With . . . delight*] written above *In cooler hours* deleted.
    38 *Or*] written over *Oer*
    54 *lifeless*] written above *languid* deleted.
    56 Left blank.
    57 *the*] written above *yon* deleted.
    59 *round*] written above *on* deleted.

29. *To Simplicity* (page 186)
    7 *weakly* deleted after *Too*
    8 Left blank.
    16 *Soft*] written over *The*
    18 *To feed thy Youth*] *Around thy couch* deleted above.
    22 *For Wisdom*] written over *From thy*
    27 *now*] written over *too*
    31 *Come Gentle Goddess Sweet* deleted above.
    33 *'midst my Cave*] written above *ever near my view* deleted.
    34 Written above *With lightest Attic lawn* deleted.
    35 *With*] written over *On all*
    40 *loveliest*] written over *Sweetest*

30. 'No longer ask me Gentle Friends' (page 188)
    1 *Gentle*] written above *Village* deleted.
    7 *wandring*] *far off* written above.
    13–16 First version deleted:

> She came and to my simple Mind
> Improv'd the blossom'd Year
> For She, Ye swains of all her kind
> Is Damon's only Dear.

    13 *Or if the*] written above *Perhaps* deleted.
    18 Written above *And scarce one thought exprest* deleted.

19 *My*] written above *Before my* deleted.

21–4 First version deleted:

> *I thought to mark her gentle Mind*
> *Tho born of lofty birth*
> *And when She left my Cot methought*
> *She mark'd my starting Tear*

25 *I saw her next by Resnel's side* deleted above.

27 *once a Bard*] written above *Otway first* deleted.

29 Written above *The thoughts which fill his tender scene* deleted.

30 *And melt*] written above *Subdue* deleted.

> After this line Collins first left a line blank and wrote *I hung* as the
> rhyme in 32; he then drafted 31–2 as below.

31 Written above *And Yet my own were fond I ween* with the first four
  words deleted, and with *But there* also deleted.

32 *Than*] written above *as* deleted.

41–2 First version, the second line deleted:

> *But Ye who know what bounds divide*
> *Our Shores or rightliest deem*

43 *is . . . little Spring*] written above *remov'd is . . . side* deleted.

49 *There too resorts*] *And near her Wonnes* written above.

53–6 After 49–52, Collins first wrote the four lines given in the note to 61–4
  below; then the following deleted attempts to begin another stanza:

> a   *From Wisdom whom she taught to please*
> b   *She sootly sung how once she heard*
>   *A Green-wood Nymph complain,*
> c   *'Twas She that sung how soft and sweet*
>   *A Green*
> d   *To Wisdom first whose Love she gain'd*
>   *The duteous Verse she paid*

Interlined with these efforts are the opening lines of the following
drafted stanza:

> *Ennobling Wisdom first she ownd*
> *And hail'd the Sacred Powr*
> *Then like a Green wood Nymph bemoan'd*
>
> *Of Melancholy last She tried*
> *To make the Virtues known*
> *Ah Why? That Theme with Love allied*
> *Belong'd to me Alone!*

In 3 of this stanza *bemoan'd* is written above *complain'd* deleted, and in 4
Of above *And*. Collins finally wrote 53–6 as in the text, headed '7', with
each line queried in the margin.

53 *They told how*] written above *The lays where of* deleted.
56 *joys*] written above *wreaths* deleted.
57 *Sweet sung that Muse*] written above *Yet sweet the Song* and *sung* above *flowd* deleted.
60 *my Laura's*] written above *Amanda's* deleted.
61–4 First version at the end of stanza 7 (see 53–6 note):

> I'll henceforth make with   Art
>   Some Garland for her Hair
>   That She who charms my Delia's heart
>   May plead for Damon there!

That She who charms is written above *Her Verse may touch* deleted and *May* above *And* deleted. There are 4 cancelled lines in the margin of stanza 8:

> I will not soil with praise the lay
>   Which soothly none can blame
> But count the Songs let all who may
>   Divine the Writers name

65 *ought*] written above *mine* deleted.

31. *Lines on the Music of the Grecian Theatre* (page 191)
  2 Written above *Obtained his old Ægyptian Throne* deleted.
  6 *humanely*] written above *too genrous and too* deleted.
  12 *They gave*] written over *Assign'd*

SELECT BIBLIOGRAPHY

SELECT BIBLIOGRAPHY

The Chief Editions of Gray's Works

Ode on a Distant Prospect of Eton College, 1747. Type-facsimile, Oxford, 1924.

Dodsley's *Collection of Poems*, Vol. II (1748, etc.) contained *Ode on the Spring*, *Ode on the Death of a Favourite Cat*, and the *Eton Ode*.

An Elegy Wrote in a Country Church Yard, 1751. Five editions appeared in 1751 and eight more were published by Dodsley in Gray's lifetime. Gray revised the third and eighth editions. The third and later editions were entitled *An Elegy Written in a Country Church Yard*. The edition by F. G. Stokes, Oxford, 1929, describes the MSS. and the printings of the *Elegy* up to 1771. A facsimile of the first edition and of the Eton MS. was edited by G. Sherburn for the Augustan Reprint Society, Los Angeles, 1951; there is also a facsimile and transcription of the Eton MS. in P. J. Croft, *Autograph Poetry in the English Language*, 2 vols., 1973.

Designs by Mr. R. Bentley for Six Poems by Mr. T. Gray, 1753. (Reprinted with the *Odes*, 1757, 1765, 1766, 1775, 1789.) Includes *A Long Story*, later omitted by Gray from his *Poems*.

Odes, by Mr. T. Gray, Strawberry Hill, 1757.

Poems, 1768. Gray's own collected edition, containing ten poems in the following order: *Ode on the Spring*, *Ode on the Death of a Favourite Cat*, *Ode on a Distant Prospect of Eton College*, *Ode to Adversity*, *The Progress of Poesy*, *The Bard*, *The Fatal Sisters*, *The Descent of Odin*, *The Triumphs of Owen*, *Elegy*. Gray's instructions to James Dodsley for the edition, sent *c.* 1 February 1768, appear in *Correspondence*, III. 999–1001, and include texts of the Norse translations. James Beattie, with Gray's approval, supervised the Glasgow edition by Foulis in 1768 and there were Irish editions in the same year in Dublin and Cork. Many London editions followed before the end of the century.

The Poems of Mr. Gray, to which are prefixed Memoirs of his Life and Writings, edited by William Mason, York, 1775; revised edn., London, 1775. The first appearance of Gray's letters, although in unreliable texts, and of several poems, including *Agrippina*, *Education and Government*, *Sonnet on Richard West*, *Vicissitude*, and other fragments.

Poems, ed. Gilbert Wakefield, 1786.

Poetical Works, ed. Stephen Jones, 1799, 1800 (enlarged).

Poems, ed. J. Mitford, 1814.

Works, ed. T. J. Mathias, 2 vols., 1814.

Works, ed. J. Mitford, 2 vols., 1816; 4 vols., 1835–7, 1857–8. Gray's correspondence with Norton Nicholls, 1843, was also published as Vol. V of this edition.

Poetical Works, ed. J. Moultrie, Eton, 1845, 1847.

Poetical Works, ed. R. A. Wilmott, 1854, 1883. (With Parnell, Green, Collins and T. Warton.)

Works in Prose and Verse, ed. Edmund Gosse, 4 vols., 1884, 1902–6 (revised).

Poetical Works, ed. J. Bradshaw, 1891, etc.

Selections from the Poetry and Prose, ed. W. L. Phelps, Boston, 1894.

Gray's English Poems, ed. D. C. Tovey, Cambridge, 1898, etc.

Letters, ed. D. C. Tovey, 3 vols., 1900–12.

Correspondence of Gray, Walpole, West and Ashton, ed. Paget Toynbee, 2 vols., Oxford, 1915.

Poetical Works (with Collins), ed. A. L. Poole, Oxford, 1917; revised by L. Whibley, 1937.

Correspondence, ed. P. Toynbee and L. Whibley, 3 vols., Oxford, 1935.

Complete Poems, ed. H. W. Starr and J. R. Hendrickson, Oxford, 1966.

Selected Poems (with Collins), ed. Arthur Johnston, 1967.

Poems (with Collins and Goldsmith), ed. Roger Lonsdale, 1969.

MANUSCRIPTS

Gray's Commonplace Book. The three volumes, at Pembroke College, Cambridge, contain Gray's transcripts of many of his poems, although they are scattered through a mass of historical and literary material. In the third volume Mason transcribed other poems and fragments which he found among Gray's papers after his death.

Eton MSS. The first draft of the *Elegy* and a MS. of the *Eton Ode* are at Eton College.

Wharton MSS. British Museum Egerton MS.2400 contains Gray's letters to Wharton, the autograph MSS. of several poems including the *Elegy*, and transcripts of others by Wharton.

Mitford MSS. British Museum Add.MSS.32561–2 are Vols. III and IV of John Mitford's Notebooks, containing his transcriptions of and notes on some of Gray's poems.

The Chief Editions of Collins's Poems

Persian Eclogues Written originally for the Entertainment of the Ladies of Tauris. And now first translated, 1742. Reprinted as *Oriental Eclogues*, 1757, 1760; type-facsimile of 1742 edition, Oxford, 1925.

Verses Humbly Address'd To Sir Thomas Hanmer. On his Edition of Shakespear's Works. By a Gentleman of Oxford, 1743. Revised as *An Epistle: addrest to Sir Thomas Hanmer, on his Edition of Shakespear's Works . . . To which is added, A Song from the Cymbelyne of the same Author*, 1744.

Odes on Several Descriptive and Allegoric Subjects, 1747 (pub. 20 December 1746). The *Ode to a Lady* had appeared in *The Museum* in June 1746; together with the *Ode to Evening* and the *Ode Written in the Beginning of the Year 1746* it appeared in a revised form in Dodsley's *Collection of Poems*, 2nd edition, 1748, i. 327–32.

Ode Occasion'd by the Death of Mr. Thomson, 1749.

*The Passions, an Ode ... Set to Musick by Dr. Hayes. Performed at the
    Theatre in Oxford, July 2, 1750*, Oxford [1750]. Similar separate editions
    for musical performance, with an altered ending by the Earl of Litchfield,
    were published at Winchester in 1750 and Gloucester in 1760.
The Poetical Calendar, ed. Francis Fawkes and William Woty, Vols. XI–XII,
    1763. Collects all the verse published in Collins's lifetime, with a bio-
    graphy (by John Hampton?) and a 'Character' by Johnson.
*The Poetical Works ... With Memoirs of the Author and Observations on his
    Genius and Writings*, ed. John Langhorne, 1765 (twice), 1771, 1776, 1781.
    Many less careful editions followed in the next half-century and Collins
    also appeared in various large-scale collections of *British Poets*, including
    Johnson's *Works of the English Poets*, Vol. XLIX, 1779; Vol. LVIII, 1790.
*An Ode on the Popular Superstitions of the Highlands of Scotland, Considered
    as the Subject of Poetry*, in the *Transactions of the Royal Society of
    Edinburgh*, Vol. I (1788). Bell's spurious separate edition appeared in
    London in the same year. An exact transcription of the MS. was first given
    by Miss C. Lamont in the *Review of English Studies* in 1968.
Eclogues and Miscellaneous Pieces, ed. Benjamin Strutt, Colchester, 1796.
Poetical Works ... With a Prefatory Essay, ed. Mrs. A. L. Barbauld, 1797,
    1800, 1802.
Poetical Works, ed. Alexander Dyce, 1827. (Includes notes by John Mitford.)
Poetical Works, ed. William Crowe, Bath, 1828.
Poetical Works, ed. Sir Egerton Brydges, 1830, 1853. (With an Essay by
    Brydges and a Memoir by Sir Harris Nicolas.)
Poetical Works, ed. R. A. Wilmott, 1854, 1883. (With Gray, Parnell, Green
    and T. Warton.)
Poetical Works, ed. W. Moy Thomas, 1858, 1866, 1894.
Poems, ed. W. C. Bronson, Boston, 1898.
Poetical Works (with Gray), ed. C. Stone and A. L. Poole, Oxford, 1917;
    revised by F. Page, 1937.
Poems, ed. Edmund Blunden, 1929.
Drafts and Fragments of Verse, Edited from the Manuscripts, ed. J. S. Cun-
    ningham, Oxford, 1956. The MSS. are in Trinity College, Oxford.
Selected Poems (with Gray), ed. Arthur Johnston, 1967.
Poems (with Gray and Goldsmith), ed. Roger Lonsdale, 1969.

Other Works Biographical and Critical

Gray

C. S. Northup, *A Bibliography of Thomas Gray*, New Haven, 1917;
    continued 1917–51 by H. W. Starr, Philadelphia, 1953.
A. L. Reed, *The Background of Gray's Elegy*, New York, 1924.
R. Martin, *Essai sur Thomas Gray*, Paris, 1934.
W. P. Jones, *Thomas Gray, Scholar*, Cambridge, Mass., 1937.
H. W. Starr, *Gray as a Literary Critic*, Philadelphia, 1941.

Lord David Cecil, *The Poetry of Thomas Gray* (Warton Lecture, British Academy), 1945.

Cleanth Brooks, 'Gray's "Storied Urn"' in *The Well Wrought Urn*, New York, 1947.

F. H. Ellis, 'Gray's *Elegy*: The Biographical Problem in Literary Criticism', *PMLA*, LXVI (1951), 971–1008.

—— 'Gray's *Eton College Ode*: The Problem of Tone, *Papers on Language and Literature*, V (1969), 130–8.

R. W. Ketton-Cremer, *Thomas Gray: a Biography*, Cambridge, 1955.

G. Tillotson, *Augustan Studies*, 1961.

M. Golden, *Thomas Gray*, New York, 1964.

P. F. Vernon, 'The Structure of Gray's Early Poems', *Essays in Criticism*, XV (1965), 381–93.

Frank Brady, B. H. Bronson, and Ian Jack, essays on the *Elegy* in *From Sensibility to Romanticism*, ed. F. W. Hilles and H. Bloom, New York, 1965.

A. Johnston, *Gray and the Bard*, Cardiff, 1966.

R. Lonsdale, *The Poetry of Thomas Gray: Versions of the Self* (Chatterton Lecture, British Academy), 1973.

Fearful Joy: Papers from the Thomas Gray Bicentenary Conference, ed. J. Downey and B. Jones, Montreal, 1974.

Collins

A. D. McKillop, 'The Romanticism of Collins', *Studies in Philology*, XX (1923), 1–16.

—— 'Collins's *Ode to Evening*', *Tennessee Studies in Literature*, V (1960), 78–83.

H. W. Garrod, *William Collins*, Oxford, 1928.

A. S. P. Woodhouse, 'Collins and the Creative Imagination', in *Studies in English*, ed. M. M. Wallace, Toronto, 1931.

—— 'The Poetry of Collins Reconsidered' in *From Sensibility to Romanticism*, ed. F. W. Hilles and H. Bloom, New York, 1965.

E. G. Ainsworth, *Poor Collins; His Life, Art and Influence*, Ithaca, 1937.

G. N. Shuster, 'Collins, Gray and the Return of the Imagination' in *The English Ode from Milton to Keats*, New York, 1940.

S. Musgrove, 'The Theme of Collins's *Odes*', *Notes and Queries*, CLXXXV (1943), 214–17, 253–5.

F. Rota, *William Collins*, Padua, 1953.

J. H. Hagstrum, *The Sister Arts*, Chicago, 1958.

M. E. Brown, 'On Collins's *Ode to Evening*', *Essays in Criticism*, XI (1961), 136–53.

J. R. Crider, 'Structure and Effect in Collins's Progress Poems', *Studies in Philology*, LX (1963), 57–72.

R. Quintana, 'The Scheme of Collins's *Odes*' in *Restoration and Eighteenth-Century Literature*, ed. C. Camden, Chicago, 1963.

P. M. Spacks, 'Collins's Imagery', *Studies in Philology*, LXII (1965), 719–36.

O. F. Sigworth, *William Collins*, New York, 1965.

P. L. Carver, *The Life of a Poet: a Biographical Sketch of William Collins*, 1967.

E. R. Wasserman, 'Collins's *Ode on the Poetical Character*', *English Literary History*, XXXIV (1967), 92–115.

A. Johnston, *The Poetry of William Collins* (Warton Lecture, British Academy), 1973.

INDEX OF TITLES AND FIRST LINES